AGAINST THE TREND

A Portrait of William Kelly

AGAINST THE TREND

The Spirituality of William Kelly (1821–1906)

Anne-Louise Critchlow
Foreword by Graham Johnson

WIPF & STOCK · Eugene, Oregon

AGAINST THE TREND
The Spirituality of William Kelly (1821–1906)

Copyright © 2016 Anne-Louise Critchlow. All rights reserved. Except for brief quotations in critical publications or reviews, no part of this book may be reproduced in any manner without prior written permission from the publisher. Write: Permissions, Wipf and Stock Publishers, 199 W. 8th Ave., Suite 3, Eugene, OR 97401.

Wipf & Stock
An Imprint of Wipf and Stock Publishers
199 W. 8th Ave., Suite 3
Eugene, OR 97401

www.wipfandstock.com

PAPERBACK ISBN: 978-1-4982-9752-3
HARDCOVER ISBN: 978-1-4982-9754-7
EBOOK ISBN: 978-1-4982-9753-0

Manufactured in the U.S.A.   07/14/16

Scripture quotations from The Authorized (King James) Version. Rights in the Authorized Version in the United Kingdom are vested in the Crown. Reproduced by permission of the Crown's patentee, Cambridge University Press.

Scripture quotations taken from the Revised English Bible, copyright © Cambridge University Press and Oxford University Press 1989. All rights reserved.

The Scripture quotations contained herein are from the New Revised Standard Version of the Bible, Anglicized Edition, copyright © 1989,1995 by the Division of Christian Education of the National Council of the Churches of Christ in the United States of America, and are used by permission. All rights reserved.

Copyright for the reproduction of the photo of William Kelly used with kind permission by Stem Publishing contact@STEMPublishing.com

In memory of my beloved parents,
Norman Douglas and Marjorie Mathie

Contents

Foreword by Graham Johnson | ix
Acknowledgements | xi
Abbreviations | xiii

CHAPTER 1
William Kelly in his Context | 1

CHAPTER 2
William Kelly—A Conservative Intellectual of the Evangelical Tradition | 30

CHAPTER 3
William Kelly as a Conservative Intellectual—His Relationship with Nineteenth-century English Theologians | 57

CHAPTER 4
William Kelly as a Biblical Literalist—His Teaching about the Afterlife | 86

CHAPTER 5
William Kelly as a Biblical Literalist—The Atonement | 118

CHAPTER 6
William Kelly and Mystic Spirituality | 146

CHAPTER 7
William Kelly's Spirituality Revealed in his Typology and Understanding of Language | 172

CONCLUSION
An Assessment of William Kelly's Contribution to Theology | 199

Bibliography | 209

Foreword

Recent years have seen a blossoming of scholarly publications into the roots and ideas of the Brethren movement in the nineteenth and twentieth centuries. Much useful work is being done with the help and encouragement of the Brethren Archivist and Historians Network (BAHN), who hold regular conferences on Brethren related themes. It always gives me pleasure, as the custodian of the Christian Brethren Archive at the University of Manchester, when approached by scholars intent on researching facets of Brethren thought in a serious and critical manner. Much Brethren historical writing is celebratory and hagiographical, and while there is a place for such writing in sustaining the Brethren tradition, I always feel that it helps to justify the place of the Archive as part of the University community when the resources of the Archive are subject to serious intellectual inquiry. This has been increasingly the case as scholars and PhD students have alighted upon the Archive. Such was the case when Anne-Louise Critchlow commenced what began as a doctoral study of William Kelly.

William Kelly is a relatively neglected figure in the history of Brethren thought. True, there are many who consider themselves "Kelly Brethren," but the resultant biographical studies tend to be hymns of praise to the "Irish Saint and Scholar" (the title of the most recent biographical study). Prior to reading this book, I thought of Kelly as a disciple and interpreter of the work of John Nelson Darby, and very much in Darby's shadow. While it is true that he was the editor of the thirty six volumes of Darby's *Collective Writings* and spent many years of his life devoted to this work, what the present book makes clear is the distinctiveness of Kelly's contribution and the unique character of his thinking. Dr. Critchlow's writing rescues Kelly from the condescension of those viewing him in Darby's shadow. She shows how he developed a theology of his own, owing a lot to Darby's, but intellectually distinct. Being associated with Darby has often led to him being

Foreword

placed among those labeled "Exclusive" with all that that entails. However, the present study focuses on the popularity of Kelly's teaching among both the "Open" and "Exclusive" wings of Brethrenism, and sees him in many respects as a bridge between the two traditions. It also emphasizes Kelly's interaction with the wider world of Christian theology, engaging in many of the controversies of the mid and late nineteenth century. Although Kelly engaged with contemporary intellectual traditions, at the same time he was critical of the religious establishment. In impressively argued chapters we have Kelly's life and thought placed into context, a detailed examination of him as a "conservative intellectual" (both in the evangelical tradition and in relation to wider theological developments), and examinations of him as a "Biblical Literalist." Two path breaking chapters consider Kelly's mystic spirituality, exploring among other things the influence of the Romantic Movement on the development of his ideas. Here, the writings of Kelly are also reflected upon in relation to developments in late twentieth century Brethren and general evangelical thought. The final result is that rather than Kelly being considered as a part of the exclusive and fundamentalist tradition, he emerges as a part of the continuum of evangelical conservative theologians whose influence extends well into the twentieth century. The resulting book is a sympathetic yet scholarly study filling a gap in the historiography of the Brethren and making a significant contribution to, and understanding of, the complexities of Brethren thought.

Dr. Graham Johnson
Archivist at Manchester University Library

Acknowledgements

This book started as a research project for a doctorate at the University of Manchester, Great Britain, and the staff at the library and at the postgraduate office have always been courteous and efficient in the help they have given. I would like to acknowledge with gratitude the patient help and advice from my former supervisor, Professor Jeremy Gregory, now a Pro-Vice-Chancellor of Nottingham University, who was unfailingly encouraging and perceptive in his comments during my six years of study. I benefitted so much from his extensive knowledge of Victorian history and religion. Professor Crawford Gribben of Queen's University Belfast, in his reading of the manuscript as an external examiner, drew my attention to the work of Steven Katz which I have subsequently used in this book. Questions posed at the Ecclesiastical History Society postgraduate symposium and the International Brethren Conference, both held in 2013, sharpened my understanding of Kelly's spirituality, and I have appreciated the interest shown by Dr. Neil Dickson and the BAHN organization. I also owe a debt of gratitude to Dr. Graham Johnson of the Christian Brethren Archives at the University of Manchester Library for his generously shared knowledge, expertise, and enthusiasm. I am grateful too to Ms. Jenny Parker, librarian at the reference section of the Central Library, Middlesbrough, for opening the room containing the Kelly library and showing me the index of the books. My thanks also go the Women's Continuing Ministerial Education Trust (part of the Church of England), for providing me with a bursary to enable me to undertake the research behind this book. I would like to record my gratitude to my husband, Dr. Mark Critchlow, for his kindness and support during times of study and manuscript preparation, especially when it came to the eagle-eyed perception needed for editing and proofreading.

Lastly, I would like to acknowledge the rich understanding of the Bible, both intellectually and spiritually, which William Kelly has bequeathed

ACKNOWLEDGEMENTS

to posterity. I hope everyone who reads this book will be able to profit from studying his works.

Abbreviations

KJV   King James Version of the Bible
RV   Revised Version of the Bible
NRSV   New Revised Standard Version of the Bible

CHAPTER 1

William Kelly in his Context

INTRODUCTION

William Kelly (1821–1906) was born in County Down, Ireland. He studied Classics and Hebrew at Trinity College, Dublin from 1836 till 1841 and he graduated with first-class honors. As he was too young to be ordained in the Church of Ireland, he obtained a tutorial post in Sark for a year, where he experienced an "evangelical conversion" and joined the Brethren movement, which had begun as early as 1827–1828, when John Nelson Darby (1800–1882), an ordained Anglican clergyman, was experiencing internal conflict about his beliefs and the nature of the established Church. Kelly spent the years 1842–1871 in Guernsey, establishing his reputation as a Bible teacher and writer.[1] While Kelly had only met Darby briefly and "by chance" in Plymouth in 1845, he had already been influenced by Darby's writing.[2] However, while Darby, John Gifford Bellett (1795–1864), Benjamin Wills Newton (1807–1899) and other early Brethren leaders were debating ecclesiology in Dublin, Oxford and Plymouth, Kelly, a generation younger than these three, was living peacefully in Guernsey, meeting with only a few like-minded Christians according to Brethren principles,

---

1. Cross, *The Irish Saint and Scholar.* , 23.

2. Pontis, Preface to *Index to the Bible Treasury*, ix. Between June and December 1856 the magazine was edited by Professor Wallace. Between 1906 and 1920 it was edited by F.E. Race. The first edition is exactly the same in page numbers as the 3rd edition, except that in the 1st edition each volume is bound separately.

rather than being involved in early Brethren debates. While in Guernsey he started to edit first *The Prospect* (1848–1850) and then *The Bible Treasury* (1856–1906), both of which were religious magazines, wrote biblical exegeses, and took part in Brethren conferences in London. In 1871, Kelly moved to Blackheath, London, where he was a revered and published teacher and author until his death in 1906.

In this book I will be concerned with Kelly's reputation as a teacher and writer both amongst the Brethren and a wider Christian public. In particular, Kelly edited and contributed many of the articles in *The Bible Treasury*. George Anthony Denison (1805–1896), Archdeacon of Taunton and High Church Anglican, spoke of it as, "the only religious magazine any longer worth reading."[3] Kelly took up controversial topics of the day such as the issues raised by "higher criticism," the inspiration of Scripture and the Atonement, and subsequently I will analyze his magazine articles and reviews, as well as his major works, in order to explore his position with regard to these controversies. Kelly not only gave his own views on these topics but he also reviewed theological and philosophical works written by scholars from a wide spectrum of belief, and especially those from the Church of England. His interest in the Church of England was due to a number of factors—the Victorian debate about disestablishment; the Anglican background of many of the early Brethren leaders; the Anglican loyalties of those who were mediating the newer theological controversies to the wider Christian public. Therefore Kelly felt he had a duty to answer and engage with Anglican divines as well as non-conformist writers. I hope to show that William Kelly had significant points to make about Victorian religious arguments and that his contribution has been unduly neglected.

Kelly wrote over one hundred exegeses of individual Bible books and also printed lectures about particular theological subjects as well as numerous pamphlets. For example, he used his *Exposition of Isaiah* (1895) to discuss the nature and object of Prophecy and argued against the "advanced and unscrupulous school of unbelief."[4] In one of his last works, *The Gospel of Luke*, he did not have time to fully edit his commentary before publication, and Edward Elihu Whitfield (1848–1911) did this task for him after his death. Whitfield used Kelly's copious notes and explained in his Preface that, in doing this task, he was using references which Kelly had made in

---

3. Pickering, *Chief Men Among the Brethren*, 108.
4. Kelly, *Isaiah*, 17.

his discussions over the years.⁵ In his exegeses there was a wide reference to nineteenth-century theologians, showing Kelly's understanding of his contemporary writers.

In this book I will show that Kelly made extensive reference to historic and contemporary theologians, demonstrating the breadth of his reading and referencing and I now introduce a few of these as examples. In *Lectures Introductory to the Minor Prophets*, he accused Edward Pusey (1800–1882), one of the leaders of the Anglican Oxford Movement and Regius Professor of Hebrew at Christ Church, Oxford, and his fellows of encouraging "a leading current of unbelief."⁶ In Part 5 of *God's Inspiration of the Scriptures*, he wrote against George Rawlinson (1812–1902), Camden Professor of Ancient History at Oxford University, in his views on Esther.⁷ In writing about a mixture of scholars and clerics, he referred to Baden Powell (1796–1860), professor of geometry at Oxford University, and Samuel Davidson (1806–1896), Irish biblical scholar, in their interpretation of the first verse of Genesis.⁸ In the same work, he noted, "This Scripture is more exact than the natural philosophy of Mr. Baden Powell or the system of Aristotle or the exegesis of Dr. S. Davidson."⁹ Later he referred to Edward Perowne (1826–1906), Vice Chancellor of Cambridge University, and, in his footnote, to Smith's Dictionary of the Bible.¹⁰ He then went back to Wilhelm M.L. de Wette's comments made in 1805 about the Fall and indeed made several references to de Wette (1780–1849).¹¹ In response to the 1860 collection of essays, *Essays and Reviews*, he discussed Baron Bunsen's views on the Flood and looked at Egyptian records.¹² In *The Higher Criticism* he commented on the views of J.S. Mill (1806–1872) and Herbert Spencer (1820–1903), the Victorian philosophers.¹³ He referred in detail to Edmund Scherer (1815–1889), the Genevan Calvinist, and his views on the divine inspiration of Scripture and the work of Christ.¹⁴ He used *The Bible Treasury* to edit and to

5. Kelly, *Luke*, vii. Whitfield was also the author of *The Plymouth Brethren* (1908).
6. Kelly, *Minor Prophets*, xi.
7. Kelly, *God's Inspiration of the Scriptures*, 201.
8. Kelly, *The Pentateuch and Its Critics*, 18.
9. Ibid., 21.
10. Ibid., 29.
11. Ibid., 32.
12. Ibid., 33.
13. Kelly, *The Higher Criticism*, 20.
14. Kelly, "Notes of the Month," 70. Between 1856 and 1857 all monthly magazines

write book reviews of theological works. In July 1856 he reviewed *New Testament Millenarianism* (1855) by Samuel Waldgrave (1817–1869).[15] In June 1895 he gave a review of *The Book of Daniel* by F.W. Farrar (1831–1903).[16] In his January 1888 edition of the magazine, Kelly wrote, "I have read Kuenen, Ewald, Bleck, Graf and looked at others."[17] In the same edition, on the subject of the Gadarene swine, he referred to Trenche, Mede, Lange, Farrar and Meyer.[18] Therefore in this one edition of his periodical, we realize the extent of Kelly's reading and referencing. Tim Grass, the Brethren historian, summed up this breadth of reference by commenting, "Kelly acquired a reputation as an exegete and textual critic of no mean ability, maintaining a correspondence with a range of biblical scholars and critics."[19]

Kelly's expertise as a translator also allowed him to argue with theologians. Kelly's individual translations were referred to with appreciation by biblical scholars from different schools of thought. It was while he was in Guernsey that he was invited to be involved with Bible translation by Samuel Prideaux Tregelles (1813–1875), a New Testament scholar associated with the Brethren.[20] Kelly's translation of Revelation was acknowledged with approval by the German critic G. Heinrich A. Ewald (1803–1875), who commented that it was "the best piece of English work of the kind that had ever come under my notice."[21] Kelly frequently made precise and insightful comments about scholarly biblical translations. In *On the Lord's*

---

include the "1st" as part of the date and belong to Volume 1. Volume 2 starts after January 1858 and thereafter the numbers run continuously.

15. Waldgrave, *New Testament Millenarianism* (1855). Waldgrave had been fellow of All Souls College, Oxford University and Bampton lecturer of 1854. Kelly, "New Testament Millenarianism," 71.

16. Kelly, "The Book of Daniel by F.W. Farrar," 352, reviewing Farrar, *The Book of Daniel* (1895).

17. Kelly, "Miracles and Infidelity," 3. Abraham Kuenen (1828–1891), Dutch Protestant theologian; Heinrich Ewald (1803–1875), German theologian; Wilhelm Bleck (1827–1875), German philologist working in South Africa; Karl Heinrich Graf (1815–1869), German Old Testament scholar and orientalist.

18. Francis Chenevix Trenche (1805–1886), English divine and author; Joseph Mede (1586–1639), English biblical scholar; Johann Peter Lange (1802–1884), German theologian; Frederic Farrar (1831–1903), school teacher, Anglican divine and author; Frederick Brotherton Meyer (1847–1929), Baptist pastor and evangelist.

19. Grass, *Gathering to His Name*, 151.

20. Cross, *The Irish Saint and Scholar*, 27.

21. Ibid., 28. Cross quotes in English translation from Ewald, *Jahrbucher* no. 11 (Gottingen: Dieterich, 1861), 247.

Announcement of Gentile Judgments, he referred to de Wette's and to David Levi's (Jewish scholar) translation of Ezekiel 38 verses 1 and 2. In "The Judgment and the Eternal State," he talked in detail about the translation of "crisis" and was not afraid to assert that "the Romish version (that is the Jerusalem Bible) is therefore much nearer the truth of God in this chapter than the Protestant Bible."[22] In making his own translation he sometimes rejected the Authorized Version and looked carefully at the Septuagint and Hebrew texts.

There is evidence that Kelly was appreciated as a writer and teacher in wider circles than the Brethren. His *Notes on the Epistle to the Romans* (1873) was recommended by William Sanday (1843–1920), Dean Ireland's Professor of Exegesis of Holy Scripture at Oxford University, and *In the Beginning* (1870), which was accepted by Gladstone for St Deniol's Library, by Archbishop Benson (1829–1896).[23] Kelly was also in correspondence with Henry Alford, Robert Scott, the lexicographer, Thomas Edwards, Sanday and other theologians.[24] In Kelly's letter of 8 September, 1897, he acknowledged that he received private letters from Archbishops Tait (1811–1882) and Benson, Bishops Ellicott (1819–1901), Westcott (1825–1901) and Wordsworth (1843–1911) and religious leaders such as Arthur Brown and Spurgeon.[25] There is also a contemporary tribute to Kelly's ability as an erudite teacher in a book by Charles Maurice Davies (1828–1910). In it the author, an Anglican clergyman, journalist and spiritualist, commented on Kelly's "critical and exegetical power," his detailed knowledge of Colenso's writing and contemporary theological controversy, and showed himself "well fitted to grapple with all its difficulties."[26] There were reviews in numerous religious and national newspapers to Kelly's books.[27]

22. Kelly, "Judgment," 290.

23. Pickering, *Chief Men Among the Brethren*, 108.

24. Ibid., 106. Henry Alford (1810–1871), textual critic, scholar and dean of Canterbury Cathedral; Robert Scott (1811–1887), lexicographer, Anglican clergyman and Master of Balliol College, Oxford University; Thomas Edwards (1837–1900), Principal of Bala College and University College of Aberystwyth and Moderator of the General Assembly of the Presbyterian Church.

25. Kelly, *Letters*, 8 September, 1897. "To P." Arthur Brown (1856–1963), American Presbyterian and missiologist; Charles Spurgeon (1834–1892), Baptist leader and preacher and theologian. Kelly wrote in this letter that he did not like to reveal the contents of letters by well-known public figures who had written to him.

26. Davies, *Unorthodox London*, 180, 182.

27. Cross, *The Irish Saint and Scholar*, 31. This refers to press notices in The Guardian and the Baptist Times.

There is a particular feature of Kelly's opus which is important to understand and which is significant for my choice of source material. Kelly did not produce books which might be appropriate for a systematic or dogmatic theologian. While he produced a few pamphlets and lectures revealing specialist interests, he generally wrote works in which he concentrated on teaching one particular biblical book. The practical reason for this approach was that many of these were either transcripts of his sermons or the development of series of lectures which he had previously given as teaching to the Brethren assemblies across London and to other members of the Christian public.[28] He expounded biblical texts, rather than followed a doctrinal scheme of teaching and this necessarily affects the way a researcher explores Kelly's theology.

The second reason for using this method of teaching was that Kelly believed that he needed to teach the whole of Scripture. Therefore a particular feature of his teaching was that he used his chosen text as a springboard to comment on several other biblical texts, which he felt clarified or modified the first. This was particularly advantageous in giving substance to his conviction about plenary inspiration, which can be distinguished from a more literalist understanding of Scripture. As a result, there is no compact, easily recognizable body of work for a researcher to use and this has necessitated a wide, general reading of Kelly's work from which relevant points have been extracted. However, when studying *The Bible Treasury*, it is clear that Kelly did write articles under specifically doctrinal titles, as well as teaching about complete biblical books in consecutive editions of the magazine. When examining his arguments and doctrines, I was able to select a particular series of articles which focused on these subjects. The relevant articles are detailed in the footnotes of each chapter, as well as in the bibliography.

The other source material which I have used consists of articles by Darby, Bellett and a few other well known Brethren teachers. I feel justified in so doing, because Kelly edited Darby's and Bellett's works and he included articles from them and other Brethren teachers in the magazine of which he was overall editor. While I have mainly concentrated on articles where Kelly is the acknowledged author, I have also used articles by others with whom Kelly was in correspondence and whose expertise he admired.

I will be making references to two other sources of information about Kelly. There is a collection of letters in the Archives of the Christian

---

28. Ibid., 55, 86.

Brethren, held in the University of Manchester, written by Kelly to friends and Brethren leaders, which give us valuable understanding of his concerns. They are dated 1844–1906 and there is a note inserted at the beginning of the collection, explaining that no one knows where the originals are but these typed copies have been made by E.B. Dolamore, (died 1948), a missionary in St. Vincent between 1896 and 1911, who knew Kelly very well. These letters have been xeroxed from the copies and have been supplied by Edwin Cross. I have used these letters, having no reason to doubt their authenticity, but being careful to use points from them which are corroborated by teachings from his wider works.

Secondly, Kelly's library consisted of over 15,000 volumes and, before he died, he bequeathed it anonymously to the Middlesbrough Public Library.[29] It included the great biblical codices, works of the Church Fathers and many works of ecclesiastical history and theology.[30] As part of my research I have visited the library in Middlesbrough and noted the many and varied works such as those of Origen and Suso and other German mystics.[31] There are also works by de Wette, and four volumes of *Tracts for the Times*.[32] I will be referring to books which were in his library and which he quoted in his work.

In justifying the subject of my research for this book, I affirm that not very much has been written about William Kelly. In Roy F. Coad's *A History of the Brethren Movement* (1976) and Tim Grass's *Gathering to His Name* (2006), there are short summaries of William Kelly's life and ministry but both books concentrate on the Open Brethren movement and Kelly was more closely associated with the Moderate Exclusive movement of the Brethren.[33] As Kelly's reputation as an outstanding Bible teacher is acknowledged by Grass and Coad, it would seem worthwhile to examine the texts of his teaching in more depth.[34] In 2004, Edwin Cross published

---

29. *Index to BT*, Preface, xv.

30. Ibid.

31. Origen, ed. Delarus, *Opera Omnia*, 7 vols, 1857; Suso, trans. Bevan, (1895).

32. de Wette, *Introduction to the Literature of the Old Testament*, 3rd ed. (1892). *Tracts for the Times*, 4 vols, 1833–1834 (1840).

33. Grass, *Gathering to His Name*, 201–06. There were various divisions of the Exclusive Brethren, after their disagreement with the Open Brethren. By the Moderate Exclusive Brethren, I mean the Glanton and Kelly Brethren. 1879 was the date of the division between Darby and Kelly over ecclesiastical matters. However, despite the division, Kelly never lost his regard for Darby as a leading theologian.

34. Grass, *Gathering to His Name*, 151.

The Irish Saint and Scholar: A Biography of William Kelly but, while this book includes some interesting anecdotes and references to Kelly's life and work, it is very much a book of personal appreciation, rather than critical, theological assessment. There has been an M. Phil thesis which has examined Kelly's writings about science and theology but it mainly looks at Kelly's response to contemporary scientific debates, whereas I intend to major on theological issues and the debates within the Victorian Church.[35] Therefore I consider that there is a need for more academic critical research into his works.

Neither has Kelly's attempt to engage with theological debate been acknowledged by Church historians. Perhaps because he has been firmly categorized as a Brethren teacher, there has not been research into his writings on subjects of important theological debate in Victorian society. Grayson Carter, in his book *Evangelical Seceders from the Church of England c1800–1850*, has looked in detail at why several early Brethren, including Darby, seceded from the Church of England but the dating necessarily excludes Kelly.[36] General histories of the nineteenth-century church, such as Owen Chadwick's *The Victorian Church*, do not consider the Brethren as being significant enough to have any mention in their histories. This is a pity as the Brethren had much more influence on the evangelical Christian community than might have been surmised from their numerical strength.[37] While the Brethren had many intellectuals and academics amongst their leaders, they did not regard academic theological argument as their primary concern as believers. In addition, as their movement grew on an *ad hoc* basis, there was no acknowledged Brethren "school of theology."

Amongst the Brethren, it is mainly Darby who has been studied, but Kelly was a much more articulate teacher and scholarly writer than Darby. Also, in terms of Brethren research, there has been a tendency to look at the polarization of the Brethren movement, through its division into the Open and Exclusive Brethren. Kelly, as part of the Moderate Exclusive movement, was admired by both the Open and Exclusive Brethren. Studying Kelly can enrich our understanding of Brethren theology and shed light on a wider movement of biblical theology which continued into the twentieth century. Contextual hermeneutics has stressed the significance of the community in

---

35. Malcolm L. Taylor, "Born for the Universe."
36. Carter, *Evangelical Seceders*.
37. Coad, *A History of the Brethren Movement*, 11, 166, 206.

the process of interpreting a text.[38] Steven Katz has argued that in defining mystic spirituality, once thought to be individualistic, the context of belief is always pertinent to understanding of the teaching.[39] Therefore it is important that we see Kelly in his context as part of the Brethren movement, as well as examining his merits as an individual Bible teacher.

KELLY IN HIS BRETHREN CONTEXT

In looking at Kelly in the context of the Brethren, I now examine the influence of Darby on his intellectual formation. Kelly had been reading Darby's teaching since 1845 but Kelly was a scholar in his own right and pursued his own theological views. After his meeting with Darby, Kelly was invited to attend a Brethren conference in London and was impressed by Darby's discourse.[40]

Kelly shared the same viewpoint as Darby on several issues. Darby was a millenarian and a dispensationalist but, in disassociation with other Victorian dispensationalists, he believed that each dispensation was not clearly defined in its transition to the next one.[41] Dispensationalism was also tied into his belief in the ruin of the church. According to Darby, each dispensation had started well but had ended in disaster. Darby's biographer explained, "Darby did not believe in restoring the primitive church, because God does not restore what is fallen."[42] Therefore Darby's admiration for the early church, as portrayed in the book of Acts, was tempered by the belief that a return to such a state was impossible and that the early Church Fathers were not to be held in uncritical veneration.

However, Darby and Kelly had some clear differences of opinion. They held different views on infant baptism, Darby being a supporter of paedo-baptism and Kelly of adult–baptism. Darby was sometimes controversial when he taught about the sufferings of Christ and included non-atoning suffering of the future Jewish remnant as part of Christ's work.[43] In contrast, Kelly's defense of orthodox Christology undergirded all his works, whether it was in the context of the Victorian Broad Church or of arguments within

---

38. Thiselton, *New Horizons*, 6, 65.
39. Katz, "Editor's Introduction," in *Mysticism and Sacred Scripture*, 3.
40. Kelly, *John Nelson Darby*, 9.
41. Weremchuk, *John Nelson Darby*, 79.
42. Ibid., 82.
43. Burnham, *A Story of Conflict*, 211–12.

the Brethren movement. Kelly and Darby also held different views about church authority, which I will explain in the next section of this chapter.

Despite these differences, Kelly expressed enormous personal admiration for Darby. Kelly later wrote that, before his first meeting with Darby, "I had conceived, because of his love and testimony to Christ, profound respect and warm affection."[44] Kelly fully supported Darby's stand against Newton in Plymouth at that time because he thought that Newton's Christology was heretical.[45] Kelly admired Darby's spiritual leadership and his modest living standards.[46] While Kelly admired Darby's ability to speak in public, he admitted that Darby's written style was difficult to understand.[47] On this subject Kelly reported that Darby had told him "You write to be read and understood. I only think on paper."[48] However, because of Darby's "unfaltering logic," and "instant and powerful grasp of the moral side" of a subject, Kelly thought that Darby's writings merited his editorship.[49] In fact, we know most of Darby's writings through Kelly's editorship. Kelly admired Darby's concern for the poor, his desire to excuse faults in others when he perceived true spiritual devotedness, his dislike of pretension and his championship of theological truth. He summed up his estimation of Darby's character with the words—"This then is my conviction, that a saint more true to Christ's name and word I never knew or heard."[50]

Newton's unorthodox Christology and his ecclesiastical position were evidenced from 1838 to 1845.[51] Although Kelly was not directly and immediately involved in the Brethren controversy which resulted, in his later writings he strongly criticized Newton's views. Kelly's ecclesiology (particularly his belief in preserving the purity of the Church) also led him at this point in his life to side with the Exclusive wing of the Brethren. Kelly rejected Newton's belief in a "presiding elder" and a more authoritarian style of leadership which was beginning to be evidenced in Plymouth by

---

44. Kelly, *John Nelson Darby*, 3.
45. Ibid., 4. Cf. a fuller account of Newton's views in chapter 5.
46. Ibid., 5.
47. Ibid., 10–11.
48. Ibid., 11.
49. Ibid.
50. Ibid., 21.
51. Ibid., 3. Newton's teaching as to order in the church was different to that of Darby. He feared disorder in the church and preferred the idea of "a presiding elder" and caution about an open teaching ministry. Cf. Grass, *Gathering to His Name*, 69.

1838.[52] Kelly later accused Newton and the assembly at Plymouth of having an independent church system, ministerialism, Judaism and a system of heterodoxy.[53] What made the division much more serious was the attitude of criticism towards Darby shown by the Bethesda assembly in Bristol, thus bringing about the division between the Exclusives and Open Brethren in 1848. Kelly later made his views quite clear when he wrote about the argument in 1896.[54] On the subject of Bethesda's acceptance of members of Newton's Plymouth assembly, Kelly thought that it was not enough to be sound in personal faith or neutral as regards evil because in such cases, "Neutrality is heinous sin, and this proportionate to knowledge."[55] This was one reason why the Open Brethren stood condemned. According to Kelly, members of the Bethesda assembly had read and condemned Newton's tracts (with their supposed heterodox views about Christ's sufferings) only after they had agreed to support the ten leaders of Bethesda, who had previously insisted that they could receive Christians from the Plymouth assembly.[56] According to Jonathan Burnham, this argument had a dramatic effect on the reputation and effectiveness of the Brethren movement, and again this restricted the influence of its key theologians. It "transformed a once-thriving religious movement into yet another example of the schismatic tendencies within nineteenth-century English and Irish Evangelicalism."[57] It is likely that because of his association with Darby and the Exclusive Brethren, Kelly's learning and teachings have not been sufficiently recognized by the rest of the Christian world.

In 1877 the Ryde assembly split about a man's marriage to his deceased wife's sister. Kelly's friend and founder-member of the Brethren, Edward Cronin, unwittingly worshipped with the rigorist faction at Ryde and Darby denounced him for promoting disunity because he thought such a division at Ryde wrong. As a result at the Central London "brothers" meeting, where such issues were discussed, the Exclusive Brethren made

52. Ibid., 221.

53. Noel, *The History of the Brethren*, vol. 1, 224–25. By an independent church system, Kelly meant not agreeing with other Brethren teachers; by ministerialism, being dominated by one or two leaders; by Judaism, clinging to what Kelly saw as a legal system of church order which he linked with forms of worship in the Old Testament; by heterodoxy, Newton's lower Christology.

54. Kelly, *The Doctrine of Christ and Bethesdaism*.

55. Ibid., 4.

56. Ibid., 5, 9.

57. Burnham, *A Story of Conflict*, 237.

the Kennington assembly excommunicate Cronin in 1879.[58] Kelly disagreed with this decision because "Ecclesiastical error even if real and grave never approaches the denial of the doctrine of Christ."[59] As a result Darby parted from Kelly in terms of church doctrine and from then on there was a division between the Exclusives (led by Darby until his death) and the Moderate Exclusives led by Kelly, lasting until the further division between the "Kelly" and "Glanton" Brethren in 1909. This division turned out to be significant because after Darby's death when the Exclusives became more extreme, Kelly was not part of them and was in fact respected as a Bible teacher by both the Open and Exclusive Brethren groups.

Despite the disagreement over Cronin, Darby made a special point before his death of claiming Kelly's friendship.[60] Kelly admired Darby but was capable of criticizing him, as shown in his letters. On 19 October 1881, he acknowledged that Darby had sometimes demonstrated that he could be untrustworthy and even when Kelly had been editing an 1832 paper of Darby's for the *Collected Writings*, he had noticed that they "betray the same extravagance of acrimony and abuse" which was later revealed in Darby's dealings with Edward Cronin.[61] In his letter to "My dear J" of November 1881, Kelly acknowledged that Darby was a danger to the Brethren because he was held in such admiration, even "idolatry." Kelly wrote about Darby's "bad tongue and spirit" and the detrimental effect it had on the Brethren.[62] When writing to "Dear H.," who was probably Heyman Wreford, in December 1881, Kelly could even affirm, "We are truly glad to be outside such a reign of evil and terror."[63]

The other two internal Brethren controversies which Kelly took part in were after Darby's death and show his concern for orthodox Christology and his disapproval of one of the more questionable teachers in the Exclusive Brethren. The Reading division took place in 1885 over C.E. Stuart (1823–1903) who "taught that Christ made propitiation by presenting his

---

58 Ibid., 54.

59. Noel, *History of the Brethren*, vol. 1, 313.

60. Ibid., 62.

61. Kelly, *Letters*, 19 October, 1881 and 2 November, 1882. These letters are addressed to "my dear brother," but follow on from a letter addressed to "Dear J.," dated 12 February, 1878.

62. Kelly, *Letters*, November 1881, "To my dear J."

63. Ibid., 1 December, 1881.

blood in heaven after his death."[64] Stuart's teachings meant that they detracted from the sufferings of Christ acting as propitiation.[65] This touched on the subject of not only the nature of Christ but also of his work of Atonement, and, as I will show in chapter 5, that subject was of supreme importance to Kelly. Kelly wrote an explicit answer to Stuart's heterodoxy and also wrote answers to it in two issues of *The Bible Treasury*.[66] He summed up his views on Stuart's teaching by calling it "the ghostly work after death and in heaven is a ghastly fable, and calls for abhorrence."[67]

The Bexhill division took place in 1890, when Bexhill refused to accept a visitor who came from the assembly where F.E. Raven (1837–1903) was teaching. Raven taught "that in person Christ was God, but in condition He was a man, a view which has been criticized as Apollinarian."[68] Raven also denied that Christ received his human flesh from Mary and that "eternal life" was not an experience of all believers, but would be entered into at some point in the future, even after death.[69] The assembly at Park Street, London, exonerated Raven and cut off all those who disagreed with him. Raven's teaching about eternal life continued until 1929 and merged into the denial of Christ's Eternal Sonship by the Taylor leadership of the Exclusive Brethren.[70] Kelly wrote numerous articles criticizing Raven's theology which appeared in *The Bible Treasury*, thereby aligning himself more clearly with the Moderate Exclusive Brethren than with the Exclusive Brethren. Again this meant that his teaching was accessible to a wider range of Brethren. I contend that the place of the Moderate Exclusives (known later as the Kelly and Glanton groups) has not been sufficiently acknowledged by Brethren historians.

---

64. Grass, *Gathering to His Name*, 204.

65. Noel, *History of the Brethren*, vol. 2, 456.

66. Kelly, *Propitiation*, and Kelly, "The Inspiration of the Scriptures," 59–61. Kelly, "Scripture Queries and Answers," 256.

67. Noel, *History of the Brethren*, vol. 2, 456.

68. Grass, *Gathering to His Name*, 205. Apollinarius was a fourth century bishop who believed that in the incarnate Christ the divine Logos took the place of a human mind or soul.

69. Ibid.

70. Noel, *History of the Brethren*, vol. 2, 563.

KELLY IN HIS NINETEENTH-CENTURY RELIGIOUS AND SECULAR CONTEXT

British Christians in the nineteenth century were influenced by what was happening in Ireland politically and theologically. The political movement to emancipate Roman Catholics in England stemmed from the desire to give freedom and education to Roman Catholics in Ireland. The Protestant reaction to this movement had an effect on evangelicals in the Church of England and the Church of Ireland.[71] Darby and Kelly came out of the Church of Ireland and their Irish background tempered their beliefs. The furor in England over the possibility of disestablishment, increasingly lay and secular influence within the church, as well as the ecclesiastical sympathies of Oxford and Cambridge students, all had an effect on the Victorians in the years 1840-70.[72] Kelly referred in his exegesis to the principles of church disestablishment and the problems of Erastianism endemic to his times.[73] In the years 1854-56, reforms took place in the Universities of Oxford and Cambridge, as dissenters claimed the right to be educated there. It was during his visit to Oxford in 1830 that Darby had a significant influence on Brethren seceders, such as Henry Bellendon Bulteel (1805-1866), Newton, Francis W. Newman (1805-1897) and George Vicesimus Wigram (1805-1879).[74]

The increasingly important place of the Roman Catholic Church in England in the nineteenth century and English consciousness and fear of this were reflected in Kelly and Darby's writings.[75] Between the years 1822 and 1825, Catholic Relief bills were being passed in London on behalf of the Irish poor. In 1829 the Catholic Emancipation Bill was passed. The position of the Roman Catholic Church in Ireland was very strong: it was feared by British Protestants there and derided by the Brethren seceders. Evangelicals in Ireland were particularly fearful when Parliament abolished two out of four Irish Protestant archbishops and eight bishops.[76] This move

---

71. Crowther, *Church Embattled*, 60. Crowther shows how the Evangelical Alliance which began in 1846 came largely from the 1845 meeting of evangelicals in Liverpool who wanted to protest against Peel's decision to give government aid to the Roman Catholic college at Maynooth.

72. Chadwick, *The Victorian Church*, Part 2, 480-81.

73. Kelly, *Matthew*, 246, 248.

74. Grass, *Gathering to His Name*, 31.

75. Kelly, *Matthew*, 231 and Darby, *Ecclesiastical*, 6 and 15.

76. Chadwick, *The Victorian Church*, Part 1, 56.

proved unsatisfactory even to the Catholics as the money saved went to the Church of Ireland rather than to the country itself. In 1834 there was considerable clamor to disestablish the Church of Ireland and this led to restlessness throughout the Church. If the Church of Ireland was considered by some to be weak in standing up to the Roman Catholic Church, Darby objected to "the pervasive Erastianism of the Church of Ireland and to its ministerial hierarchy, the Church's secularity and its apparent indifference to the leading of the Spirit."[77] Darby was angry with the "unwarranted state intrusion" of Archbishop Magee, but also felt frustrated with his evangelical clerical contemporaries in the Church of Ireland, who were more interested in the threat of Catholic emancipation than in Darby's objections to Erastianism.[78] In 1827 he wrote in "Considerations addressed to the Archbishop of Dublin and Clergy who signed the petition to the House of Commons for Protection," stating that "the Charge is a mere substitution of the Civil sovereign for the Pope."[79] In 1832 he wrote a scathing attack on Richard Whately (1787–1863), the Archbishop of Dublin, for cooperating with the Roman Catholics about education. Carter observed, "by the mid 1830s, Darby seems to have regarded himself as being outside the established church."[80] However, Kelly, while sympathizing with Darby's frustrations over the established Church, did not have to fight those historic battles himself and was therefore more measured in his rhetoric against the Catholic and Anglican churches than Darby.

Kelly reacted strongly against the developing views of the Broad Church faction within the Church of England. The views of these more liberal theologians were expressed in *Essays and Reviews* which was published in 1860.[81] Darby had written a critique of the work but Kelly inserted comments about the authors' views in a more diverse manner in his exegeses. That Frederick Temple (1821–1902), one of the contributors to *Essays and Reviews*, became Archbishop of Canterbury in 1896 confirmed Kelly in his suspicion of the orthodoxy of the Anglican Church.

---

77. Carter, *Anglican Evangelicals*, 211.
78. Ibid., 212.
79. Darby, *Considerations*.
80. Carter, *Anglican Evangelicals*, 217.
81. These involved essays by Frederick Temple (1821–1902), Rowland Williams (1817–1870), Baden Powell (1796–1860), Henry Bristow Wilson (1803–1888), Charles Goodwin (1817–1878), Mark Pattison (1813–1884) and Benjamin Jowett (1817–1893).

The Broad Church movement was supportive of the development theories of the nineteenth century which took two main forms. One was expounded by Thomas Arnold (1795–1842), who wanted to minimize dogma, increase the part played by the laity, provide moral leadership and saw the Scriptures on a par with other ancient texts.[82] Samuel Taylor Coleridge (1772–1834) was one of the key influences of the Broad Church movement and he rejected plenary inspiration.[83] Frederick Denison Maurice (1805–1872), scholar, Anglican priest and Christian socialist activist, thought that "every man could apprehend God, and that every man possessed a spiritual vision."[84] The views of Arnold, Coleridge, Connop Thirlwall (1797–1875) and Julius Hare (1795–1855) were based on those of Bartold Georg Niebuhr (1776–1831) and Ferdinand Christian Baur (1792–1860), German historians who believed that civilization was progressing both materially and morally. Baur was influenced by the German philosopher Friedrich Wilhelm Joseph von Schelling (1775–1854), "the idealistic philosopher of history" and by Georg Hegel's idea of progress.[85] German philosophical and religious works were not well known in the first half of the nineteenth century in England but this changed in the second half of the century, which accounts for Kelly's concern for them in *The Bible Treasury* during that period. The Broad Church theologians were, to begin with, more influenced by the theories of historical development, than theological challenges.[86] Temple's essay "The Education of the World" adopted and made more widely known the idea that humanity was gradually developing its moral faculties and that this entailed spiritual progress.[87] This idea of development was strenuously opposed by Kelly.[88] Wilson used his belief in development of the "clerisy" to follow Coleridge's original idea and stress with Arnold the importance of education.[89] This belief in development led to the idea that the Old Testament was not a perfect guide

---

82. Jay, *Faith and Doubt*, 27.
83. Ibid., 53.
84. Chadwick, *The Victorian Church*, Part 1, 350.
85. Reventlow, *History of Biblical Interpretation*, vol. 4, 276, 281.
86. Crowther, *Church Embattled*, 72.
87. Ibid., 73.
88. Kelly, *Pentateuch*, xxiv–xxv.
89. Crowther, *Church Embattled*, 107.

for nineteenth-century Christians.[90] Kelly's teaching on the Old Testament opposed this Broad Church view.

The other theory of development which was important was the theory of religious development advocated by John Henry Newman (1801–1890), showing that the church had to be the contemporary interpreter of the Bible and that there needed to be an acceptable doctrinal development. Newman argued that Christianity must develop according to the way it related to the world around it.[91] The history of the Tractarian movement, especially its beginnings between 1833 and 1841, was also an important time for the early Brethren.[92] Timothy F. Stunt, a Brethren historian, has already pointed to key similarities and differences between the two movements.[93]

Stunt reminds us that Darby had some background as a high churchman, just as Newman had an evangelical background.[94] He explained that intense spiritual exercise was at the basis of both movements—"it began as a reaction like the Oxford Movement to the worldly and material values of an Erastian church."[95] Stunt also pointed out that, just as the Brethren rejoiced in their lack of centralization, "in the case of the Oxford Movement, there was no official 'line' and the writers of the Tracts wrote quite independently and did not always agree."[96]

Newman and Pusey emphasized the visible church (through apostolic succession) rather than the invisible church. As Brethren assemblies became more established, Darby and Kelly came to believe in the visible church (as in the Brethren assemblies), although Kelly always had a more measured view of a clearly defined line dividing the two and both of them rejected the Anglican doctrine of apostolic succession. Kelly acknowledged in his writings that there might well be members of the true church both in the Anglican and Roman Catholic churches.[97] On the subject of apostolic succession and papal authority, Stunt made an interesting observation about the two movements:

---

90. Ibid., 73.

91. Newman, *An Essay on the Development of Christian Doctrine*, 58.

92. *90 Tracts for the Times* were written by a variety of High Church clergy between these dates.

93. Stunt, "Two Nineteenth-century Movements," 221–31.

94. Ibid., 225.

95. Ibid., 227.

96. Ibid., 231.

97. Kelly, *Lectures on the Book of Daniel*, 104.

> The papal view of authority has always laid emphasis on the succession and authority handed down, while, very broadly speaking, the conciliar theory has maintained that the Church collectively, or through her various delegates, is the ultimate sanction of authority ... Darby and his followers took a more "conciliar" view, regarding the voice of the local church as a whole to be the voice of authority ... the authoritarian leadership in the exclusive development.[98]

Thus Kelly, writing about the authority of the church, apostolic succession and right decision-making in the church, did so against the background of Tractarian as well as Darby's views on the subject. However, rather than wanting to return to reformed Catholicism, he did not believe that the Reformation had gone far enough, especially with regard to church doctrine—"The Reformation never touched the true question of the church."[99] Kelly also had a far lower view of the Church Fathers than the Tractarians did.

Stunt astutely remarked about the interpretation of Scripture and authority within the Brethren,

> The Brethren's interpretation of Scripture was their own, but the question still remained: where was the authority going to be within their own churches? Just as Calvin replaced the authority of Papal interpretation with the authority of the interpretation of the consistory of Geneva, so sooner or later the Brethren had to decide where their authoritative interpretation was to be found.[100]

That is why it is so important that Kelly edited Darby's works and often endorsed them in his teaching. Napoleon Noel (1853–1932) in his history of the Brethren movement, said that Kelly and Darby's works were often referred to as "the ancient landmarks."[101]

There were other similarities and differences between the Tractarians and the Brethren to which Stunt has not drawn attention. Chadwick has shown that it is not easy to define the essence of the Tractarian movement and I would suggest that is also true for the Brethren movement. Both were born against the background of politics and religion in Ireland; the Reform Act and Erastianism in England; the significant Arminianism of eighteenth-century evangelical fervor; the release of imagination and a new sensibility

---

98. Stunt, "Two Nineteenth-century Movements," 229.
99. Kelly, *Matthew*, 233.
100. Stunt, "Two Nineteenth-century Movements," 228.
101. Noel, *History*, vol. 1, 257.

about the history of the early church.[102] Chadwick has shown that the Tractarian movement was about worship and moral needs, "an impulse of the heart and conscience."[103] Even the doctrine of reserve, which is normally associated with the Tractarian movement, had some parallels with Exclusive Brethren belief.[104] Paul Ricoeur (1913–2005), the linguist and philosopher, has shown that revelation shows a tension between showing and hiding and such a tension revealed the power of symbol both for the Tractarians and the Brethren.[105] Paul Ricoeur has identified symbol as "a double-meaning linguistic expression that requires an interpretation and interpretation is a work of understanding that aims at deciphering symbols."[106] I will explore Kelly's use of symbolism in chapter 7 of this book. Kelly as well as Newman was cautious about the "superficial" evangelism of some groups in which emotion was made public and, indeed, of "light" emotion in worship.[107] Both had an interest in tradition but also a desire for reform.[108] For Newman, worship was paramount but he was also "rigorously intellectual."[109] That and his desire for holiness and obedience are mirrored in Kelly's writings. Pusey, in a similar way to Brethren writers, had a mystical sense of the individual's incorporation into the body of Christ. Like Kelly, his language was often mystical in his sermons.[110] Both movements were opposed to theological liberalism in all its forms.

What set them apart was the issue of Tractarian support for the traditional church creeds, though the Brethren endorsed the orthodox belief behind those creeds. The Brethren were far more critical of the early Church Fathers than were the Tractarians.[111] The Tractarians were devoted to liturgical forms but, even though the Brethren shunned these, their own liturgical traditions developed within the "breaking of bread" service. However, while High Church worship appealed to the senses, the Brethren worship halls had a simple decor. While the Brethren pursued the Reformation

102. Chadwick, *The Spirit of the Oxford Movement*, 148.
103. Ibid., 1, 2.
104. Ibid., 26.
105. Ricoeur, *Freud and Philosophy*, 5, 8.
106. Ibid., 9.
107. Kelly, "The Types of Scripture V1. The Priesthood," 184.
108. Chadwick, *Spirit of the Oxford Movement*, 29.
109. Ibid., 33.
110. Ibid., 39.
111. Toon, *Evangelical Theology 1833–1856*, 15.

ideal of the individual Christian interpreting the Scriptures, the Tractarians claimed that only the Church could take on that role.[112] Both were purist in their attitudes to doctrine. It is interesting that Peter Toon, in writing about the evangelical response to the Tractarians, has not mentioned the Brethren movement. I suggest that such parallels that I have briefly noted here indicate more similarities between the two movements than Stunt has explored in his article and that both responded to Victorian culture, politics and religion in diverse, but also in similar, ways.

THREE KEY CONVICTIONS WITHIN KELLY'S THEOLOGY

I will shortly be explaining the subject matter of each chapter, but, before doing so, it is worth noting three of Kelly's key convictions because they inform all his theological understanding. These were—particular eschatological convictions; belief in the "Fall" of mankind; and belief in a high Christology. In my view, these beliefs undergirded not only Kelly's understanding of the biblical text but also his use of language, which I will explore in more detail in chapters 6 and 7.

In terms of eschatology, the concepts of millenarianism, dispensationalism, and the return of Christ known as "the rapture," were fundamental to the understanding of Kelly's theology and it is necessary to have some understanding of them when assessing Kelly's works. The "millennium" was the thousand year period of Christ's reign over the earth and the "rapture" was identified as Christ's coming for his church, before that time. Pre-millenarianism was the belief that Christ was going to come for the church before the great "millennium" took place; post-millenarianism was the belief that Christ would come again after this period. Dispensationalism was the belief that each period of human history was complete in itself and that God had a unique purpose for each period. Millenarianism was a popular theology in the nineteenth century and has been considered to be a panic reaction to world events, especially the French Revolution, the rise of Napoleon and the weakening of Britain's hold over Ireland.[113]

The identification of the Pope with the anti-Christ was a common Victorian Protestant assumption.[114] This linked with expectations of the end times and the identification of Rome as the Babylon of Revelation.

112. Ibid., 29.
113. Bebbington, *Evangelicalism*, 83.
114. Dickens, *Barnaby Rudge*.

This explains the paranoia surrounding Archbishop William Magee's (1766–1831) "charge" in Ireland and the Victorian fear that Peel would allowing the establishment of the Roman Catholic hierarchy in England.[115] However, it should be noted that, while Darby referred outspokenly to the place of the Pope in end time prophecy, Kelly, while rejecting Catholicism as a religious system, was much more circumspect in his denunciations of the Pope, and much more accepting of the individual's genuine belief, whatever his church.[116] He was also cautious about the ultimate importance of prophecy. He warned, "Prophecy never does really deepen our souls in the ways of God."[117] Kelly's avoidance of arguments about prophecy ensured that his writings had a longer lasting significance because they were not narrowly sectarian in their tenor. However, he was in agreement with the pre-millenarian point of view and supported Darby's position.

In the nineteenth century millenarianism was part of the evolving continuum of theological belief which took on particular characteristics within evangelicalism. At the beginning of the Evangelical Revival in 1743 in America, Jonathan Edwards had believed that the millennium, the perfect thousand years of Christ's reign on earth, would start in America and would be ushered in by the conversion of the heathen.[118] In the early nineteenth century in England two schools of thought became more popular, the "historicist school" of pre-millennialists, which was the general Church of England evangelical position, and was supported by the Prophecy Investigation Society and by the Bampton Lectures of 1854, given by Samuel Waldgrave, the future Bishop of Carlisle, and reviewed critically by Kelly who had a more futuristic view.[119] I make particular reference to this school of thought and some interesting contrasts and parallels with Kelly's work in chapter 5. Secondly there was the futuristic school, represented by Edward Irving's (1792–1834) Apostolic Church, and Darby.[120] Darby believed in

---

115. Bebbington, *Evangelicalism*, 103. Archbishop Magee used his regular exhortation to his clergy in Ireland (known as "the charge") to point out the dangers of the Roman Catholic Church gaining ascendancy and the necessity of guarding the Protestant Church in Ireland. He opposed the movement for Catholic emancipation.

116. Kelly, *Matthew*, 96. This broader acceptance of Roman Catholics was also shown in John Wesley's theology.

117. Kelly, *Pentateuch*, 72.

118. Bebbington, *Evangelicalism*, 63.

119. Ibid., 84. I have already referred to these lectures earlier in the chapter.

120. Cf. Stephen C. Orchard, "English Evangelical Eschatology 1790–1850," for a fuller discussion of this subject.

"the secret rapture of the saints, the tribulation and Christ's coming with the saints to reign over the earth after the tribulation."[121] This view led to a marked dispensationalism, which is also evident in Kelly's works.

Pre-millennialism, with its detailed working out of biblical prophecies, also encouraged a higher view of Scriptural interpretation. Evangelicals were also influenced by the teaching on literal inspiration of the Scriptures by the Scottish evangelical, James Alexander Haldane (1768–1851), and by Henry Drummond (1786–1860), Tory M.P. and Irvingite, who became Vice President of the The Jews Society in 1823.[122] Until Darby's time many evangelicals had argued that Old Testament prophecies should be taken spiritually not literally, but literalist views on prophecy gave a new significance to prophecies about Jews. The literal interpretation about the place of Jews in the future was an important part of Kelly's theological paradigm. Although Paul Wilkinson has shown that belief in separate dispensations was part of traditional evangelical theology and cannot just be attributed to Darby, Darby's emerging belief in pre-millennial rapture had a marked effect on the nascent Brethren movement and this was shown in his involvement in conferences on eschatology.[123]

Where these three beliefs came together was in Powerscourt, Ireland—an important place for Darby's development and for the views of the early Brethren on prophecy. It is undeniable that such teaching had a long lasting influence on Kelly, even though he was not present. Robert Daly (1783–1872) was the evangelical rector of Powerscourt, the future bishop of Cashel and Darby's mentor. From 1826 he became interested in the prophetic movement and in miraculous gifts.[124] Regular Christian conferences were held at Powerscourt, the home of Theodosia Wingfield, Countess Powerscourt (1800–1836), in order to discuss the two subjects. In 1831 Daly invited thirty-five clergy, one hundred and fifty-one laymen and twenty women from all denominations. This gathering transcended parish and denominational boundaries.[125] Darby's interaction with the delegates proved him to be a powerful leader and gave him an ecclesiastically wide sphere of influence. The divergence between the evangelical Anglicans and the Brethren can be demonstrated in the aftermath of Powerscourt.

121. Carter, *Anglican Evangelicals*, 223.
122. Bebbington, *Evangelicals*, 84, 82.
123. Wilkinson, *For Zion's Sake*, 100.
124. Carter, *Anglican Evangelicals*, 201.
125. Grass, *Gathering to His Name*, 26.

When Darby went on to lead a new movement, Daly stayed in the Anglican Church.[126]

Prophecy which was a subject of discussion at Powerscourt continued to be a major teaching point for the Brethren. In the conference of 1832 there was much conflict and Darby emerged as a leader of the extreme millennialists. By the time of the third conference in September 1833, the possibility of separation and secession from the Anglican Church was a major topic. Newton later saw these conferences as the start of the Brethren movement and also believed that they planted the problems and divisions which were to come.[127] As Darby became more dominant, evangelical Anglican ministers such as Daly increasingly distanced themselves from his views. Later those meeting in Powerscourt started to align themselves with the early Brethren meeting in Aungier Street, Dublin. At the time of the conferences Lady Powerscourt seceded as did several leading Anglican families. The last three Powerscourt conferences, held between 1834 and 1836, were firmly under the authority of Darby.

The doctrine of the Fall and its pivotal place in the interpretation of the rest of the Bible was made clear in Kelly's teaching. He taught its truth using unequivocal language:

> Leave out the Fall; fail to keep it before you and test all with that in mind, and you will be wrong about every result. Next to Christ Himself, and what we have by and in Him, there is nothing of greater importance than the confession of the truth, both that God created, and that His creation is in ruins. Your judgment alike of God and man will be falsified; your estimate of the past and your expectations of the future will all be in vain, unless you steadily remember that God now in all His dealings with man acts on the solemn fact of sin—original and universal sin.[128]

However, considering the variety of interpretations the Fall has received in church history, we need to ask about the particular emphasis of Kelly's interpretation.[129] He referred to the Vincentian Canon of the accep-

---

126. Ibid., 27.

127. Ibid., 28. Grass quotes from Newton's notebooks, in which, many years later, he looked back at the start of the Brethren movement.

128. Kelly, *Pentateuch*, 45.

129. According to Williams, *The Ideas of the Fall and of Original Sin*, 246, there are five key questions to be asked about the Fall:
  (i) the literal or allegorical interpretation of Genesis 3,
  (ii) the original state of man before the Fall,

tance of a doctrine by the church—*ubique, semper et ab omnibus*.[130] Kelly would have agreed with Norman P. Williams in his 1924 Bampton Lectures about the Fall that the Church Fathers had not always accepted the doctrine of original sin but, according to him, that did not take away from the truth of this doctrine, which he regarded as vital. While Kelly's paradigm relied on the dogmatic assertion of the early chapters of Genesis, he employed allegorical and typological ways of reading the text as well. He criticized Davidson and German biblical critics for treating the Fall as "a national mythos" because he felt that such an attitude detracted from its universal truth.[131] According to Kelly, the biblical account was "historical in the strictest and fullest sense."[132] He therefore rejected the full allegorization of Clement and Origen.[133] However, on other occasions he used the moral principles of the story of Genesis chapter 3 to go back to the principles of earthly choices and sometimes his writing came very near to acknowledgement of allegory, as when he saw the two named trees in paradise as representing the principles of obedience and life.[134]

For Kelly the story of the Fall was above all about the failure to acknowledge God's authority and the necessity of obedience, rather than simply "grave moral evil."[135] In his lectures he appealed, not only to correct interpretation of the text but also to practical Christian experience in showing the truth of the Fall and in his view this doctrine should never be weakened by the influence of modern biblical criticism. He was against what might be considered to be Pelagian error in teaching the frailty of human nature in consequence of the Fall and instead enjoined total corruption of human nature, in harmony with Augustine's views.[136] As he felt that the Fall affected the condition of succeeding generations, the doctrine of

---

(iii) of the exact nature of the disastrous consequences flowing from the first man's sin,
(iv) how these consequences were perpetuated—physiological or social hereditary—and
(v) present condition of human nature, whether grave or slight.
Kelly's works answer all these questions.

130. Ibid., 186 and Kelly, *John*, 47.
131. Kelly, *Pentateuch*, Introduction, xli.
132. Ibid., 23.
133. Kelly, "The Early Chapters of Genesis. Chap. iii. 1," 129.
134. Kelly, *Pentateuch*, 22.
135. Ibid., 19.
136. Cf. Williams, *The Fall*, 395, for a clear distinction between the Pelagian and Augustinian view of the state of human nature after the Fall.

recapitulation was developed in his writing.[137] As man's nature had changed through the Fall, spiritual rebirth and the gift of a new nature were absolute necessities in order to know God.[138] According to this paradigm, all biblical history had to be read as part of the consequences of the Fall and technical knowledge of the text without renewal of heart was no advantage to the reader.[139]

In his implicit and explicit interpretations of the Fall, Kelly was quite clear about what it did not mean. He believed that the pre-Fall state of man was one of innocence, rather than righteousness. He taught against the idea of gradual change in man according to the theory of evolution, which advocated the idea that moral defects were only stages in man's development.[140] He thought that contemporary theologians had wrongly confused the idea of man being created in "the likeness of God" with "the image of God."[141] He also rejected an exclusive emphasis on the sins of the flesh meaning sexual sin, because he believed that the sin of disobedience was far more crucial.[142] Kelly was careful to guard against Gnosticism, which had been acknowledged as one of the heresies of the New Testament church and also of using Platonic philosophy to reinterpret Christianity. Gnosticism had always been essentially dualistic in nature and had forced the early Church Fathers to consider the origin of evil. In his lectures on John's Gospel, Kelly argued against the Jewish Gnostic philosopher, Philo, and against Platonism and the belief in eternal matter and against Manicheism.[143] Kelly rejected the idea that God could be an agent of evil, and for him, the narrative of the Fall was a clear example of positive theodicy.[144] While Kelly observed that the Church Fathers such as Origen and St. Gregory of Nyssa (335–395) were influenced by Gnosticism and even early Indian thought patterns on God's

---

137. Kelly, "The Fall of Man," 57.

138. Kelly, "The Serpent and the Woman's Seed," 128.

139. Kelly, *Romans*, 10.

140. Y. O. D., "Drummond on Evolution (Second Letter)," 334.

141. Kelly, *Pentateuch*, 38. For Kelly, the "likeness of God" meant true righteousness (which Kelly rejected in his understanding of human moral ability), and "the image of God" meant human ability to discern between good and evil, which he accepted as true.

142. Kelly, "The Early Chapters of Genesis Chap. iii 6, 7," 161.

143. Kelly, *John*, 16. Kelly went on to argue against the Christology of Basileides and the threat of Gnosticism.

144. Williams, *The Fall*, 265. Williams shows how at several points in church history and in Jewish theology, the Fall story of Genesis 3 is used as a theodicy to guard against the possibility that God could have created the evil "yecer" or imagination of man's heart.

all-encompassing nature, Kelly rejected the philosophy of "Hinduism," as making God the author of evil.[145] He explained that although the nature of the serpent was only disclosed by Scripture later, evil did not have the same place as in the Persian myth, when Ahriman was in conflict with Ormuzd. He concluded in one of his articles on Genesis 3, about the nature of Satan as a fallen angel, "Scripture knows no dualism but a rebel against the true God."[146] He vehemently denied that God could have been the agent of evil. There was a strong Pauline eisegesis into the Fall narrative and therefore the idea of inherited guilt was affirmed.

The Augustinian interpretation of the Fall necessitated harsh judgment of anything which man by himself could achieve. Kelly believed that mankind, before and after the Fall, possessed an immortal soul, which, as I shall show in chapter 4, was important to Kelly's understanding of the afterlife.[147] Through the Fall, according to Kelly, mankind acquired an increased moral capacity, which also made him miserable.[148] In the early chapters of Genesis there is an increasing sense of moral degradation which was shown particularly in Genesis chapter 6 and which Kelly linked with Greek mythology.[149] The judgments of God against Israel in the Old Testament were assumed by Kelly still to apply to Christianity in the nineteenth century and he gave the New Testament warnings against heresy as his justification for this view, as well as the criticisms he had against the established Church and the Roman Catholic Church.[150]

If the ruin of man was foundational for Kelly, so was his high Christology and therefore the cryptic words spoken by God at the end of the story of the Fall were interpreted as the promise of the Christ to come.[151] Kelly's high view of Christology characterized his arguments with any writer, Brethren or otherwise, who failed to uphold that standard. The significance of that view will be apparent in every chapter of this book for different reasons, but the subject was of central concern for the Victorians and that

---

145. Kelly, *John*, 13. Here we must accept Kelly's own definition of Hindu thought, though that description might not be acceptable to scholars of Hindu thought.

146. Kelly, "The Early Chapters of Genesis Chap. iii. 1," 130.

147. Kelly, *Pentateuch*, 18–19.

148. Ibid., 34.

149. Ibid., 40.

150. Kelly, *Romans*, 10.

151. Kelly, *Pentateuch*, 30–31. The cryptic words are found in Gen 3:15, "he will strike your head and you will strike his heel."

is why Kelly continually came back to the subject in his articles from 1890 onwards. This date coincided with the publication of Charles Gore's *Lux Mundi* which included the debate about Christ's self-awareness. Ironically Kelly sided with the Tractarians such as Henry Parry Liddon (1829–1890) and Pusey who opposed Gore and who opposed higher criticism. Kelly's high Christology was central to his objections to theologians of the Broad Church tradition. In defending his position, Kelly was in the tradition of the Church Fathers who always saw Christ as the center of biblical texts.[152]

A BRIEF SUMMARY OF THE PURPOSE AND CONTENTS OF THIS BOOK

Kelly's stated concern was not only to teach the Bible within the Brethren movement, but to help all those who were struggling with theological challenges and those who were confused. He wrote, "I wish to aid the feeble entangled by snares of the devil."[153] He also felt that those who had been "friendly to revelation" had also been feeble in their ability to defend biblical inspiration. He judged that evangelical scholarship had been weak and naïve. From this it seems that Kelly was an evangelical scholar who thought it worthwhile to answer the skeptics, but I would like to suggest that he was far more than this. The writer of the Preface to the Index of *The Bible Treasury* said of Kelly, "he desired neither to form nor belong to any school of thought, doctrine or interpretation."[154] It is because it is difficult to define his theology narrowly that Kelly's works are interesting and important. Based on my understanding of Kelly, I have chosen to pursue the description "conservative intellectual" first because Victorian arguments about the nature of inspiration were significant for Kelly and provide the background to his spirituality. Therefore I will be spending chapter 2 looking at his beliefs in biblical inspiration, concentrating on his response to the school of higher criticism in Germany and also looking at his awareness of philosophical viewpoints. In chapter 3, I shall examine Kelly's response to English theologians—the writers of *Essays and Reviews* and *Lux Mundi* and, in particular, Davidson of the non-conformists, John William Colenso (1814–1883) of the Anglican Church and F.W. Newman, who, having been part of the Brethren movement, became a Unitarian. In these chapters I will

---

152. Thiselton, *New Horizons*, 155.
153. Kelly, *Pentateuch*. Preface.
154. Pontis, Preface to *Index BT*, xii.

show that Kelly can reasonably be called "a conservative intellectual" in the continuum of evangelical spirituality because of his ability to give reasoned arguments for his belief in plenary inspiration. In chapters 4 and 5, I shall look at Kelly's views on the afterlife and the Atonement, and, as a result, define him as a biblical literalist, meaning his belief in "inerrancy and verbal inspiration of the Bible."[155] I also follow John Barton's definition of literalism as meaning "not sensitive to literary genre" and concern with "canonical scholarship."[156] Chapters 6 and 7 will be devoted to Kelly's response to the Church Fathers and the later mystics, and, through highlighting his symbolic and typological analysis of Scripture, I will suggest that he can also be defined by his mystic spirituality. By mystic I mean, not just visionary, but one who sees the "authentic reading of (a particular) Scripture" as being significant, who gives "normative value to the literal text," and who is concerned with the "mystical exegesis of canonical texts."[157] Such a description is perhaps a surprising part of his theological identity. This will lead to my overall conclusions about how we can assess William Kelly and his place in church history.

At the end of this introductory chapter, I should like to suggest why Kelly might be described in part as a biblical literalist. Kelly had a view of Scripture as infallible; prophecy was interpreted literally and had particular links with the Jews; evangelical conversion was seen as essential; he interpreted the Old and New Testaments through his particular paradigm of dispensationalism; belief in the Fall was essential to his theology; biblical critics who disagreed with him were seen as "rationalists." However, while these views are the hallmarks of a biblical literalist, I contest that Kelly was far more than this. Through his considered and scholarly study of the Bible, he was able to enter into dialog with the different theological views of his day. He had studied the works of the German critics in particular in some depth and made his own translation of the original biblical texts. While defending the fundamentals of the faith, he also opened the way to the more serious scholarly criticism of much later conservative evangelical theologians. I also consider him to show evidence of revealing a spirituality with mystic tendencies—perhaps having more in common with this tradition of the Church than the Brethren would normally acknowledge. Indeed we should be wary of having too monochrome a definition of mysticism

155. Bebbington, *Evangelicalism*, 14.
156. Barton, *The Nature of Biblical Criticism*, 23, 152.
157. Katz, ed., *Mysticism and Sacred Scripture*, 17, 56.

as it reveals widely different beliefs and is not only "the expression of transcendent experience."[158] In my conclusion I will consider Kelly's place in the continuum of theologians, and, in defining the nature of his theology, come to some evaluation of his contribution.

---

158. Ibid., 3.

CHAPTER 2

William Kelly
A Conservative Intellectual of the Evangelical Tradition

INTRODUCTION

According to James Barr and Ernest Sandeen, Darby and the millennialists were at the root of the fundamentalist tradition, which was at the heart of literalist readings of the Scriptures.[1] However, they make no reference to Kelly and in this chapter I will show that, while following the theology of dispensationalism and millennialism, Kelly cannot be merely categorized as a literalist theologian. In this chapter and the next I argue that he does much more than give a literalist interpretation of scripture, and that his basis of interpretation is a much wider one. In looking at the Bible as "the word of God," Kelly had a broader definition than Barr would allow a "fundamentalist" and therefore I suggest that Kelly might rather be described as a conservative intellectual of the evangelical tradition.[2]

That Kelly made references in his work to writers other than Brethren ones, including those from the Broad Church position and those who did not see themselves as believers, shows how willing he was to debate and that

---

1. Barr, *Fundamentalism*. Sandeen, *The Roots of Fundamentalism* also saw the start of fundamentalism in the millenarian views of Darby and other Brethren teachers.

2. The different definitions of "fundamentalist" and "conservative evangelical" are dealt with helpfully in Harris, *Fundamentalism and Evangelicals*, Introduction.

he was intellectually capable of dealing with a broad spectrum of views. The question of the basis of biblical authority was a particularly important one because it underpinned the whole of his theology. In the word "inspiration" he perceived the whole text as "God-breathed;" he did not see it as a literary response to human searching after God. Kelly desired to demonstrate the truth of plenary inspiration in his teaching, instead of analyzing the exact meaning of "inspiration." The integrity of the whole text was essential to his understanding. Between 1898 and 1903 Kelly wrote a series of articles on "God's inspiration of the Scriptures" which covered material on every book of the Bible and which was later gathered together into a book of that name.[3] In the first half of this chapter I will be looking at Kelly's interpretation of this key word "inspiration" through these articles and the book, as well as in his other works of biblical exegesis and afterwards I will explore his response to the German school of higher criticism and some of its foundational philosophy. I will end this chapter by questioning whether Barr's definition of fundamentalism is too rigid for an adequate understanding of Kelly's attitude towards the Bible.

KELLY AND BIBLICAL INSPIRATION

As an acknowledged lower, or textual, critic of some distinction, Kelly knew the importance of accuracy in linguistic knowledge, but he also recognized that the point of view of the translator was significant too. This was especially so when translating and interpreting key verses which gave the scriptural understanding of inspiration, such as 2 Timothy 3:6 and 17.[4] He disagreed with the recently published Revised Version of the Bible (1881–85) in its translation of these verses.[5] Kelly argued for "every scripture is inspired by God" (his own translation), rather than, "every scripture, inspired by God, is profitable for teaching" (the Revised Version). For Kelly, this was a significant difference, because he saw his translation as affirming plenary inspiration as opposed to the looser interpretation which acted as a description rather than a definition. He explained, referring to preparatory work by Henry Alford (1810–1871) which had preceded the new trans-

---

3. Kelly, *God's Inspiration of the Scriptures*.

4. 2 Tim 3:16, 17 (KJV), "All Scripture is given by inspiration of God, and is profitable for doctrine, for reproof, for correction, for instruction in righteousness. That the man of God may be perfect, thoroughly furnished unto all good works."

5. Kelly, *God's Inspiration*, 28.

lation: "None of the constructions within or without the New Testament cited by Dean Alford approaches the one before us."[6] His justification of his position shows that it was crucial for Kelly that the accuracy of his translation was vindicated by scriptural precedent, rather than because he supported a particular theological interpretation. He revealed that he was aware of different strengths of different translations and quoted Origen to support his own. "The RV, whether intentionally or not, is ambiguous," he concluded.[7] In his essay Kelly also discussed an unidentified "learned dignitary" who understood the phrase "God inspired" as not comprehending any verbal error or possible historical inaccuracies, as well as problems of transcription and transmission. The latter were always a matter of concern for Kelly, as a lower critic. However, concerning the former objections, he stated: "The imputation really leaves God out, as every measure of skepticism does."[8] Here we see that theological attitude to the text was important for Kelly but that did not mean that the problems of the text could not be discussed.

As well as demonstrating his abilities as a lower critic, Kelly justified his textual views theologically. For example, when he examined the verse in Malachi, "Jacob have I loved, Esau have I hated," (Mal 1:2–3) he did not look at Hebrew linguistic conventions, but chose to examine the biblical ideas of predestination and choice.[9] At the same time he used precise analysis of language to support his points. When writing of God's promise to Jacob, he noted that it included the sand, not the stars of heaven, because Jacob "is the type of the earthly Jew."[10] He saw here a choice of language which upheld his theology. He added the comment, "He (Jacob) was the object of grace, but no way established in grace."[11]

In interpreting scripture, Kelly allowed for the investigation of textual and historical issues concerning scripture. He had in essence a

---

6. Ibid.

7. Ibid., 30. It is interesting to note that the recent NRSV gives Kelly's translation for the text, and puts the other one as a possibility in a footnote: *Holy Bible NRSV* (Oxford: OUP, 1995), 210.

8. Kelly, *God's Inspiration*, 33.

9. Kelly, *Pentateuch*, 20.

10. Ibid., 94–96. This refers to the apparent unmerited favor by God towards Jacob rather than Esau. This verse, with its clear paradox, which might be explained as a Jewish exaggeration of contrast in order to make a point, is interpreted and justified by Kelly in terms of predestination alone.

11. Ibid.

straightforward reading of Genesis, which he appreciated as unique in all ancient literature, and he and other writers whom he used in his magazine, believed that there was no comparison between other pre-historic books and the Bible.[12] Genesis was exceptional, he felt, because it started with facts rather than notions and ideas and there was no attempt to explain who God was. Interpretation of Genesis was a key focal point for him because he declared that creation was the most important doctrine after redemption.[13] He demanded of its readers either unqualified acceptance or rejection of its theological viewpoint. He wrote: "Its first words are necessarily either a revelation or an imposture."[14] The act of God resting after creation in Genesis 2:3 he also saw as very significant because he regarded it as a parallel with Christ having completed the work of salvation. Kelly was always far more critical of contemporary theologians than he was of scientists, partly because he saw theologians as having responsibility towards God which could be abused. However, he was humble in accepting that he did not always understand, as in his commentary on the story of the sun standing still at Gilgal.[15] In such matters he advised trust.[16] He also believed that Scripture was open to investigation, something he accepted, for example, in his comments on the first two verses of Genesis, where he believed that the first two verses referred to a different era than the rest of the chapter. He also encouraged thoughtful doubt, rather than a mere traditional acceptance of everything taught by Christendom.[17]

A distinctive feature of Kelly's doctrine of scripture was that, while being an advocate of plenary inspiration, he always had a broad conception of the nature of God. God was beyond the word of God (a position often taken by theologians both in the nineteenth century and today against "fundamentalists"). Kelly wrote: "The word of God, blessed as it is, is not everything. We need the God of the word as well as the word of God. What weakness if God himself be not with us?"[18] Kelly was also aware that it was easy to turn from God to rely on ourselves for interpretation.[19] He was also

12. Beacon, "The Impregnable Rock of Holy Scripture," 112.
13. Kelly, *Pentateuch*, 3.
14. Kelly, *God's Inspiration*, 9.
15. Kelly, *the Earlier Historical Books*, 77.
16. Ibid., 150.
17. Kelly, *Pentateuch*, ix.
18. Kelly, *BT*, 1 January, 1863, 56.
19. Kelly, *Earlier Historical Books. Joshua*, 63.

acknowledging the "mystery" of God beyond the written word. Although he used his magazine to review books on the subject of inspiration with which he did not agree such as W.E. Gladstone's *The Impregnable Rock of Holy Scripture* (1890), he felt that the Brethren should be willing to listen to accusations of not following the Scriptures, even when those accusations came from a non-Brethren source, thus showing his open-mindedness.[20] Kelly was never "literalist" in the plodding sense; therefore he was able to evade the problems which surfaced in Bishop Colenso's controversial views on the authorship and dating of the Pentateuch.[21] Theological understanding as a whole was important in interpreting the Bible. He sought to look behind the text and understand the scheme of theological thinking which undergirded it. When looking at genealogies, for example, he did not just look at possible errors and difficulties, nor did he ignore them. He used them to expose the purpose and viewpoint of the writer. For example, on the subject of genealogies in Genesis chapter 46, he was able to write, with an ironic use of litotes:

> It may be worthwhile to observe in this and other genealogies not often the object of infidel attack that the difference between Genesis, Numbers and Chronicles in their form are due to the motive for their introduction in each particular connection, that the differences clearly spring from design, in no way from error in the writer but, in fact, because of ignorance in such readers misapprehend them, and that both the differences and the difficulties are the strongest evidence of their truth and inspired character, for nothing would have been easier than to have assimilated their various forms and to have eliminated that which sounds strange to western ears.[22]

Kelly believed that there was danger in any falsehood being taught because "it will work evil in various ways."[23] By this he meant not merely textual inaccuracies, but the moral consequences of misunderstanding Scripture. For him unity of truth was important and he made no distinc-

---

20. Beacon, "The Impregnable Rock," 110.

21. Cf. chapter 3 where I examine Colenso's objections to the Pentateuch, which were often pursued from a literalist's point of view. Colenso tried to show that the historic nature of the Pentateuch was inadmissible.

22. Kelly, *Pentateuch*, 118. Immediately after this passage he goes on to examine why Stephen quotes the LXX version in Acts and argues against the skepticism of contemporary biblical critics.

23. Kelly, *Earlier Historical Books*, 393.

tion between the essential and the apparently circumstantial. Kelly showed this all-embracing understanding in many places in his work, including his interpretation of the numbers seven and twelve in Genesis 8 in the description of the Flood.[24] This approach has proved to be in step with a more modern understanding of biblical narrative, and different to that of literary formalism.[25] Luther's idea of a canon within the canon had no persuasive power for the Brethren. All scripture became part of their paradigm of understanding.

Kelly's own definition of infallibility was nuanced. As early as October 1863 he published an article "On Inspiration." He used the word "infallible" of the Scriptures to mean them "having all the infallible certainty of what God says."[26] But he contrasted the infallible movement of the Holy Spirit in the Scriptures with the fallibility of the writers, such as the apostles. He also maintained that in what they wrote they were "conformed to the state of the dispensation."[27] Clearly Kelly felt that there was greater truth implicit in the writing than what the limited consciousness of the writer knew. He wrote of the Holy Spirit working on "the affections" rather than "the intelligence" of the writer. Therefore he considered that his task as interpreter was to reveal the full intentions of the biblical discourse in the light of the whole Bible.

Although Kelly did not accept the idea of the canon within the canon, he explored the Jewish tripartite division of scripture into the "Gradus Mosaicus . . . and the Gradus Propheticus and Bath Kol," and seemed to approve of the distinction in the varied character and purpose of the different sacred writings.[28] "This did not touch the authority but the character of the writings," he explained.[29] He proceeded to argue that omniscience was not necessary on the part of the scriptural writers but compared their task "to the spout which gives a form to the current that flows from it, and so may transmit the water as pure as it flows in."[30]

He also wrote against the Broad Church position of Benjamin Jowett with his suggestion in *Essays and Reviews* (1860) of treating the "Bible like

---

24. Kelly *Pentateuch*, 41.

25. Thiselton, *New Horizons*, 478.

26. Kelly, "On Inspiration," 350.

27. Cf. chapter 1 where I show that each part of the Bible is strictly relevant only to a particular "age" of God's revelation.

28. Ibid., 351.

29. Ibid.

30. Ibid., 352.

any other book."³¹ Kelly did not condone bibliolatry but, instead, had a complete faith in the God who had allowed the Bible to be written. On the other hand his conception of authors not being conscious of the implications of what they wrote, but of succeeding generations being capable of interpretations not available to the original writers, concurs with the ideas of postmodern literary criticism.³² Concerning Matthew's account of the transfiguration he wrote, "I do not pretend to say how far the inspired writers knew all the mind of God in such a thing: they wrote as moved by the Holy Ghost."³³ In his *God's Inspiration of the Scriptures* (1903), he was quite clear that skepticism about the Scriptures was a precursor of the full apostasy to come, so that their faithful interpretation was very important to him. Although he did not gainsay the established Church's creeds, he thought it was more important to go back to the word of God, than to refer to the creeds.³⁴ He felt that subjection to the authority of Scripture was essential to right understanding of its text. He noted: "It is evident that the rationalist approaches Scripture, not as a believer and learner, but as a judge, and that his criticism is captious, to say nothing of irreverence."³⁵ For example, he affirmed that understanding of Genesis chapter 3 (The Fall narrative) was by faith alone and that it was not easy to meet objections. He advised, "the great point, my brethren, is to hold fast the truth."³⁶ This shows us Kelly's objectives in his own writings and his sense that other members of the Brethren movement, learned or unlearned, who had access to the Scriptures, were on an equal footing with himself. While maintaining his own authority as a teacher, this attitude preserved him from arrogance and also gives a sense of Kelly being a representative of the interpretative community.

---

31. Shea and Whitla, *Essays and Reviews*, 503.

32. There are some links here with Newman's Doctrine of Development (cf. my references in chapter 3) but certainly not in terms of agreeing with Newman's acceptance of Roman Catholic dogma which departed from the biblical text.

33. Kelly, *Matthew*, 269.

34. Kelly, *Earlier Historical Books; 1 Samuel*, 391. The way in which theological statements have been placed in a different context in ecclesial creeds has been studied by the philosopher Richard Swinburne; cf. Thiselton, *New Horizons*, 36.

35. Kelly, *Pentateuch*, 106.

36. Ibid., 21.

KELLY AND NINETEENTH-CENTURY UNDERSTANDING OF LITERARY TECHNIQUES

In his understanding of the term "inspiration," Kelly's writing shows that he was aware of literary techniques employed by biblical writers. In the later nineteenth century, theories of literary techniques and schools of literary criticism were developing in the area of classical studies and the newly recognized discipline of English Literature.[37] For Kelly, plenary inspiration was not the sole criterion for interpreting the Bible correctly. In addition to this criterion, knowledge of the unity of the Bible, a "right" theological understanding according to Brethren paradigms and a fruitful spiritual life were the most important means of understanding the Scriptures. Literary criticism became the tool for a "correct" theology. Frequently using the conventions of literary criticism, Kelly showed his deeper understanding of the text, which was far from a straightforward literalist reading. My aim in this next section of the chapter is to demonstrate this understanding.

An essential key for interpreting the Bible was an understanding of its unity of revelation. Thus, eisegesis, which was a frequent practice of Kelly's, was entirely justified, because it contributed to his understanding of the unity of the Bible.[38] "There is a profound design," he wrote, "which runs through the works of God and more especially through His word."[39] For example, in his writing about the early books of the Bible he traced the way man's evil drew out the love and knowledge of God, which would be revealed in the prophets and the Gospels.[40] Like many Brethren and Victorian evangelicals, he was interested in prophecy but he saw its limitations. He wrote, "Prophecy, admirable as it is, is always short of the fullness of grace and truth which is in Christ . . . it neither looks up at the heights of God's glory, nor again does it in any way go down into the depths of His grace."[41]

Kelly was aware of focused editorial in biblical narratives. For example in his work on the Gospels there was a strong sense of the overriding purpose of each separate Gospel account. In his comments on Genesis chapter

---

37. Crews, *Literary Criticism*. Literary criticism owed much to the work of Wordsworth, Coleridge and the German Romantic Movement and philosophers such as Hegel and J.S. Mill.

38. Kelly, *God's Inspiration*, 5.

39. Kelly, *Daniel*, 25.

40. Kelly, *Pentateuch*, 265.

41. Ibid., 66–67.

15 he accepted that a literary account was organized in a certain way to present a truth.[42] He gave this as the reason why Abram was justified after he had been called out and had worshipped acceptably—"in order to form our souls according to His own mind."[43] It was Kelly's role as interpreter and teacher to demonstrate the theological significance of that order, and to relate it to his fellow believers, as is seen in the change of reference from Abram to "our."

The book of Hebrews, with its discourse relying heavily on reinterpretation of the Old Testament, had great significance for the Brethren. Discussing Numbers chapters 18 and 19, Kelly talked about the Christian's whole rest under the Messiah, not just the believer's rest through salvation in Christ.[44] He asserted that this was the true meaning of Hebrews chapter 4. Therefore it is clear that Kelly was more interested in the underlying spiritual truth conveyed by the Old Testament text than in its narrative details. Numbers came to have great significance for him. The intended meaning of numbers was far more important than the literalist understanding. Therefore, in talking about thirteen young bullocks used for sacrifice or burnt offering in the book of Numbers, he posed the question, "Was this not intended to exercise our spiritual thought as to the truth of God? Are we not to infer that it is the all but fullest expression of Christ known on the earth?"[45] Kelly saw the New Testament as a hermeneutical commentary on the Old and I will explore this in detail when I write about his understanding of typology in chapter 7. Kelly's understanding of the Bible was Christologically focused in his reading of every part of the text. This approach was more significant for him than a literalist reading.

Symbolism does not prove or disprove inspiration, but in interpreting symbolism, Kelly moved away from a more pragmatic treatment of the text. Ricoeur has pointed to the creative value of the symbol and how it impinges on the reader and Kelly was aware of this creative value.[46] Whatever he taught, he would link the symbolism of the passage to other parts of the Bible, as for example in Daniel, when he traced the symbols of the tree and the vine to Psalm 80, Jeremiah chapter 2 and Ezekiel chapter 15.[47] When

---

42. Ibid., 63.
43. Ibid., 64.
44. Ibid., 407.
45. Ibid., 409.
46. Thiselton, *New Horizons*, 5.
47. Kelly, *Daniel*, 76.

writing about Exodus, he gave a detailed interpretation of the rod of Moses as meaning "power" and of the serpent, which was construed as some sort of satanic creature, and, in so doing, he made careful cross references to Genesis.[48] For Kelly symbolism was a more important way of interpreting the Bible than literalism and intertextual understanding was significant for him. Leprosy, even in the Old Testament, stood for sin as defilement, and palsy meant paralysis and the weakness of humanity.[49] Kelly saw the symbolic worth of the words as more important than the literal reading. He took biblical interpretation out of the historical and into the conceptual realm. Symbolism was explained so that there could be a depth of understanding in reading the Bible. In writing about the Passover meal, he commented:

> Leaven represents iniquity in its tendency to extend itself by assimilating what was exposed to its action ... The flesh of the lamb was to be eaten not raw or sodden, but roast with fire, the strong and evident sign of fierce unsparing divine judgment. It must and ought to be so, for herein Christ's death met our sins and God's judgment.[50]

Often, within his own sentences, he moved quickly from a historical comment to a symbolic Christian interpretation, thus presenting a tension between the two. In writing about the deliverance from the Red Sea, he affirmed that historically the Passover started in Egypt because "they could not have been delivered across the Red Sea without the blood of the Lamb. First, the death of Christ is the necessary and only possible foundation for any blessing from God."[51]

While a dispensationalist view of the Bible could have led to a purely literalist understanding of the text, Kelly looked beyond this. For example, circumcision was not just seen as a ritual within the dispensation of the law. Not only had it existed before the giving of the law, but it had symbolic meaning for Christians now. In teaching about the Pentateuch Kelly examined the deeper meaning of circumcision for the Christian of his own

48. Kelly, *Pentateuch*, 142.

49. Ibid., 143.

50. Ibid., 159. The symbol of leaven was also used later by the Brethren to justify judgment of particular Brethren groups who were considered to be erring and the need to exclude them. They were even referred to as "the new lumpists"—that is expanded lumps of dough which contained leaven.

51. Ibid., 340. At one point in the sentence "the blood of the Lamb" acts as a referent to the lamb which was killed at the Passover and to Christ, symbolized as the Lamb of God in John chapter 1, shedding his own blood.

time. He saw it as representing the mortification of the flesh. In addition he warned that in concentrating on prophetic eschatology it was very easy to enter into "the bias of our own minds . . . but rather (prophetic eschatology) leads them on in lower lines and earthly principles."[52] Prophecy was only useful if it had a spiritual effect on the life of a Christian, as could be seen in the biblical account of Sodom and Gomorrah. In that instance, the foreknowledge of the destruction of the city did not help the inhabitants, because they were spiritually deaf to the warnings.

Kelly not only interpreted symbols as he found them in the text but also read their meanings into other narratives. When talking about the language of Daniel, he replied to a correspondent designated by the initials GHL that he could not

> for a moment allow that to deny symbols in the prophecies is a help to understanding them . . . The truth is, that in almost all the prophets there is a mixture of figures with ordinary language. The source of mistake as to scripture lies in the truths communicated far more than in the words which convey them.[53]

He pleaded for an understanding of symbolism rather than a superficial literalist reading of the text—"A symbol, if clearly and certainly understood, is quite as determinate as any other mode of expression. . . those who profess to be literal interpreters exhibit a very large amount of conflict and inconsistencies in their schemes."[54] I will examine Kelly's understanding of symbol in greater depth in chapter 7.

Kelly also showed a strong sense of the text being crafted for literary purposes rather than being chronologically precise. He did not see plenary inspiration as being inconsistent with the different purposes and forms of the text. When he discussed the Sermon on the Mount in the Gospel of Matthew, he wrote, "it need not be considered historically, as one continuous discourse, but may have been divided into different parts."[55] He noted that this understanding gave "a key to the difficulties in the gospel," thus showing himself to be capable of considering problems in the text.[56] Kelly paralleled the literary shaping of the Sermon on the Mount with a similar grouping of the miracles of Christ, even though the miracles might have

52. Ibid., 16.
53. Kelly, "To Correspondents," 223.
54. Ibid.
55. Kelly, *Matthew*, 70.
56. Ibid., 71.

been divided by space and time.[57] Therefore his position as a literalist was always tempered by his understanding of literary crafting.

Kelly observed that words also worked as signifiers of change and age in documents. Thus, in Genesis chapter 15, the phrase "after these things" was recognized as an indicator of another age.[58] He "read" a passage through historical clues, textual nuances, symbolic associations, Christological inferences and spiritual application. He was able to acknowledge genre, for example, talking about Job as a poetical book and distinguishing it from the previous historical books.[59] He saw a different purpose in the genealogy of 1 Chronicles compared to other Old Testament genealogies.[60] Within the whole canon he recognized literary parallels: for example, the order of Daniel is paralleled with the order of the parables in Matthew chapter 13.[61] He also saw literary continuity throughout the Bible, so that Babylon was seen as a continuous type of religious corruption.[62] He also acknowledged the biblical writers' understanding of human psychology. Commenting on Moses's first attempt to mediate a quarrel between the Hebrews, he observed, "There may be, I grant you, the mingling of that which is of nature along with faith . . . The great work of which he [Moses] had a certain anticipation no doubt vague and dark, in his soul."[63] Through this sentence Kelly was "reaching in" to the human motivation of the narrative.

In Kelly's writing about Matthew in relation to the other Gospels, there was a marked understanding of literary crafting, very different from a literalist reading. *Lectures on the Gospel of Matthew* was written in 1868 and he was able to write of the "alienation of the Jews from such a Messiah as their own scriptures portray."[64] Rather than seeing the Gospels as copying from sources, he discussed the dispensational purpose of Matthew and the moral purpose of Luke.[65] The question of eye-witnesses of the life

57. Ibid., 72.
58. Kelly, *Pentateuch*, 13.
59. Kelly, *God's Inspiration*, 202.
60. Ibid., 188–89.
61. Kelly, *Daniel*, 24. Matthew chapter 13 gives a series of parables which can be linked with teaching on "the last times" and therefore can be seen in parallel with the prophecies of Daniel.
62. Ibid., 100. Babylon recurs as a motif in Daniel and Revelation.
63. Kelly, *Pentateuch*, 130.
64. Kelly, *Matthew*, v.
65. Ibid., vii.

of Christ was considered and the reasons why John would choose not to give the Olivet discourse, even though all the other Gospel writers placed John as being there. Change in form for a purpose was accepted by Kelly. Geographical placing was not just literalist but had a theological intention, so he discussed the post-resurrection appearances placed by Matthew in Galilee and Luke in Jerusalem. Matthew's account was in accordance with the geographical location when Jesus was rejected by the Jews.[66] Thus the symbolism of the place became more important than the geographical reality. The fourth and later gospel, John, was connected with Jesus in glory, not the sequence of events and their location in the approach to the Crucifixion. Understanding of different time schemes was carefully explained. He wrote: "In Matthew, the mere order of history is here neglected and the facts are brought together that took place months apart."[67]

KELLY'S ENGAGEMENT WITH THE GERMAN SCHOOL OF HIGHER CRITICISM

While he clearly defended a plenary view of the Scriptures, Kelly nonetheless relished intellectual discussion, engaging over his career as a writer and teacher with the viewpoints of theologians of the school of higher criticism and showing evidence in his editorship of *The Bible Treasury* of his wide theological and philosophical reading by providing book reviews. He saw the school of higher criticism and trends in German philosophy as a threat to the acceptance of the Bible as divinely inspired. The word "inspiration" can be interpreted in many ways but in the nineteenth century new hypotheses about the nature of the biblical texts were perceived by evangelicals as a threat to plenary inspiration. Kelly deliberately tackled the challenges which came from these new schools of thought.

The fifty years in which Kelly consistently taught the Bible was a particularly significant era for the emergence of higher criticism because within this period *Essays and Reviews* (1860) and *Lux Mundi* (1890) were published in England and there was a strong response to both these publications on the part of the Anglican and non-conformist Churches. The *Bible Treasury* editions of 1890 onwards show a marked increase in Kelly's engagement with the arguments of this school. This dating is in keeping with Chadwick's observation that "until about 1882–1892 the churches as

66. Ibid., 134.
67. Ibid., 133.

a whole were not reconciled to biblical criticism and paid little attention to the new scholarship."[68] However, in his earlier works and magazine articles between 1856 and 1890, Kelly also revealed extensive wider reading on this issue. For example he wrote a long article in *The Bible Treasury* about the Double Document Theory in 1867.[69] Also Kelly's own works, *Lectures Introductory to the Study of the Pentateuch*, and, *Rationalism and the Pentateuch*, were advertised in *The Bible Treasury* no. 177, January 1st 1871. Kelly maintained that the German school of higher criticism was not original: it had come out of the writing of the deists and therefore from the premises first laid down by the Enlightenment thinkers.[70] John Rogerson, while clearly not sympathetic to conservative evangelicalism, agrees with Kelly about the philosophical origins of German higher criticism.[71] Rogerson pointed to Jean Astruc writing in 1753 in France about the two sources of Genesis, and to Johann Gottfried Eichorn (1752-1827), whose work *Introduction to the Old Testament* (1780-1788), was a foundational work to the later documentary hypothesis.[72] De Wette himself admitted that he owed much to Eichorn's research.[73] When Kelly frequently referred to the higher critics as "rationalists," he was knowingly linking them with the earlier Deists, and assessing them to be part of the Enlightenment movement of the eighteenth century, and therefore suggesting that they were opposed to Christianity by aligning them with the Deists.

Kelly chose to reference the ideas of de Wette because he rightly discerned de Wette's significance for biblical criticism. Rogerson confirmed that de Wette's *Contributions to Old Testament Introduction* (Halle, 1806-07) was the first work of Old Testament scholarship to use the critical method in order to present a view of the history of Israelite religion that

---

68. Chadwick, *Victorian Church*, Part 2, 74.

69. Kelly, "The Double Document Theory," 356-60. The "Double Document Theory" was an early theory, proposed by Jean Astruc (1684-1766) and largely supported by the work of Johann Gottfried Eichorn (1752-1827). The latter suggested that the use of two main divine names in Genesis could be attributed to two different sources. Cf. Reventlow, *History of Biblical Interpretation*, vol. 1, 293.

70. Kelly, *Pentateuch and its Critics*, 4. Kelly shows how the viewpoint of German higher criticism came out of the work of Spinoza, Hobbes, Bolingbroke and Hume. Interestingly, this has been confirmed by 21st century biblical such as John Barton, *The Nature of Biblical Criticism*, 119, 123. Barton himself does not fully agree with this and thinks that this view comes particularly from those critics who are interested in semantics.

71. Rogerson, *Old Testament Criticism in the 19th century*, 19.

72. Rogerson, *W.L.M. de Wette*, 50.

73. De Wette, *A Critical and Historical Introduction*, vi and 77.

was radically at variance with the view implied in the Old Testament itself.[74] He also claimed that "De Wette raised all the main questions that were to be of concern to nineteenth-century scholarship."[75]

In view of the fact that the German school of higher criticism looked at the possibility of a variety of documents being incorporated into the Old Testament, particularly into the text of the Pentateuch, I will now explore Kelly's views on this matter. This appeared to be a threat to the notion of plenary inspiration, due to the German questioning of Mosaic authorship, as well as the German assertion of multiple documents behind the supposedly Mosaic manuscript. Kelly wrote several articles about the names of God and how they were used in the biblical text. Many of these contributions were very short.[76] In an article in January 1871, he made distinctions between the Hebrew title Elohim (where the article Ha is added) and where Eloah was used as the singular of Elohim.[77] As the biblical use of these titles was being studied by the German school of higher criticism, Kelly showed that he was able to analyze their usage. Kelly was honest in his writings and showed a sense of his own limitations—"I can say nothing satisfactory to my own mind as to Jah (a term used for God in places in the Old Testament)." While acknowledging his perplexity, he used this article to criticize "the senseless scissors" of the German theologians.[78]

His general attitude was one of extreme skepticism towards German theories. In his article entitled "The Double Document Theory," he criticized them as "narrow-minded" in codifying too easily the ethical tendencies of a particular book and placing it in a later period of Israel's history, "pettifogging" and displaying "a plodding diligence."[79] He accused German theologians of reducing the text "to some imaginary documents, which none of them know anything about but suppose."[80] He said that such a system of multiple documents was too mixed up to prove anything important

---

74. Rogerson, *Old Testament Criticism*, 29. Rogerson meant that de Wette looked at the possibility of varied authorship from different times for the Pentateuch, rather than accepting the Old Testament's testimony to its own authorship.

75. Ibid., 34.

76. Kelly, "Names of God in the Psalms," 48. (Untitled article) *BT* 20, no. 458, 107.

77. Kelly, "Scripture Queries and Answers," 207–8.

78. Ibid., 208.

79. Ibid., "The Double Document Notion of Sceptics," 356.

80. Ibid., 358.

and condemned what he called the German practice of "mechanical separation of parts of the text."[81]

Kelly spent time in this article noting the different names of God and explaining their gradual revelation in the Bible. He said that the title "Elohim" was always used of the Creator God, while Jehovah was the personal name whereby God made himself known to Israel.[82] He placed Psalm 14 and Psalm 53 alongside each other, and explained why they were similar in thought but used different names for God. Using this method, he went through the books of Psalms, explaining why one or another name was used.[83] Kelly taught that although multiple documents had not been proposed for the book of Jonah, the same difference in the way God related to the Jews and the Gentiles could be seen. Here Kelly was considering the dating of the text rather than genre. He made it clear that within the Jewish system of writing, the use of different names was consistent and appropriate.[84] He showed himself not to be necessarily against the idea of editing having taken place within the text but affirmed that differences in divine names were not necessarily a proof of editing. He explained why the name Jehovah had been used in Genesis but was not personally revealed to Moses and the people until the time of the Exodus—a supposed inconsistency which had been previously hailed by the German critics as evidence of later manuscripts.[85] Repetition in Scripture, he claimed, was not because of multiple documents, but the need to consider facts under new light, such as the list of Benjamin's progeny and Saul's royal court family.[86]

Through the use of names, Kelly traced Israel's special relationship to God and then the gradually revealed developing purpose of the Messiah to come and how He would relate to God the Father, the Jews and the Gentiles. Thus Kelly explained that all of the first book of Psalms, up to Psalm 41, was addressed to Jehovah except for Psalm 16 "which is quoted by Paul and Peter as proof of Christ's humanity and resurrection. By using Elohim, Christ is taking the place of human subjection—the servanthood position."[87] In Psalm 91, Christ takes on the names "Elion Shaddai," the

81. Ibid., 359.
82. Ibid., 356.
83. Ibid., 357.
84. Ibid.
85. Ibid., 358.
86. Ibid.
87. Ibid., 357.

words which were used by Melchizedek to bless Abraham.[88] Then in Psalm 108, "Christ is brought out as Jehovah in the most astonishing way." Kelly used these points to stress the validity of the Trinitarian position. "The healing of the paralytic is a distinct allusion to Jehovah's name in Psalm 103 verse 3."[89]

As Kelly interpreted the names of God prophetically and dispensationally, he made the use of God's names tie in with his own theological paradigm. Looking at the first two books of Psalms, he explained, "I have no doubt that, prophetically, the first book refers to the Jews in the latter-day returned to Jerusalem and enjoying *outwardly* their hoped for advantages there, and the second has its application when they are driven out in the time of the great tribulation mentioned in Matthew xxiv."[90]

This teaching followed Kelly's tendency to oppose the document theories by revealing different theological purposes within the text and making them cohesive rather than differentiated in time. He explained that it is not "even rational to seek imaginary causes, when the real reason lies within the system."[91] He thought that just as he believed in an Almighty God, the Germans had their own philosophical reasons for their beliefs.[92] Kelly not only acknowledged motivation in the way scholars looked at text, but he observed that it was important because it changes, not what we find in the text, but how we interpret it. "I would just add here, that it is perfectly indifferent to me, if Moses used five hundred documents, provided what in result he gives me expresses exactly, perfectly and completely what God meant to communicate to me."[93] Kelly's attitude was in fact much more in tune with a twentieth-century understanding of biblical narrative than the source-critical approach of the nineteenth century.[94] When we understand Kelly's more fluid attitude to editorship and dating, literalism, meaning inflexibility of accepting different documents, does not seem an appropriate term for Kelly's views. Acceptance of plenary inspiration seems more accurate. There was also in his writing a sense of successive revelations for different purposes. "From the first calling out of the world to be separate

---

88. Ibid., 359.
89. Ibid., 357.
90. Ibid.
91. Ibid., 358.
92. Ibid.
93. Ibid., 358.
94. Thiselton, *New Horizons*, 479.

from it, *God Almighty, Jehovah, Father,* characterized successively the position which God assumed for faith."[95]

Although Kelly criticized de Wette, there were certain strands of the German critic's thought which, surprisingly, Kelly came near to agreeing with. Kelly not only referred to de Wette's works but also his library shows his ownership of these works.[96] De Wette had argued that it was difficult to know what Moses gave the Jewish people in terms of his instructions and how these were practiced in the wilderness, and the account was in no way proof of Mosaic authorship.[97] Kelly had no hesitation in pronouncing Moses as the original author of the Pentateuch, but, in his answer to Colenso's later objections, he did agree that there was no evidence that Moses' instructions were practiced in the wilderness.[98] Rogerson commented that de Wette "had arrived at a comprehensive understanding of the nature of religion and of the way in which religious narratives, symbols and worship grasped and expressed external ideas."[99] This is remarkably similar to the way in which Kelly saw Old Testament narratives as saying something deeper about human understanding of religion, eternal values and ultimately about the church. Fries's notion of "Ahnung" used by de Wette—hunch, feeling, premonition, something instinctive in understanding—had similarities with Kelly's idea of ongoing revelation and the use of symbolism. This fits in with the German critical understanding of the Bible being a history of religious ideas.[100]

Kelly also had some interesting agreements with some of the later German Higher Critics after de Wette. C.P.W. Gramberg (1797–1830) looked at the dating of religious ideas and saw seven periods in the history of religion in the Old Testament.[101] Kelly and the Brethren also identified this number of periods which they worked into their theory of dispensationalism.[102] Rather than viewing Ezekiel and Leviticus as contemporane-

95. Kelly, "Double Document," 360.

96. De Wette, *Die Heilige Schrift des Altes und Neuen Testament,* vols 1, 2, and 3, and ed. De Wette, *Synoptici Evangelisti.*

97. De Wette, trans. Theodore Parker, *Introduction to the Old Testament,* vol. 2, 72.

98. Kelly, *Pentateuch,* 421.

99. Rogerson, *OT Criticism,* 43.

100. Howard, *Religion and the Rise of Historicism,* 9, 46. This philosophical notion came from the work of Jacob Friedrich Fries (1773–1843) to whom I shall refer later in this chapter.

101. Ibid., 58.

102. Darby's and Kelly's works abound with references to dispensationalism.

ous manuscripts due to their concern with holiness, as Gramberg did, Kelly saw the subject of holiness as an important unifying subject throughout Scripture. Sometimes the same observations on the content of the biblical text were explained differently by Gramberg and Kelly. Therefore the literary observations were the same, but the explanations different.

While de Wette promulgated the idea of the falling away of Jewish religious principles during the Hebrew monarchy, Wilhelm Vatke (1806–1874) championed the idea of religious development during Old Testament times.[103] Both ideas were present in Kelly's interpretation—the gradual development of God's revelation over time and the increased degeneration of the human condition, leading to the hardness of heart and the blindness of religious Jews in the Gospels and, in another dispensation, the apostasy of Christendom. Both these notions are related to different philosophy and historical ideology, not to a simplistic interpretation of higher criticism.

Therefore we see in Kelly's views on the inspiration of Scripture, on the one hand the promotion of the idea of plenary inspiration, which might be expected from a Brethren teacher, and on the other hand, a wider and more nuanced approach to the biblical text. There is not only a sense of the ability to argue with the German school of higher criticism in Kelly's writings but the suggestion of a wider approach than we would necessarily expect of a theologian of his background, time and convictions.

KELLY'S RELATIONSHIP TO PHILOSOPHY

All theologians make "a priori" assumptions about the biblical text and so their work must be placed within a continuum of philosophical and social understanding. Thus it is important to acknowledge the stance of the German critics within their historical, intellectual and sociological context. At the beginning of his study on nineteenth-century German criticism, Rogerson does this in a particularly helpful way. He argues that different ways of approaching language had an effect on Old Testament scholarship.[104] This helps to explain the clash between the German critics and the conservative evangelicals of the nineteenth century. Nationality was also an important indicator of divergence. Britain produced specialists in philology and

---

103. De Wette, *Old Testament*, 39. De Wette writes about the "idealo-poetic" element in religion. Rogerson, *De Wette*, 34. Rogerson shows how de Wette was influenced by Schelling who rejected the idea that the primitive in religion was crude and barbaric.

104. Rogerson, *OT Criticism*, 4.

textual criticism and this was Kelly's area of expertise. The Germans were more interested in the purpose and structure of the whole biblical narrative. As David Law explains in his book *Inspiration*, they were more concerned with non-verbal, than with word-centerd, theories of inspiration.[105] As a result of their rejection of verbal inspiration, a rejection made most explicitly by Semler (1725–1791), the German critics sought to expose the idea of a divine "word of God" within a text which might otherwise be errant or not inspired.[106] In contrast Kelly was particularly keen to reject this duality because he saw the whole Bible as a unity intentionally revealing Christ and the position of the Church.[107] Therefore Kelly's understanding of what was meant by "the word of God" was different to that of the German Higher Critics. However I also propose that his approach cannot easily be catalogued as that of literalism. Kelly was concerned with the purpose and structure of the biblical narrative as well as with the minutiae of the text.

Kelly's own philosophical influences are interesting. While not agreeing with the conclusions of Enlightenment philosophers, he was firmly conditioned into the patterns of thinking of the Enlightenment, as shown by his reading of the Enlightenment deists and his references to writers such as William Paley (1743–1805). Kelly was influenced by the distinctions made between rational and irrational argument and understanding of what "knowledge" is and how it is acquired, as Enlightenment thinkers had demonstrated. Henning Graf Reventlow has shown that most movements which affected theological thinking in the nineteenth century had their roots in the previous century.[108]

FOUNDATIONAL PHILOSOPHY IN THE WORK OF KELLY AND IN THE GERMAN SCHOOL OF HIGHER CRITICISM

In chapter 1 I showed that Kelly's admiration for Darby caused him to edit Darby's *Works* and to use them for individual articles in *The Bible Treasury*. I now show how Kelly printed Darby's articles on German philosophy to grapple with the philosophical basis of German higher criticism. These articles were included in *The Bible Treasury* between 1866 and 1869 when

---

105. Law, *Inspiration*, 99–145.

106. Ibid., 17.

107. For developing views on the inspiration of Scripture within Protestantism, including Luther's views on Scripture, cf. Alister McGrath, *Christianity's Dangerous Idea*.

108. Reventlow, "The Role of the Old Testament," 132.

the Victorian Christian public were becoming more aware of German higher criticism and the inclusion of these articles shows that Kelly thought that the philosophical basis of higher criticism was important and that his magazine was intellectually rigorous enough in outlook to tackle this subject. He also made use of J. E. Batten's articles in *The Bible Treasury* issues of January 1st 1857 and July 1st 1868 to look at the link between Hegel and Hinduism. The inclusion of these articles is particularly interesting as Batten had been a colleague of Newton, had been involved in the dispute with Darby in 1845, and had sided with the Bethesda view of the dispute, which Kelly disagreed with.[109] Later Kelly wrote his own articles between 1887 and 1889 about the shortcomings of British philosophy though he often made links between them and German philosophers. These articles acted as fore-runners to his attacks on English evangelicals in the Church of England who he saw as falsely espousing the premises of higher criticism. I shall look at these in detail in chapter 3.

In April 1866 Darby linked what he considered to be the dangers of Friedrich Daniel Ernst Schleiermacher (1768–1834) with the philosophy of Kant.[110] He wrote, "The great blunder of Schleiermacher and the source of the worst infidelity now is that he has taken the Holy Ghost's work in us—very likely in "himself"—for intuition or specially *collective* Christian consciousness. This is, I suspect, the key for the whole system itself, probably the fruit of Kantian philosophy and its offsets."[111]

In linking this philosophy with theories of inspiration Darby explained that Schleiermacher's theories made Scripture "the mere history of partial apprehension of truth."[112] He asserted that Scherer and Bunsen were saturated with Schleiermacher's philosophy and therefore, by his own understanding of Scriptural inspiration, he was rejecting this philosophy. Darby understood that acceptance of revelation itself depended on a particular philosophic viewpoint. In entitling his article "The Absolute," Darby not only referred to the influence of Kant and Hegel but asserted the objectivity of God beyond the mind of man.[113] He followed his own line of reasoning in asserting "where God is not known objectively, this centers

---

109. Grass, *Gathering to His Name*, 73.
110. Darby, "The Absolute," 53–56.
111. Ibid., 55.
112. Ibid.
113. Ibid., 54.

in self and centering in self is the perfection of degradation."[114] Darby used this line of argument to point to the absolute nature of Christ's perfection. "I get absolute moral absolutes glorified in God at the cost of abnegation of self in man (i.e. In man who was the Son of God) love, righteousness, majesty and truth. God was glorified in Him."[115] Like Kelly, Darby and J.E. Batten showed themselves to be learned in ancient philosophy. In his article of January 1st 1867, J.E. Batten linked the theology of Hooker and the teaching of Pusey with the philosophy of Plato and Aristotle.[116] In his article written on January 1st, 1869, Darby linked Aristotle, Origen and Johann Gottlieb Fichte (1762–1814).[117]

Darby and Kelly were able to link German philosophy with the new English schools of philosophy, particularly that of Henry Longueville Mansel.[118] Darby criticized Mansel when he wrote, "But when Mr. Mansel accepts Hegel's dictum that the Absolute must include all that is actual, even evil, I deny it."[119] He accused Hegel and Mansel of having "a want of moral discernment": he did not believe that moral discernment and philosophical understanding could be separated.

For Kelly and Darby it was very important that it was not a theory of biblical inspiration which was the bedrock of truth. Instead, Christ Himself was the truth and, in that the truth was embodied in a person, it could not be fully intellectually explained. In his article included in *The Bible Treasury* of 1869, Darby wrote, "Christ is the truth (it is not the revelation which is truth). Hence no theology is the truth." In the same article he attacked pantheism: "Pantheism reduces existence to matter, and so denies absoluteness and unchangeableness."[120]

Kelly also included articles by J. E. Batten to look at the further influences of German philosophy. In an article from *The Bible Treasury*, dated January 1st, 1857, Batten examined the ideas of Hegel and Strauss and linked them with Hinduism and the teachings which were going on in Germany as a result of the influence of the great German philosophers.[121]

114. Ibid.
115. Ibid.
116. Batten, "Modern Hegelianism," 133.
117. Darby, "The Relative and the Absolute," 201.
118. Mansel (1820–1871), Dean of St. Paul's Cathedral.
119. Darby, "Relative and Absolute," 198.
120. Ibid., 201.
121. Batten, "Modern Hegelianism," 133.

In July 1868, Batten wrote an article in which he argued that Hegel, in asserting that everything is logical, drew another false conclusion, "namely, that there is no sin or guilt, no accountableness, no personal responsibility. What men call sin is regarded as only a step to further development and greater improvement."[122] For the Brethren, sin was axiomatic to their philosophical understanding and therefore they rejected the premises of German higher criticism, but they were aware of this intellectual influence. Batten went on to make another point which was important. "The third point in which this modern philosophy coincides with Hinduism, is the distinct denial of a personal existence after death."[123] In one of his own articles Kelly supported Batten's viewpoint. "If you deny [evil], you say that either God is everything—pantheism—or that God does not exist—atheism."[124] In Batten's article on Spencer he linked Spencer's views with those of Kant and the Upinashads and the Bhagavat Gita.[125]

Darby and Kelly considered the enormous effect of Kant, Hegel and Schleiermacher on the German school of higher criticism. Barr states that Kant's theory of knowledge was consistently ignored by conservative evangelicals of the nineteenth century.[126] However, it might be more accurate to say that Darby and Kelly consciously rejected those views rather than consistently ignored them. De Wette was greatly influenced by the philosophy of Jakob Friedrich Fries (1773–1843) and Schleiermacher.[127] De Wette, influenced by Fries's concept of "ahnung," saw a contrast between the more instinctive Hebrew religion which was life-giving and the later Judaism which he saw as slavery to the letter of the law. This division informed his understanding of dating and authorship of the Old Testament.[128] *Leben Jesus* by David Strauss (1808–1874) was published in 1835 and, in particular, its English translation by George Eliot in 1846 had an enormous influence on English thinkers.[129] Strauss was against both the supranaturalist

---

122. Ibid.
123. Ibid.
124. Kelly, "The Word of God," 98.
125. J.E. Batten, "What is a Succession a Succession of or the Apostasy," 266–67.
126. Barr, *Fundamentalism*, 274.
127. Howard, *Religion and the Rise of Historicism*, 9.
128. Rogerson, *de Wette*, 66.
129. Ibid., 241. De Wette came to be seen as influencing Strauss. Cf. Howard, *Religion and the Rise of Historicism*, 8. George Eliot, the famous novelist and intellectual, in translating Strauss into English, brought his ideas to the attention of the Victorian public.

interpretation but also the rationalist interpretation of Christ's life. Instead he gave a "mythical" reading, which majored on the Gospels as an early Church interpretation of Messianic expectations.[130] Strauss elevated "the idea" and transposed it onto the person of Christ, and therefore an immanent relationship between God and man became more important than a transcendent one.[131] Strauss's book had a large influence on the Romantic school of literature in England, which in turn had an enormous influence on the Anglican Broad Church theologians such as Hare, Thirlwall, Arnold and Milman, who became the leaders of "liberal Anglicanism."[132] Darby and Kelly rejected the philosophical premises of Strauss and the Anglican Broad Church.

A CRITIQUE OF BARR'S DEFINITION OF FUNDAMENTALISM IN THE LIGHT OF KELLY'S VIEWS OF INSPIRATION

Kelly shows a more nuanced approach to biblical inspiration than Barr would lead us to expect from his criticism of fundamentalism. (The Brethren have often been seen as proto–fundamentalist even though this description is anachronistic.) Rogerson identified the difference in philosophical influence between those of the German school of higher criticism and the Pietists. "From the end of the 1820s, we find the beginning of the polarization brought about by the renewal movement, as well as the divisions among critical scholars and, later, among the Confessionalists."[133] However, Barr turned this difference in philosophical influence into a condemnation of those who had different motivations for their biblical scholarship. The question we might ask about Kelly is whether that motivation stopped him accepting different sources for the biblical narrative or whether it was other scholarly considerations which stopped him doing so.[134] Postmodern criticism has shown us that we cannot avoid considering the motivation of any literary scholar because neutrality is impossible and not even desirable.[135]

130. Larsen, *Crisis of Doubt—Honest Faith in Nineteenth-century England*, 79.
131. Grafe, "The Old Faith and the New," 226, 229.
132. Clements, "The Intellectual Background of H.H. Milman," 252.
133. Rogerson, *OT Criticism*, 139.
134. Barr, *Fundamentalism*, 61.
135. Eagleton, *Literary Theory: An Introduction*. This book gives an overall understanding of postmodern criticism.

Barr went on to say that the link between inspiration and inerrancy had no rootage in the Bible and belonged to purely speculative philosophical assumption, but Kelly showed that the idea of plenary inspiration was firmly fixed in the Bible. Of course, Kelly was influenced by materialism, just as Barr has accused all fundamentalists as being.[136] However, I would argue that Kelly was a far broader scholar, who was able to consider philosophical motivation quite carefully. Barr has shown that fundamentalists quarreled not with science but with historians and literary critics. However, *The Bible Treasury* shows Brethren writers such as J.G. Bellett, to have been much more aware of different views of history than Barr would allow. For example, Bellett reviewed A.P. Stanley's book *Sinai and Palestine in connexion with their history* (1856) and commented that, "even though there was much that is valuable and masterly," he has "an habitual exaggeration of secondary causes."[137] Barr has also contended that fundamentalists disliked mysticism.[138] However, Kelly's theology was connected with his mystic spirituality and so there is always a tension between his spirituality and his conservatism. I propose that Kelly was influenced by the Romantic movement of his day and by the Hegelian "ideal" through his strain of mystic spirituality rather than through his idealization of Scripture as the Word of God. I disagree with Barr when he asserted that conservative scholars wanted their readers to think that they were only attached to facts and that they had no ideological point of view. Darby and Kelly were fully aware of having an ideological point of view. Barr also maintained that fundamentalists were influenced by Plato rather than Aristotle, but they turned the idea of the perfection of God to the perfection of the Bible. Again Darby and Kelly considered the philosophy of the ancient Greeks and also of the Church Fathers in their writings. Absolute inerrancy, according to Barr, was a development of the nineteenth century and came about as a reaction to critical scholarship.[139] Barr observed that "there is an absence of history in fundamentalism which allows it to live in a fictitious past."[140] Therefore the past is always idealized, as we see when fundamentalists pointed back to the early church and to the reformation. Although this was partly a feature of Brethren theologians who intentionally went back to the "simplicity" of

---

136. Ibid., 85, 93.
137. Kelly, "People and Land of Israel," 191, referring to Stanley, *Sinai and Palestine*.
138. Barr, *Fundamentalism*, 98.
139. Ibid., 172.
140. Ibid., 181.

the Acts of the Apostles in their ecclesiology, Kelly was able to be critical of the early church and of the Reformation. Belief in the ruin of the church was central to Brethren teaching. We should also remember, in addition to Brethren contributions to scholarship, that there were some conservative evangelicals who agreed with the critical documentary hypothesis of the Pentateuch, such as W.F. Albright (1891–1971), who was part of the Princeton Seminary. Therefore we see that, despite Barr's assertions to the contrary, fundamentalists were not just a homogenous group when it came to biblical scholarship and that Kelly cannot be stereotyped as "a fundamentalist," while ignoring his wider spirituality.[141]

SOME CONCLUSIONS ABOUT KELLY'S VIEWS ON BIBLICAL INSPIRATION

Darby and Kelly were particularly aware of philosophical influence down the centuries, and in the articles printed in *The Bible Treasury*, they consciously rejected the philosophical basis of the school of higher criticism in Germany. Kelly did fit into David Bebbington's "quadrilateral of priorities" for an evangelical Christian—conversionism, activism, biblicism and crucicentrism.[142] I would also like to place Kelly in an extensive continuum of conservative, intellectual, evangelical theologians. He would have agreed with Beacon's observation, "There are many dangers to beware of in interpreting Scripture, but perhaps a bald literalism of mind is not the least."[143] He did not just fit into a narrow definition of "fundamentalism," and we can see that the philosophical influences—pre-Enlightenment, Enlightenment and Romantic—were varied and led him to a unique contribution to biblical exegesis.

Kelly made his own views on higher criticism very clear in his article on "The Higher Criticism" (1906) in *The Bible Treasury*. He called it "the revived superstition and infidelity of our day" and linked it to the rationalist, Tom Paine, who came out of the Enlightenment tradition.[144] In *Introduction to the Pentateuch* (May 1870), he noted that we must accept revelation, even though there are difficulties because, "it is better to be in lack of knowledge than in unbelief." The fact that the Scriptures were not all understood was

---

141. Ibid., 148.
142. Bebbington, *Evangelicalism*, 3.
143. Beacon, "Truth Absolute and Relative," 31.
144. Kelly, "The Higher Criticism," 12.

greater proof to Kelly that they were of God. "Revelation is the mind of God in the language of man, but perfectly guided and guarded by the Spirit."[145]

In conclusion, we can recognize Kelly to have been a major Bible teacher in the Victorian conservative evangelical tradition, but he was not limited by Barr's narrow definition of fundamentalism. He had read the works of the German school of higher criticism and consciously argued against their theories. When Barr described "fundamentalism" as a school of thought, arising at the end of the nineteenth century, but with its roots in dispensationalism, we can see a parallel to Kelly's theological position. Dispensationalism did indeed have a varied influence on Kelly's theology but it did not necessarily lead to fundamentalism, as Barr has suggested. The Brethren were prominent in their defense of biblical inspiration, and Kelly was one of their foremost Bible teachers. Some of the ideas associated with higher criticism—historical progress, comparative religion and literary theory—became an important part of nineteenth-century thinking and crossed the barriers of different academic disciplines. Thus we see the same ideas arising in the schools of history, philosophy, literary criticism as well as theology. Kelly not only engaged with these theories but he saw clearly the "results" in terms of linked theological understanding. Although he rejected wider theological interpretations of the Bible, he consistently engaged with them in his writings. Even though Kelly might be regarded superficially as a literalist and nascent "fundamentalist"—a precursor of the Princeton Seminary school of thought—his views on inspiration suggest a wider and more nuanced approach. In my next chapter I will look at Kelly's engagement with the English theologians of the Broad Church, the Tractarians and the non-conformists, whose writings had an influence on the established Church of England. Kelly had something to say about all of them.

145. Kelly, *Pentateuch*, xii.

CHAPTER 3

William Kelly as a Conservative Intellectual
His Relationship with Nineteenth-century English Theologians

INTRODUCTION

In this chapter I will look at Kelly's response to the English theologians who followed the German school of higher criticism and who had influence on Victorian thinkers. Kelly mainly used his exegesis of the Pentateuch (1871) to do this. Then I will include articles from *The Bible Treasury* used and edited by Kelly in the light of the publication of Gladstone's *The Impregnable Rock of Holy Scripture* (1890) and *Lux Mundi* (1890), which represented the later Tractarian views on the debate and which moved from consideration of the Old Testament to the New. Lastly I will consider Kelly's concern with the arguments of the academic Anglican evangelicals, A.F. Kirkpatrick (1849–1940) and S.R. Driver (1846–1914), and his series of articles in *The Bible Treasury* which opposed their views.

Kelly used his periodical *The Bible Treasury* to review contemporary English religious books. As well as writing articles himself, he also included reviews by trusted Brethren writers, J.N. Darby, J.G. Bellett and William Trotter (1818–1865), and encouraged younger Brethren writers, such as William J. Hocking (1864–1953) and Richard Beacon (junior) (dates unknown), to do the same. A pattern becomes clear when we look at the progression of these articles. In the 1850s there is a criticism of Davidson's contribution to the tenth edition of Thomas Horne's *Introduction to the Old Testament*, vol. 2, a review of the 1854 Bampton lectures by Waldegrave and a review of Baron Bunsen's *Signs of the Times* on the subject of biblical inspiration.[1] Kelly wrote a response in 1885 to Henry Drummond's *Natural Law in the Spiritual World* (1883), which had advocated social optimism and made love the object of evolution.[2]

Later, in the 1890s there was a clear increase in the number of articles written about English attitudes to biblical criticism after the publication of *Lux Mundi* in 1890. Kelly also published a review by Beacon in July 1890 of Gladstone's popular work, *The Impregnable Rock of Holy Scripture* which had itself been published in April 1890.[3] There were five articles about *Lux Mundi* (1890) and the subject of Mosaic authorship of the Pentateuch between 1890 and 1898 by Hocking as well as many articles on the early chapters of Genesis between 1892 and 1895.[4] This suggests that, although Kelly had always written about biblical criticism in his exegeses and had reviewed current theological works in his periodical, his particular concern from 1890 onwards was to counteract the influence of more liberal Broad Church theologians and later the more open evangelical Anglicans, whom Kelly considered to have capitulated to the position of the liberals.

It was the publication of *Essays and Reviews* (1860) which was the first piece of widely circulated and influential English writing on inspiration and which had an impact on the ongoing nineteenth-century discussion about biblical criticism. It might seem surprising that Kelly made little reference to this publication, though he continually came back in his writings to the subject of inspiration and made implicit references to the controversial ideas found in its essays.[5] There were several reasons for this. Firstly, the

---

1. Kelly, "Charges against Mr. Davidson," 182. Bunsen, *Signs of the Times*. Thomas Horne (1780–1862)—Thomas Horne, *Introduction to the Old Testament*, vol. 2; cf. footnote 8 for further details of this volume. Samuel Prideaux Tregelles (1813–1875); Samuel Waldegrave (1817–1869), conservative theologian and Bishop of Carlisle; Christian Josias, Baron Bunsen (1791–1860), German diplomat and theologian.

2. Kelly, "Drummond's Natural Law," 220–23; Henry Drummond, *Natural Law in the Spiritual World*.

3. R. Beacon, "Impregnable Rock," 110–12; W.E. Gladstone, *The Impregnable Rock of Holy Scripture* (1890).

4. Beacon, "On Biblical (O.T.) Criticism," 79–80; Hocking, "The Lord's Testimony to the Mosaic Authorship," 58–60; 72–75; 90–92; Kelly, "Scripture Questions and Answers," 175.

5. For example, in writing about Gladstone's book in *BT* 18, no. 410 (July, 1890), 110, Beacon tackles Jowett's idea that the Scriptures should be treated like any other book and

date of *Essays and Reviews* was right at the beginning of Kelly's editorship of *The Bible Treasury* and we have already noted that his references to books about biblical criticism become more numerous in later years. Secondly, as a work edited by Anglican divines, it was attacked by the Church of England itself and two of its writers had been taken through the ecclesiastical courts; therefore, as a member of the Brethren, Kelly would not have felt the same duty to expose its arguments.[6] Thirdly, within the Brethren, J.N. Darby had already given his own forthright reply in *Dialogues on the 'Essays and Reviews'* (1862), and Kelly acted as Darby's editor.[7]

THREE KEY ENGLISH THEOLOGIANS AND THEIR VIEWS ON THE PENTATEUCH

The three key authors on the subject of biblical inspiration in England between 1850 and 1880 were Samuel Davidson (1807–1898), John William Colenso (1814–1883) and Francis W. Newman (1805–1897). All three came from different theological backgrounds and were important for different reasons and, after a brief introduction to their points of view, I explain how Kelly reacted to them mainly in his exegesis on the Pentateuch. All three were praised by German scholars for opening up the debate about biblical infallibility in England and in particular the dating and composition of the Pentateuch. Davidson wrote mainly for biblical scholars, Newman for professional literary men, while Colenso opened up the whole subject to the intelligent and questioning layman. Davidson wrote as a Presbyterian who became a Congregationalist and then later a Unitarian. Colenso continued to be a bishop of the Church of England. Newman seceded from the Church of England to follow Darby into the Brethren and later became a Unitarian. Colenso and Newman were influenced by their experiences as missionaries in Natal and the Middle East respectively.

Samuel Davidson started his career as an orthodox believer who, during the course of his professorship at the Free College in Manchester, started to study the German School of biblical criticism. In the 1820s he was asked by the publishers of *An Introduction to the Critical Study and Knowledge of the Holy Scriptures* by Thomas Hartwell Horne (1780–1862) to produce a

---

also that the Bible only "contains" Scripture. (Ibid., 112).

6. Attacks by Archbishop Tait and Oxford professor Rawlinson are analyzed in Shea and Whitla, *Essays and Reviews*, 41, 45.

7. Darby, *Dialogues on the "Essays and Reviews."*

further edition along with S.P. Tregelles (1813–1875) and all three eventually contributed the second volume of four.[8] As Davidson's contribution gave a more liberal view to dating and authorship of the Old Testament than that of Horne and Tregelles, Davidson's fitness as Professor in the Free College was called into question "partly occasioned by a letter written by Dr S.P. Tregelles, the third co-author with Horne and Davidson, to *The Record* newspaper, in which it was indirectly alleged that Davidson had not upheld the plenary inspiration of the Bible."[9] Davidson felt betrayed by Tregelles.[10] In his *Autobiography* (1899), which is a useful record of his changing beliefs over the years, he explained his attitudes to the doctrine of biblical infallibility. Davidson appealed to the Church Fathers, and quoted Justin Martyr, Origen, Chrysostom and Augustine, showing that these well respected divines had rejected verbal infallibility. He then passed to Luther, Calvin, Erasmus, Grotius, Lowth, Baxter, Howe and many more recent theologians "of acknowledged authority," who also had wider views on the subject.[11] He acknowledged the presence of genuine Christian faith amongst critics—"A deeply religious man may be highly sceptical."[12] Davidson was extremely critical of any bigotry or unfair judgment of critics: for example he spoke disparagingly of Tregelles's translation of Wilhelm Gesenius (1786–1842) as being inaccurate.[13] He also bewailed the lack of influence of philosophers such as Kant and Schleiermacher in England.[14] He came to believe in the progression of religion from polytheism to monotheism, and opposed what he saw as the "bibliolatry" of the orthodox believer.[15]

Colenso can be assessed not only for his views on biblical inspiration but also for his understanding of cultural context. Colenso's book, *The Pentateuch and the Book of Joshua Critically Examined, Part 1* (1861), caused considerable disturbance because it was published in the wake of *Essays and Reviews* (1860) and because it pursued the line of criticism which questioned the infallibility of Scripture.[16] It raised objections from the Archbish-

---

8. Horne, *An Introduction to the Study and Knowledge of the Holy Scriptures*.
9. Rogerson, *OT Criticism*, 202.
10. Davidson, *Autobiography*, 57.
11. Ibid., 58.
12. Ibid., 210.
13. Ibid., 216.
14. Ibid., 219.
15. Ibid., 232.
16. Larsen, "Bishop Colenso and his Critics," 71.

op of Canterbury, Charles Longley and from the *Christian Remembrancer* (a High Church publication) of January 1863, as well as from evangelicals.[17] Although Larsen and Rogerson have disputed the legacy of Colenso, David Jobling maintains that Colenso has not been understood within his colonial context.[18]

On examining recent German criticism, Colenso was not convinced by the Confessionalist School represented by Karl Hengstenberg and Johann Heinrich Kurtz (1809–1890).[19] When he confided in Wilhelm Bleek (1827–1875), a German linguist who was a specialist in South African languages and son of an eminent theologian, he observed that he was aware that his work on the Pentateuch would cause uproar.[20] Colenso received positive feedback on his work from German and Dutch scholars, Kalisch, Ewald, Hitzig and Kuenen. Thomas Kelly Cheyne (1841–1915), writing in 1896, thought that Colenso had made a significant contribution to biblical criticism.[21] Jobling commented that Kuenen admired Colenso's stand within the established Church, had written in the spirit of Reformation freedom and had had a major influence on his own work when he was looking for the dating of the *Grundschrift* or P document.[22] Colenso had translated the work of German critics for the English public.[23]

In Colenso's work there was an interesting link between his views on the Pentateuch and his views on salvation which he considered might be understood culturally. Colenso saw large gaps in the understanding of post-Enlightenment Europe.[24] The importance of seeing Colenso in his context is explained in the subtitle of his 1861 *Commentary on Romans*, "explained from a missionary point of view."[25] Colenso was not prepared to push answers he did not believe in, or to preach hell or penal atonement like other missionaries in South Africa. He worried about separating the Zulus from their own culture and that Westerners could not distinguishing

---

17. Ibid., 51.
18. Jobling, "Colenso on Myth or Colenso as Myth," 71.
19. Guy, *The Heretic*, 104.
20. Ibid., 106.
21. Larsen, "Colenso and his Critics," 42.
22. Jobling, "Colenso on Myth," 84, 88, 89.
23. Ibid., 94.
24. Ibid., 108.
25. Colenso, *St. Paul's Epistle to the Romans*.

between good and bad morality within that culture.²⁶ Even before he had gone to Africa, Colenso had read broadly and greatly admired Maurice, appreciated Arnold and Benjamin Jowett and was an admirer of Francis Newman's work on biblical criticism and his autobiography, *Phases of Faith* (1850).²⁷ Draper has pointed out that Colenso was far ahead of his time in recognizing the importance of language in interpreting ideas and that he understood that the perception of the Bible was a "dialectical process."²⁸

Newman was less influential than Colenso because he was not ordained in the Church of England. He was less revered as a Bible scholar than Davidson because he was an amateur. His relationship with the Brethren was an interesting one. He had been part of the first Brethren missionary expedition to the Middle East when he had attempted to join A.N. Groves and his family in Baghdad.²⁹ Various misfortunes beset them and Newman eventually returned to Britain by himself, thoroughly disillusioned with his experiences. Previously, he had met Darby on a visit to Ireland as an Oxford undergraduate and, as a result of that influence, had seceded from the Church of England and joined the Brethren movement.³⁰ After his failed missionary journey, he became more heterodox in his beliefs and was eventually excommunicated by the Brethren. He became a Unitarian. His writings about the Pentateuch did not attract the same notoriety as Davidson's because he did not take the position of theological teacher. As Professor of Latin at London University, he was a respected academic and gifted amateur with a strong sense of the contemporary movement in historical development and the ways in which ancient texts might be read. His academic career in classics and his previous association with the Brethren made him little known as a theologian and his work was less accessible to the general public. Therefore Kelly did not identify him in the same way as he did Davidson and Colenso. Newman's autobiography, *Phases of Faith* (1850), shows the influence of Darby over him as a young man: he was later condemned by Darby for his heterodoxy.³¹ However, his ideas are worth

---

26. Ibid., 113, 114.
27. Ibid., 71.
28. Draper, "Colenso's Commentary on Romans," 105.
29. Newman, *Phases of Faith*, 37. Despite his later rejection of the missionary enterprise, he expressed great admiration for Groves and what he considered to be Groves' loving and inclusive spirit.
30. Grass, *Gathering to his Name*, 31.
31. Newman, *Phases of Faith*, 17, 18.

examining because Kelly makes reference to them in *The Bible Treasury* and his exegeses, even though he only occasionally refers to him by name.

Some of Newman's theories about the Pentateuch were similar to those of Colenso but his main critical book was published some years before Colenso's work in 1847. Kelly did not start to edit *The Bible Treasury* until 1860 and at that time Newman was not the main protagonist in the theological arguments in England or in the controversies which ensued. Colenso acknowledged Newman as a personal inspiration in his own research. Rogerson has claimed that Newman, although an amateur, was one of the original English biblical critics who brought the work of the German biblical critics to the notice of the Victorian public.[32] Bernard Reardon has also drawn attention to the influence of Newman on his contemporaries, exploring his influence on biblical criticism in England, his contribution to "the erosion of belief" in the Victorian era, and his understanding of religious temperament and language.[33]

KELLY'S DETAILED RESPONSE TO THEIR ARGUMENTS

Kelly responded to these three scholars by accusing them of lack of originality and he derided Davidson as a "neologist," who showed "a lack of Biblical foundations in his work."[34] One example of this was, when he saw that Davidson and Colenso were trying to separate the supposed influence of the Levites and the priests in the Pentateuch, he accused them of merely following the lead of the earlier deists.[35] Davidson himself paid tribute to the work of de Wette from 1811 onwards and admitted that all English biblical critics relied heavily on their German colleagues.[36]

Kelly felt able to challenge the English critics because of his expert knowledge of Hebrew grammar. Of the three, only Davidson had a scholarly knowledge of Hebrew. Kelly argued against Davidson, who said that Genesis 1:1 was a summary of the remaining verses. In contrast Kelly believed that there was a deliberate gap between two different types of creation—the original creation of the universe and a recreation after the fall of Satan—which were described in verses one and two. Kelly justified his own

---

32. Rogerson, *OT Criticism*, 195.
33. Reardon, *From Coleridge to Gore*, 261–65.
34. Kelly, *Pentateuch and its Critics*, 31.
35. Ibid., 459.
36. Davidson, *Autobiography*, 186.

view by explaining that "the copulative *van* connects each verse, but of itself in no way forbids an immense space, which depends on the nature of the case where no specification of time enters."[37]

Kelly disputed Davidson's dating of many Old Testament books including the Pentateuch, the history books, the Psalms and Daniel. There were specific parts of these books where Davidson questioned traditional dating. In his *Lectures Introductory to the Study of the Pentateuch* (1871), Kelly answered Davidson's objections which involved the post-dating of the instructions about the spies and the help given by Jethro. Kelly referred in detail to the text of Davidson's *Introduction to the Old Testament*.[38] According to Kelly, Davidson "ventured to set portions of this chapter in juxtaposition with two from elsewhere in order to show that God's speaking to the inspired writer was simply his own mind."[39] In answer Kelly compared the circumstances of Exodus 18:23 and Deuteronomy 1:9 and saw the difference between "a historical statement and the use a legislator made as he addressed a new generation."[40] Kelly discussed the possible contradictions between Exodus and Deuteronomy in laying out the commandments.[41] He often judged the confusion about dating to be a misunderstanding of the moral purpose of the passage and the social habits of different generations being recorded.[42] While following the German lead, Davidson was cautious about dating problems. He admitted that there were some wild ideas amongst critics in the dating of the Pentateuch and admired the cautious attitude of Newman.[43] Newman had noted that Deuteronomy had been found by Hilkiah, the chief priest, but he had been wary of asserting the process of compilation. As a secular historian not a theologian, Newman wondered whether Josiah's self-styled "discovery" had in fact been an invention, because, claimed Newman, "no unconquered nation loses the books of its religion."[44] Newman traced the likelihood of the Pentateuch being piecemeal works made from pre-existing fragments, in accordance

---

37. Kelly, *Pentateuch and its Critics*, 18.
38. Davidson, *Introduction to the Old Testament*, 235.
39. Kelly, *Pentateuch*, 428.
40. Ibid., 432.
41. Ibid., 449.
42. Ibid., 459.
43. Davidson, *Autobiography*, 306.
44. Newman, *The History of the Hebrew Monarchy*, 334.

with the parallels he saw as a classical historian.[45] Kelly's view was of the divine maintenance of the texts for divine purpose. Newman was aware that his views would give extreme offence to the religious but felt that in all honesty he should propose them.[46]

In the nineteenth century much had been made about the witness of the use of different divine names to the dating and authorship of different manuscripts in the Pentateuch and Kelly consistently argued against this perspective. Similar ideas to Kelly's have been argued more recently by evangelical scholars, who have shown no awareness of Kelly as an earlier authority, suggesting that as a conservative scholar his ideas were thoughtful and worthy of consideration but also that he was not known to later generations of evangelical scholars.[47] Kelly remarked that Edward Perowne thought that it was difficult to examine closely the use of the Divine names as the German critics had done consistently, but Kelly disagreed. "Not so; it only seems to fail, I venture to say, for want of a searching analysis."[48] Kelly made a point of making the sort of analysis which he felt was lacking in other studies.

In writing about Genesis Kelly argued with Davidson on the subject of the name of God being revealed to Abraham, because Davidson had found the story in Genesis inconsistent with Exodus 6:3.[49] Kelly explained that the same name had been used in Abraham's time but not understood until the time of Moses, adding, "Hence on the *hypothesis* of one and the same writer of the Pentateuch, and the correctness of the alleged explanation, we argue that the contrast between the acquaintance of Abraham with the name of Jehovah, and full knowledge of that name first made known to Moses is groundless."[50] Here Kelly uses Moses as a theological interpreter of previous events and he also explains that the particular name of God is used in this passage in Exodus for moral motives. He explained that the same motivation exists in the use of Jehovah in Psalms 42 and 83. The idea of theological interpretation of text was a particularly important one for

---

45. Ibid.

46. Ibid., 335.

47. Cf. *The New Bible Commentary*. Kelly is not acknowledged by the editors but nevertheless the possible ways of interpreting the critical passages in the Pentateuch are similar to his.

48. Kelly, *The Pentateuch and Its Critics*, 29.

49. In Gen 16 God appears to Abram (before his name is changed to Abraham) and uses the name El-Shaddai. In Ex 6:3 the same name is used but another one is added.

50. Kelly, *Pentateuch*, 148 (italics in the original).

Kelly, though for him it was connected with God's choice of revelation for a particular time, rather than with man's gradual religious understanding as the Broad Church would have claimed. Kelly gave detailed reasons why he dismissed Davidson's views on the Jehovistic and Elhoistic manuscripts which had been explained in Davidson's *Introduction to the Old Testament* 1.[51] He gave as a parallel the use Jesus made of the title "Father" for God in the New Testament. In his view this was proof of a new attitude, a new understanding rather than a new name and was not due to diversity of authorship.[52] Davidson had also suggested that there was a contradiction between Exodus 4:31, where the people appear to accept God's desire to save them and Exodus 6:9 and 12, where the text shows that they did not listen to Moses.[53] Kelly answered Davidson's accusation by explaining that the first verse talks about the elders accepting Moses and his signs from God, whereas the verses in chapter 6 are about the ordinary people being so burdened by slavery that they were unable to embrace the promise of deliverance.[54]

Kelly frequently quoted at length from Davidson before arguing against him and showing his understanding of Davidson's points. When referring to Davidson's plea to "the redactor who was not Ezra... the unfortunate Deuteronomist in the reign of Manasseh, who employed the innocent fictions, which an uncivilized age rendered easy," Kelly counteracted by calling Davidson's idea, "the Christian or unchristian mythology of the nineteenth century."[55]

The Genesis narrative of the Flood was an area of dispute for a number of biblical scholars. Kelly acknowledged that Colenso treated the subject in some detail, following the German critics and Davidson in his views on varied authorship and manuscripts.[56] However Kelly surmised that it was one historian who presented everything from more than one point of view. In looking at the different names for God in Genesis chapters 6 and 7, Kelly explained that one was consistently used for creation and the other for the development of God's relationship with Noah. Kelly showed understanding of Colenso's viewpoint but rejected his conclusions. He felt that the choice

---

51. Davidson, *Introduction to OT*, vol. 1, 65.
52. Ibid.
53. Ibid., 65.
54. Kelly, *Pentateuch*, 147.
55. Davidson, *Introduction to OT*, 47–51, quoted in Kelly, *Pentateuch*, 10.
56. Ibid., 42, 43.

of "two" animals was about generation, but the "seven" was about "marked completeness for sacrifice."[57] Interestingly this accords with twentieth-century hermeneutical understanding of narrative techniques.[58] Although there is no specific mention of the number seven indicating sacrifice in the Genesis accounts, what we see in Kelly's commentary is that he took the numbers as ancient signifiers and therefore understood language as pointing beyond literal meaning. Here his understanding of language use conflicted with Colenso's literalist interpretation. The so-called "Brethren literalist" can be seen as the literary interpreter—one who understood what was appropriate in a text revealing different purposes. Kelly appeared to do this instinctively through his experience of interpreting ancient texts and his mature sense of the text as a whole rather than concentrating on a small part of the manuscript.

All four theologians looked at problems in the wilderness narratives and the history books. Davidson frequently examined contradictions between passages in 1 and 2 Kings; he posited not only different source material but also the addition of "the mythical and miraculous in them."[59] In answer to chapter 18 of Colenso's *The Pentateuch and the book of Joshua critically examined: part 6* (1872), Kelly discussed the problem of the increase in the population in the wilderness.[60] Kelly mixed a belief in the miraculous with justification from secular sources: he quoted in justification of his views Malthus's *Essay on the Principle of Population* and Short's *New Observations on Bills of Mortality*.[61]

Colenso had looked at the origins of the Passover and disputed the biblical account.[62] He thought that the Passover had emerged out of Egyptian tradition and that in earlier times the Israelites had sacrificed the first born son in honor of the sun god. This was a variation of the view of other scholars that the Passover had come out of a harvest celebration of the Canaanites which had been taken over by the Israelites: there too the original religion of the Canaanites was associated with child sacrifice.

57. Ibid., 42.
58. Moberley, *At the Mountain of God*, 29–30.
59. Davidson, *Autobiography*, 229.
60. Kelly, *Pentateuch*, 128.
61. Malthus, *Essay on the Principle of Population*, 190; Dr Short, *New Observations on Bills of Mortality*, vol. 8, 259. Malthus (1766–1834) had been made popular by Archbishop Sumner and Edward Copplestone, Professor of Oriel College, Oxford and Bishop of Llandaff. Cf. Norman, *Church and Society in England 1770–1970*, 43.
62. Colenso, *The Pentateuch and the Book of Joshua Critically Examined*, part 6, 427.

Kelly, in considering the absolute divine ban on child sacrifice in the Old Testament, called such ideas, particularly those of Colenso, "as weak as they are malicious."[63] He argued against Colenso's specific objection to the idea that in one day the instruction and the keeping of the Passover could have taken place as related in Exodus. Kelly explained, "Everyone knows the habit in Hebrew and indeed in other languages, for the speaker to throw himself forward into the chief event in question, even if there had been no express preliminaries which evince the futility of the statement."[64] Here we see Kelly using his authority and experience as a Hebraist to good effect and showing up Colenso's amateur status in that specialty. Colenso, though adept at mastering languages for himself, was a mathematician by training and profession.

Against Colenso's objection to the number of priests needed in Exodus chapters 20 and 21, Kelly stressed that it was a family feast and probably was so in the wilderness as well. He believed that the Israelites were not circumcised in the desert and that therefore there would not have been the appropriate work found for Aaron, the priest, and his sons. He went on to argue in detail against Colenso's translation of the word "harnessed" as "armed." According to Colenso, this led to there being 600,000 men armed. In answering, Kelly, in justifying his own interpretation, referred to Gesenius and August Knobel (1807–1863) as well as Onkelos (35–120), Abraham Ben Meir Ibn Ezra (1089–1167) and Alexander McCaul (1799–1863). Supported by his references to these scholars, Kelly translated the word "girt" or "in regular order," thereby overcoming Colenso's objections to so many men being armed in the wilderness.[65] Later in the same work he referred to Colenso's comments on Leviticus 4:11 and 12. Colenso commented on the practical impossibility of Aaron carrying the bullocks for six miles.[66] Kelly argued back from the Hebrew that "carried" meant "caused to be carried." He explained, "For a tyro in Hebrew knows that verbs are susceptible of a change in form which gives a causative force."[67] Another example of Kelly looking at Colenso's specific objections to the text is found when he spoke against Colenso's claim that each family must have had forty-two boys on average. Kelly claimed that Colenso had copied his claim in Part 1, chapter

63. Kelly, *Pentateuch*, 158.
64. Ibid.
65. Ibid., 161.
66. Colenso, *The Pentateuch*, part 1, 4th ed., chapter 6.
67. Kelly, *Pentateuch*, 243. "Tyro" means a beginner or novice.

13 from Bishop Patrick.[68] Kelly replied that the greatest number must have been eight, and that Colenso had overlooked several details in the record. He drew the reader's attention to Exodus chapter 6 and explained that many of the instructions were not carried out in the wilderness.[69]

All four theologians wrote about the apparent discrepancy between Saul not knowing David when he came to fight Goliath and having already met him when he came to play music to soothe his depressed mood. As a result of this supposed discrepancy, Davidson tried to assess the relative dating and source material of 1 Samuel and both books of Kings. He explained, "The two sources were put together by a writer who did little to harmonize them though he showed some skill in interweaving the contents." Newman, in working through inconsistencies, was much less literalist than Colenso, and had a much clearer understanding of literary perspective. He was also less dogmatic and argumentative in tone than Colenso and this probably drew him up against fewer critics. Like Colenso, Newman questioned the authority of the account of David and Goliath. Along with Davidson, he suggested the possibility of different source material. He said that the episode bore the marks of romance rather than history.[70] While Newman explored possibilities, it was always Kelly's task to defend what he saw as the unity of Scripture. He justified the inconsistency by writing,

> I am convinced that all this arises from not apprehending the very lesson that God teaches in the scene. The truth is that Saul might have loved David for his services but there never was a particle of sympathy and where this is the case we readily forget. It is the very spirit of the world towards the children of God.[71]

In this comment we see Kelly's psychological justification of the Scriptural story and order, his assumption that either original writers or redactors did not easily make mistakes but also his reading of all Scripture as pointing to the truth of Christ and the church; here Saul is the type of the worldly man who has no sympathy with the Christian.[72] Kelly's views have in part been upheld by twentieth-century hermeneutics. Robert Alter

---

68. Ibid., 320–21.
69. Ibid., 422.
70. Newman, *Hebrew Monarchy*, 54.
71. Kelly, *Daniel*, 92. It is interesting that Kelly's answer to the critics on this subject comes unexpectedly in his exegesis of the book of Daniel—another example of Kelly's scope of reference within one book.
72. Ibid.

has affirmed that the different accounts of David's anointing and coming to power were not about dual sources but about two points of view, focusing on divine election and activities of the hero.[73]

Newman boldly asked questions about different points of view in Chronicles and Kings, and came to a similar understanding as de Wette did as to the historical inaccuracy of Chronicles.[74] Newman thought that Samuel was earlier than Kings and that Chronicles was much later, and he found his evidence in the genealogies.[75] In contrast, Kelly looked at the purpose of the genealogies and, when looking at the apparent discrepancies which Newman pointed out, attributed them to divine purpose.[76] However, in linking the genealogy with the identity of the writer and the dating of the manuscript, Kelly was careful to point out that there was no evidence of Ezra being the author of Chronicles or Kings. Authorship of the history books was a different matter for him than authorship of the Pentateuch, because of Christ's precise reference to Mosaic authorship in the New Testament.

The English theologians had cause to argue about the moral problems found in the Old Testament and Kelly was careful to consider these problems. In answering Davidson about the free will of Pharaoh in hardening his heart against Moses, Kelly asserted that Pharaoh could not trust God because he found that God interfered with everything he liked. "Hardening is a judgment which comes when man persists in unbelief in the face of repeated and distinct testimony from God."[77] In his *Introduction to the Old Testament*, Davidson criticized the behavior of the Children of Israel for taking Egyptian jewelery before they left the country but Kelly said they were justified in doing so because they were slaves.[78] However Kelly did acknowledge that there were some difficulties in affirming the moral judgments of the Bible. When talking about the killing of the Canaanites, he acknowledged that some critics had encountered ethical difficulties in this.[79] He solved the problem by evading the problem of historical reality and instead, having recourse to typology, with the Canaanites representing

---

73. Alter, *The Art of Biblical Narrative*, 47, 154.
74. Rogerson, *OT Criticism*, 30, 31.
75. Newman, *Hebrew Monarchy*, iv.
76. Kelly, *God's Inspiration*, 188.
77. Kelly, *Pentateuch*, 152.
78. Kelly, *Pentateuch*, 141. This refers to Davidson, *Introduction to OT*, 237, 258.
79. Ibid., 487.

"the emissaries of Satan, the spiritual wickedness in heavenly places."[80] In the same passage he pointed out that the harshest judgments were made against the Children of Israel, who failed to enter the Promised Land.

Newman saw weak moral arguments as evidence not only for religious development over the centuries, as Davidson had done, but also for varied authorship and different political views of writers and editors.[81] Two illustrations make this clear. The argument between Samuel and Saul which led to Samuel's rejection of the king, was seen by Newman as "the misconception of a later time" and evidence of priestly political power in later Israel. He also questioned the morality of the biblical author's views of Saul's curse of Jonathan. Kelly saw a spiritual point in the story. "Here he (Saul) receives a holy rebuke of his own son, who alone was in the secret of the Lord."[82] On the subject of the sacrifice of the Amalekites, Newman said that the writer had to find a spurious reason why Saul was rejected as King and so this was invented—"the factiousness of all this is transparent."[83] Newman's assertive language in relation to problems of manuscripts and authors is general. Kelly again argued back, not on the question of technical theories, but on the question of spiritual truth. He counteracted with the language of spiritual devotion.[84]

Davidson and Colenso had a wider understanding of social context than Kelly and this affected their biblical interpretation. Davidson was outspoken in his criticism of the actions of the British Empire as a supposedly Christian power. He observed a blatant contrast between its attitude and that of Jesus. Colenso was a more prescient and purposeful critic of the Empire, even suggesting that the heathen showed more "Christian" values than the white invaders, whether from Britain or the Transvaal. Newman had not only appreciated the integrity of Muslims he had met in the Middle East, but also admired the moral effects of Cicero and Boethius.[85] Kelly had a narrower world view than any of them. Judgment in the Old Testament was not so much the narrow judgment of an emerging monotheism

---

80. Ibid., 488.

81. Newman, *Hebrew Monarchy*, 42, 43, for some of his views about Saul's reign in Samuel.

82. Kelly, *Earlier Historical Books*, 264–65.

83. Newman, *Hebrew Monarchy*, 48.

84. Kelly, *Earlier Historical Books*, 270–71. Kelly wrote about quick confessions being genuine and the law of defilement in the Pentateuch.

85. Newman, *Phases of Faith*, 33, 98.

or priestly caste, but a sign of God's judgment throughout history. As a Victorian, he saw the role of the sons of Noah in Genesis chapter 10 as "a little key to the world's history" and as possibly explaining if not justifying a colonial or racialist view of history.[86] In this way, Colenso's questioning of hegemony could be understood though for Colenso it had more practical significance as he was experiencing the realities of power and authority in politics and the way beliefs had practical and disastrous consequences.

Newman also observed the intolerance of monotheism in the early biblical historical books.[87] Unlike Colenso and Davidson, who saw monotheism developing out of polytheism, Newman said that the Hebrew religion did not deny the existence of other gods, but demonized them, thereby leading to dualism. Kelly acknowledged the presence of other gods from the Canaanite traditions, saw their reality as evil, but denied their ultimate power, just as Elijah opposed the supporters of Baal on Mount Carmel. Newman saw the priestly system gradually developing in Israel and imposing its view in earlier, more primitive accounts, such as those of the earlier "history" books of the Bible. In line with this, he showed that Samuel was the founder of the school of the prophets but not of the priests.[88]

While Davidson quoted Ewald, Knobel, and Bleek to back up later dating of supposedly Mosaic documents, Kelly used Paul as an authority, in declaring that Deuteronomy 32:21 was the language of Moses.[89] This was also linked to Kelly's views on Christology which made his position at variance with those of Davidson, Colenso and Newman. In the Victorian debate about Christ's knowledge of Himself and His times, Davidson took the position of negative accommodation. In his *Introduction to the Pentateuch*, Kelly showed that he was keen to protect Christianity from Davidson's argument.[90] Davidson's argument about the possible readings of Exodus chapter 15 and the subject of the water brought out of the rock had consequences, in Kelly's view, for the understanding of Christ as the Messiah.[91] In other words, if the original story was suspect in its authenticity, then any typological reading of the story as a revelation of Christ, the perfect Messiah, would also be less authoritative.

86. Kelly, *Pentateuch*, 49.
87. Newman, *Hebrew Monarchy*, 29.
88. Ibid., 31.
89. Ibid., 518. Paul refers to this verse in Rom 10:19, "Thus Moses saith . . ." (KJV).
90. Ibid., 12–13.
91. Ibid., 169.

Kelly combined defending the conservative interpretation of the Bible and interpreting the Scriptures figuratively and this helped him to be authoritative about his interpretation of the Old Testament text. According to Kelly, Colenso was always asking questions about likelihood and practicality, but Kelly always came back to the subject of communion with God.[92] Colenso published a letter in 1860 using the Church Fathers to justify his own skepticism.[93] Kelly always looked to the Old Testament to exemplify his reading of the New Testament, and so had the same attitude as the writer of the book of Hebrews—"The fact is that, no matter what might be the measure of carrying them out in the wilderness, God was setting forth by them the shadow of good things to come. This was their real object."[94]

Newman also linked his rejection of plenary inspiration to that of the Church Fathers. He made a very similar defense of his views to that of Colenso. He wrote, "Early Christian Fathers believed the law of Moses to have been destroyed and lost in the Babylonian captivity, yet to have been *rewritten* by Ezra under divine inspiration. This did not startle their imagination or embarrass their faith."[95] What was important for Newman was not the question of whose pen had written it, but whether God had inspired it. He wrote, "Such topics as 'genuineness and authenticity' never dawn on the minds of spiritual persons except where a literature exists which is beyond the cognizance of the national religion."[96] Like Kelly, he acknowledged the presence or absence of genuine spiritual understanding but he felt that it was important to explore the history and the compilation of the documents. Newman's belief in spirituality led him to be unafraid to question the manuscripts; Kelly's led him to affirm their authenticity.

THE RESPONSE OF RICHARD BEACON'S ARTICLE (1890) IN THE BIBLE TREASURY TO GLADSTONE'S THE IMPREGNABLE ROCK OF HOLY SCRIPTURE

Beacon, a valued contributor to the magazine, followed Kelly in being particularly critical of "those writers who profess Christianity," while defending

---

92. Kelly, *Pentateuch*, 243.
93. Larsen, "Colenso and His Critics," 55.
94. Kelly, *Pentateuch*, 422.
95. Newman, *Hebrew Monarchy*, 337.
96. Ibid., 337.

the attitudes of the school of higher criticism.[97] However, like Kelly, Beacon was careful not to judge Gladstone's own faith. In his view, in Gladstone's case, the "affections of the writer's heart are in conflict with the infidelity of his intellect."[98] Beacon also pointed out Gladstone's apparently deceptive use of language, particularly in his title, which seemed to defend inspiration of Scripture. In this way, Beacon shows that the book is "really built on sand" and the promise of orthodoxy in the title is "illusory" and language has been used "to conceal thought and deceive."[99]

Beacon was critical of Gladstone's belief that the Scriptures are "as corresponding by their contents to the idea of a Divine revelation to man."[100] Beacon observed that, "This *idea* is then outside and independent of the Scripture."[101] He attacked the formulation of *idea* which was at heart both Hegelian and a key concept for nineteenth-century higher criticism. He was skilled in attacking what he perceived to be Gladstone's lack of logic. According to Gladstone, human beings understand the correspondence between Scripture and the *idea*, through "known divine operations in other spheres."[102] However, Beacon argued that, apart from the Bible, we cannot know that there are divine operations in other spheres and he pointed out that pagans, in observing nature, thought that it was eternal.[103] He challenged Gladstone's logic in moving from the assertion that through the Bible we know that these things are from God to the conclusion that these divine operations are a proof that the Bible is a divine revelation.[104] Instead, Beacon claimed that the only fixed point is faith in God's Word, and that Gladstone's belief in divine revelation and its imperfections did not come from the Bible itself and therefore Gladstone should question the origin of this belief. He attacked Gladstone's championship of Jowett's assertion that the Bible should be treated like any other book.[105] However, it is worth noting that neither of them finished the rest of Jowett's statement, which went on to say that the Bible would reveal itself to be different. According

---

97. Richard Beacon, "Impregnable Rock," 111.
98. Ibid., 112.
99. Ibid., 110, 111.
100. Ibid., 110. Gladstone, *Impregnable Rock*, 4.
101. Beacon, "Impregnable Rock."
102. Gladstone, *Impregnable Rock*, 4, 12, 13.
103. Beacon, "Impregnable Rock," 110.
104. Gladstone, *Impregnable Rock*, 13.
105. Ibid., 7–8 and Beacon, "Impregnable Rock," 110.

to Beacon, it was the revelation of man's sin and ruin which made the Bible unique.[106]

Beacon objected to Gladstone's idea that other documents of pre-historic literature are "witnesses and buttresses to the office of Holy Scripture."[107] Beacon argued against the notion of the "imperfect comprehension" and "imperfect expression" of divine revelation.[108] He argued that such an expression must be a denial of God's wisdom and love and used 2 Peter 1:21 and 1 Corinthians 2:13 to back up his argument. He picked out inconsistencies in Gladstone's argument about Scripture containing divine revelation and asked how we should know which parts of the Scripture contain this divine revelation.[109] While Gladstone saw contradictions in the variant Greek and Hebrew versions of the Old Testament, Beacon saw a different purpose in the Septuagint being deliberately quoted in the New Testament.[110] In this he was following Kelly, who always saw changes in the Hebrew version as showing an intentional change.[111] Beacon also followed Kelly in that he saw Gladstone's assessment of Scripture as being in line with the later evangelicals, Driver and Kirkpatrick, and we shall see in this chapter that Kelly was particularly critical of such views.[112]

KELLY'S RESPONSE TO GORE'S LUX MUNDI THROUGH HIS EDITORSHIP OF THE WRITINGS OF WILLIAM JOHN HOCKING (1864-1953) IN THE BIBLE TREASURY

Kelly and Gore had much in common. Neither believed that free enquiry should be feared.[113] Both thought that real understanding of the Scriptures came through spiritual, rather than intellectual, understanding.[114] Both had a sense of typology and its spiritual significance.[115] Both believed in

106. Beacon, "Impregnable Rock," 111.
107. Ibid., 111. Gladstone, *Impregnable Rock*, 5.
108. Ibid. Gladstone, *Impregnable Rock*, 10.
109. Beacon, "Impregnable Rock," 112.
110. Ibid.
111. Kelly, *An Exposition of the Gospel of Mark*, 16. This is an example of Kelly showing how the prophecy in Mark 1:2 had the variant wording of Mal 3:1.
112. Beacon, "Impregnable Rock," 111, and Gladstone, *Impregnable Rock*, 13.
113. Gore, *Lux Mundi*, 327, and Beacon, "On Biblical (O.T.) Criticism," 79.
114. Gore, *Lux Mundi*, xv.
115. Ibid., xxxv.

the inter-dependence of the Old and New Testaments.[116] Both had a high Christology and thought that it was difficult to articulate this in rational argument.[117] Both believed in a spiritual idealism in the Old Testament. Gore identified this as the priestly strand of writing, while Kelly gave this concept a prophetic and Christological interpretation and Gore admitted that the books of Joshua through to the Kings were always seen as prophetic by the Jews.[118] Kelly, Hocking (an amateur but learned theologian who appreciated Kelly's theological work) and Gore all acknowledged that it was impossible to define the incarnation adequately. Gore referred to St. Gregory of Nazianus in claiming that the incarnation transcended human reason and power of expression.[119]

However, Gore differed from the Brethren writers in some significant ways. Gore, unlike Kelly, believed in the sacraments and the apostolic succession.[120] While Kelly saw variety in church history as spiritual degeneracy, Gore recognized and valued the variety of ecclesiastical expression of the early Church.[121] While the Brethren saw the visible Church as a small, exclusive group of Christians, Gore accepted the outward church, while at the same time admitting its imperfections and lack of the Holy Spirit's work in parts of it.[122]

The articles in *The Bible Treasury* revealed different views of inspiration and the theory of Christ's adaptation and limitation. Gore believed in the "spiritual use of the Old Testament" as did Kelly, but for Kelly this did not negate the historical accuracy of the Scriptures. Both believed that a human being needed the work of the Holy Spirit to understand Scripture but Gore, in contrast to the Brethren, thought that is did not matter if there were errors in the text.[123] Neither did the Brethren agree with Gore's views that there were various degrees of inspiration.[124] Gore believed that the Church did not need a dogmatic view of what inspiration entailed.[125]

---

116. Ibid., xxii–xxiii.
117. Ibid., 334.
118. Ibid., xxv.
119. Ibid., 334.
120. Ibid., 322.
121. Ibid., 323.
122. Ibid., 317, 332.
123. Ibid., 341.
124. Ibid., 342.
125. Ibid., 356.

Hocking's articles, written in May, April and June 1892, disputed Gore's views. Hocking, quoting John 8:25 to assert Christ's uniqueness, worried that *Lux Mundi* called into question the character of Christ.[126] He argued against what he saw as Gore's defamation of Christ, even though he was careful to explain that the Bible was "significantly silent as to the secrets of that incomprehensible mind."[127] In *Lux Mundi*, Gore suggested that Moses was a "dramatic hypothesis" and that Christ, in apparently quoting Moses, had endorsed "the Jewish views of their own history."[128] Hocking counteracted this view by explaining that in the Gospel, Moses had been mentioned as a spiritual authority independently of his writing.[129] He went on to say that Christ had reprimanded the Pharisees about their interpretation of Scripture, not about their understanding of authorship.[130] Hocking felt that the adaptation and self-limitation theory were attacks on Christ's moral character and His person.[131] While Gore said that Christ operated within the limitations of contemporary knowledge, Hocking pointed out that Christ did not accept the current opinions of the Rabbis and that He could have used the term "the law" instead of Moses, had he so wished.[132] Christ's knowledge, wrote Hocking, was "personal and intuitive, not rabbinical."[133] He pointed out that even Gore had acknowledged that Christ saw clearly into men's hearts.[134] Hocking went on to give many examples of Christ knowing more than anyone else about people's backgrounds, and apparently without being informed of them by human sources.[135] While Gore talked about Christ emptying Himself of prerogatives, Hocking taught that in Philippians chapter 2, it was clear that Christ emptied Himself of form, not prerogatives.[136] Further, in arguing against Walter Frederick Adeney (1849–1920), Hocking explained that Luke 2:52, about Jesus increasing in wisdom and stature, was about how it appeared to an observer, not about

126. Hocking "The Lord's Testimony to the Mosaic Authorship," 58 and 74.
127. Ibid., 92.
128. Gore, *Lux Mundi*, xxix, 359.
129. Hocking, "The Lord's Testimony," 58.
130. Ibid., 60, arguing against Gore, *Lux Mundi*, xxii and 261.
131. Ibid., 74.
132. Ibid., 75, and Gore, *Lux Mundi*, 360.
133. Ibid., 90.
134. Gore, *Lux Mundi*, 265.
135. Hocking, 91.
136. Ibid.

Jesus' limitations.[137] When Jesus said that He did not know the time of His coming again, this was only about his teaching in the servant position, not about the limitation of His divine knowledge.[138]

Despite these critiques of *Lux Mundi*, in what Gore said about inspiration we can see much in agreement with Kelly's method of Bible exposition—"the mystical method, as a whole, tended to the depreciation of the historical sense, in comparison with the spiritual teaching which it conveyed."[139] Surprisingly, Gore, the later leader and theologian of the Tractarians, and Kelly, the teacher and theologian of the Brethren, had much in common.

KELLY'S RESPONSE TO ANGLICAN EVANGELICALS IN THE EARLY TWENTIETH CENTURY

In contrast, there was a clear divergence between Kelly and the evangelical scholars of the late nineteenth and early twentieth centuries who were able to accept the German school of higher criticism. Kelly's criticism of Driver and Kirkpatrick was clear. They had moved to accept compromise with liberal critics.

A.F. Kirkpatrick (1849–1940), Lady Margaret Professor of Divinity at Cambridge University, and S.R. Driver (1846–1914), Regius Professor of Hebrew at Oxford University, wrote three papers on this subject between the years 1902 and 1904, and these were published together in 1905.[140] Their writing represented a softening of the evangelical Anglican clergy towards the subject of higher criticism and, in response, in November 1905, December 1905, and January and February 1906, Kelly wrote a series of four articles in *The Bible Treasury* vigorously contesting their position theologically. It is interesting that at the end of his life (he died in March 1906) he thought it still worthwhile, having contested the ideas of de Wette, Colenso and Davidson and the writers of *Lux Mundi* from 1859 onwards, to argue against the wider Anglican acceptance of higher criticism. He believed that it was important to defend his theological position. The articles

---

137. Ibid.—arguing against Adenay in *The Thinker*, 138. Walter Frederick Adenay was Professor of New Testament exegesis and Church history at the Lancashire College, Manchester.

138. Hocking, 92.

139. Gore, *Lux Mundi*, 358.

140. Kirkpatrick and Driver, *The Higher Criticism*, (1912).

proved to be detailed, questioning and he frequently quoted the original lectures. Parts 1 and 3 of the published book had originally been delivered as lectures at the Church of England Congress in Northampton in 1902 and at New College, Hampstead in 1900, and their publication in book form offered them to a wider Christian audience. In the Preface, Kirkpatrick and Driver stated that they had both held these views for a long time.[141]

Kelly felt that Kirkpatrick and Driver's book was particularly significant because it concerned the inspiration of Scripture. He went to some trouble to answer their points in detail. For example, in his article in December 1905 Kelly dealt logically with three ways that Kirkpatrick had shown that modern criticism affected theology—mode of revelation, character of prophecy and nature of inspiration—and I would like to show Kelly's response to them.[142] In his article of January 1906 Kelly looked in detail at Driver's questions about the possible authorship of Moses, Joshua and Samuel.[143] He was able to partially agree with and applaud some of Driver's points, particularly his practical suggestions.[144] Kelly did not deal with the last lecture in the book so fully, partly because he considered that the magazine, *The Interpreter*, had already answered its points.[145]

In so far as Driver and Kirkpatrick drew on some of Jowett's arguments from *Essays and Reviews* Kelly showed his understanding of the Broad Church's terminology in criticizing the literalist approach to Scripture. He took the term "bibliolatry" and argued against its use. He said that this word and also "verbal inspiration" had been invented to bolster the arguments of higher criticism and to denigrate those who had a different view of inspiration.[146] He resisted the attempts of writers in the tradition of Jowett to "pigeon-hole" and "stereotype" those theologians who like himself had a particular regard for the inspiration of Scripture. He also argued against Kirkpatrick's assertion that inerrancy of Scripture was nowhere taught in Scripture itself.[147] He used Bible passages to show that it was.[148] He also argued that the way that higher critics argued against inerrancy was no

141. Ibid., Preface, v.
142. Kelly, "Higher Criticism," 374.
143. Kirkpatrick and Driver, *Higher Criticism*, 20. Kelly, "Higher Criticism," 8.
144. Kirkpatrick and Driver, *Higher Criticism*, 37–43. Kelly, "Higher Criticism," 26.
145. Kelly, "Higher Criticism," 43.
146. Ibid., 27.
147. Kirkpatrick and Driver, *Higher Criticism*, 31.
148. Kelly, "Higher Criticism," 27.

new phenomenon, because there had been a long established tradition to establish allegory rather than history in the reading of Genesis. He rejected what he saw as the stark alternative of *a priori* and *a posteriori* judgments in coming to the text and explained that there was a third way of looking at Scripture, a way of faith.[149] It is interesting that Kelly managed to do this through a rational and intellectual argument. While maintaining a position of belief in the authority of Scripture, he showed himself able to refute arguments and explain his own position cogently.

Kelly also touched briefly on Driver's arguments about science negating the scientific beliefs of previous centuries and thereby negating the accuracy of Scripture considering the scientific progress in the nineteenth century.[150] Kelly maintained that it was a false argument because there was no science in Genesis.[151] According to him, the truth of God as Creator was more important than any scientific discovery.[152] In addition he was able to quote from Lord Kelvin's Glasgow speech about the limitations of science.[153] The development of human knowledge, which Kelly did not deny, was not the same as the need for human beings to deal with their moral dilemmas.[154]

Kelly, Kirkpatrick and Driver discussed the importance and the dangers of the claims of higher criticism and they were all concerned about the finding of "truth," though they gave different meanings to this term. Driver and Kirkpatrick wanted to find the "truth" about the dating and the provenance of the text, while Kelly claimed that they confounded love of doubt and love of truth.[155] In contrast Kelly wanted to stress the "truth" of Jesus Christ and he believed that the only way of discerning the text rightly was by a "spiritual" existentialist experience, which resulted in being filled with the Holy Spirit.[156] To be spiritual was to be full of joy and, according to Kelly, the higher critics did not demonstrate this quality.[157] Instead Kirkpatrick stressed the need for the clergy and the laity to understand

---

149. Ibid.
150. Kirkpatrick and Driver, *Higher Criticism*, 37.
151. Kelly, "Higher Criticism," 45.
152. Ibid., 375.
153. Ibid., 7.
154. Ibid., 11.
155. Ibid., 14.
156. Ibid., 26, 27.
157. Ibid., 366.

the origins of the text.[158] Kelly, while agreeing with Driver that we cannot know how God communicated with the writers of Scripture, objected to having a particular theory of literary structure imposed on him.[159] Kelly used 1 Corinthians 3:13–15 to show that the Holy Spirit had a variety of operations and also that the natural man (including the academics) could not receive the wisdom of God. Kelly looked at all the possible translations of "*sugkrinontes*" and was favorably impressed by the Revisers' marginal translation.[160]

Kelly did not agree with Driver and Kirkpatrick's assessment of past theories of inspiration, nor did he see any significance in the title of the third lecture, "The Old Testament in the light of today," as though the word "today" were bound to mean progress in understanding. Kirkpatrick asserted that up to fifty years before he had written, there had been a rigid theory of inspiration.[161] Kelly showed that he disagreed with this assessment of the history of understanding of inspiration and Kelly rejected this monochrome view of inspiration. Driver justified his interpretation of "inspiration" through the formularies of the Church of England, which he believed gave freedom to interpret that word in a variety of ways.[162] In contrast to both these points of view, Kelly was only interested in defining it biblically. Therefore Driver's criticism, "that formerly believers in inspiration have framed theories without basis," was not true for Kelly, who justified his theory of inspiration meticulously.[163] Driver said that readers should distinguish between different degrees of probability in the Old Testament narrative.[164] Kelly argued against this and drew particular attention to the claim of higher criticism that the book of law in Josiah's day had been a fabrication of the writer.[165] However, it is true that Kelly was happy to look at more than one possibility of editing, but he did not believe that

---

158. Kirkpatrick and Driver, *Higher Criticism*, 1.

159. Kelly, "Higher Criticism," 26.

160. Ibid., 27. The word could be translated as comparing, combining, interpreting or communicating.

161. Kirkpatrick and Driver, *Higher Criticism*, 26.

162. Ibid., 47.

163. Ibid., 48.

164. Ibid., 60.

165. Kelly, "Higher Criticism," 14.

hypotheses of the critics helped them to make progress in analyzing the text of Scripture.[166]

As we have already seen in chapter 2, Kelly had a limited sympathy with the idea of a progressive element of revelation throughout the Old Testament but generally felt that the understanding of the whole text as a unity was more important. He also argued vigorously against a progressive interpretation since the Canon of Scripture had closed. Driver argued that a progressive revelation and interpretation could "only be accomplished by criticism."[167] He also spoke about the "relatively immature stage in the spiritual education of mankind" during the early part of the Old Testament.[168] In contrast Kelly believed that there were no immature stages of religious belief.[169] He used the Messianic prophecy of Genesis chapter 3 to question the idea of progressive revelation and he also believed that the apostle Paul refuted the progressive theory.[170] Referring to work of Paine and Charles Bradlaugh (1833–1891) and quoting from J.S. Mill and Herbert Spencer, Kelly gave a thoughtful refutation of theories of progressive history.[171] While Driver explained that higher criticism helped to explain the theory of progression, Kelly dealt with the subject in an entirely different way. He described Driver and Kirkpatrick's ideas as "the fashionable craze of development."[172] Kelly argued against Driver's views on the progression of history in general by explaining that there could not be restitution of all things without God's intervention.[173]

Driver entitled the last article of his booklet, "The permanent religious value of the Old Testament," and the epithet "religious" implied the value of a generalized human spirituality and also a historical perspective, neither of which Kelly shared.[174] It is clear that Driver rejected the historical truth of the Old Testament narrative and Kelly responded by describing Driver's ideas as "current theories" based on the "neo-critical principal," which are

---

166. Kirkpatrick and Driver, *Higher Criticism*, 61.
167. Ibid., 59.
168. Ibid., 60.
169. Kelly, "Higher Criticism," 44.
170. Ibid., 367.
171. Ibid., 367, 375.
172. Ibid., 365.
173. Ibid., 45.
174. Kirkpatrick and Driver, *Higher Criticism*, 71.

"arbitrary, unbelieving and excessively artificial."[175] Kelly believed that by questioning the form of literature, it was natural to question its truth, while Kirkpatrick and Driver maintained "different degrees of inspiration" within the Scriptures.[176] While Kirkpatrick called the earlier books of the Old Testament "a lower stage of religious history," Kelly used typology to show that this was not true.[177] Driver felt that through the prophets "spiritual perceptions were enlarged," while Kelly felt that this was a different strand of God's revelation and a further explanation of the law.[178]

There were two particular re-readings on the part of the Higher Critics which Driver and Kirkpatrick saw as important for an understanding of the Bible and which Kelly argued against in his articles. The first was seeing "prophecies" as only moral messages rather than predictions.[179] Driver rejected Joseph Butler's definition of prophecy as given in his *Analogy*: "the history of events before they come to pass."[180] Kelly believed that critics had no right to dismiss the predictive aspects of prophecy.[181] He asserted that apostasy had always been predicted in the Old and New Testaments.[182] Understanding of typology must be connected with prophecy.[183]

Whereas Kelly saw the revelation to the Jews as being unique, Driver and Kirkpatrick saw that revelation as being influenced by other near Eastern civilizations and therefore not unique.[184] According to Kelly the emphasis on the need for the literary man to be looking for sources had been wrong.[185] He refuted the idea that the biblical writer had needed to borrow from Babylonian stories, though he did not deny that there were similar narratives in the history of the Near East.[186]

---

175. Kelly, "Higher Criticism," 27.
176. Ibid., Kirkpatrick and Driver, *Higher Criticism*, 33.
177. Ibid., 13.
178. Ibid., 76.
179. Ibid., 1, 11.
180. Ibid., 111, 44. Joseph Butler (1692–1752) was Bishop of Durham and eminent theologian.
181. Kelly, "Higher Criticism," 374.
182. Ibid., 365.
183. Ibid., 14.
184. Kirkpatrick and Driver, *Higher Criticism*, 42.
185. Kelly, "Higher Criticism," 29.
186. Ibid.

Kelly anticipated twentieth-century arguments about New Testament source material, although Driver and Kirkpatrick said that they would never be in question. Kelly argued that there might be other manuscripts which were correct and interesting but that did not mean that they should have been included in the Canon. He gave as an example the fact that John was the only one of the Gospel writers who was present at the agony in the garden of Gethsemane, but he was the only one who did not record it.[187] Kelly argued here that it was not enough for the biblical narrative to be good history. He looked at the first verses of Luke's gospel in a different way from those who used it to justify a sound modern historical process. When looking at the Old Testament he showed that a decision about the dating of the manuscripts was not at the heart of the problem when dealing with the texts. Understanding God's mind and design was.[188]

Kelly argued against the use of the "ideal" and the "realizing genius" view of the Old Testament. Kirkpatrick said that the Bible gave an ideal rather than the actual picture of national life.[189] Driver asserted, rather than using real proof, that spiritual types were idealized as heroic figures of the past. This was true both for the patriarchs and David and this fitted in with the Old Testament stress on a pure and spiritual religion.[190] Therefore, according to Kirkpatrick in his second lecture entitled "The Inevitability and Legitimacy of Criticism," the elevation of religious commitment described the "realizing genius of the Hebrews" and "its tendency to embody ideas in a concrete historical form."[191] Kelly acknowledged and dealt with Kirkpatrick's argument. He asked how such an idealism could have a bearing on the inspiration of the Old Testament, how it might affect our estimate of its moral and doctrinal values, and what practical conclusions might be deduced, and he came to his own conclusions which were different from those of Kirkpatrick and Driver who, according to Kelly, had "turned from the light of God's word."[192]

Lastly, there was a clear parallel which Kelly made explicit in his articles between the divine/human argument about the inspiration of the text and the divine/human argument about the nature of Christ. Kelly

---

187. Ibid.
188. Ibid.
189. Kirkpatrick and Driver, *Higher Criticism*, 6.
190. Ibid., 81, 85.
191. Ibid., 24.
192. Kelly, *Higher Criticism*, 13.

intentionally related the argument to his understanding of Christology and the sacred nature of the biblical text. The Brethren's high Christology and their desire to defend it against "rationalism," the Church Fathers and perceived "heterodox" teachers in their own midst, was vital to their identity. Therefore in his articles in *The Bible Treasury* Kelly contributed to this intention. He maintained that the human element of the Scriptures was in the style not in error and, although there were partial truths revealed along the way, the whole was needed to give "the full truth."[193] He agreed with Driver about the "double element" of Scripture but disagreed about how to place it and contended that the Higher Critics "lower Christ as much as the Scripture."[194] In his February 1906 article he highlighted the parallel between the two issues, which was one of the reasons he pursued his concerns over the inspiration of Scripture.[195]

Thus Kelly, as late as 1906, thought it worthwhile to oppose the gradual evangelical acceptance of higher criticism. As early as 1892, he had revealed in a letter that he saw their university spokesmen as "far weightier for harm than a score of Newmans and Colensos."[196] In agreeing with Gore's "experience" of Christ he appeared to have more in common with the Tractarians than with the later evangelicals. While opposing Davidson and Newman, he had sympathy for their dislike of dogma.[197] Kelly was often open-minded in the way he looked at the compilation of ancient manuscripts but he would never consider any place other than the very highest for his Christology. This led him to a possible contradiction between his intellectual and literalist position, which was resolved by his spirituality.

193. Ibid.
194. Ibid.
195. Ibid., 27.
196. Kelly, *Letters*, "My dear J," 25 November, 1892.
197. Davidson, *An Introduction to the Critical Study*, Preface, vii. Newman, *Phases of Faith*, 37.

CHAPTER 4

William Kelly as a Biblical Literalist
His Teaching about the Afterlife

INTRODUCTION

In the previous two chapters I have examined Kelly's belief in the plenary inspiration of Scripture and have shown that he is better seen as a conservative evangelical theologian who was aware of literary techniques rather than as a narrow literalist. However in this chapter, I shall explore Kelly's position as a literalist with regard to his Christian understanding of the afterlife. Kelly's exposition of this subject included his understanding of the subject of hell and the mortality of the soul. These were particular Victorian concerns which were linked to contemporary debates about the reliability of the Bible. Kelly himself made that link when he suggested that anxiety about future punishment in the Victorian era gave doubt to "the authenticity of revelation."[1] Other related subjects, particularly judgment, the context of pre-millenarianism, and the centrality of Christ were very important for Kelly and affected his writing about the afterlife. I will explain Kelly's teaching in relation to that of his contemporaries, coming to some conclusions about Kelly's place as a theologian within these debates. What

---

1. Kelly, *Brief Notice of G. Cox*," 8. The only author who seems to be relevant here is Samuel Cox (1826–1893), a Baptist minister who wrote about universalism and the afterlife. He was president of the Baptist Association in 1873. His *Expository Essays and Discourses* were published in 1877. George Cox (1827–1902) was a clergyman, historian and supporter of Colenso.

is distinctive about Kelly's teaching about the afterlife is his emphasis on future enjoyment for the believer and the way that it is always Christocentric and pre-millennial in its focus. What is distinctive about Kelly's teaching on the subject of hell is that he neither attempts to imagine the horrors of hell nor to threaten non-believers with its reality, but neither does he seek to minimize its significance nor to treat it as if it were an illusion. As it was a focus of theological dispute in the Victorian era, I will major on Kelly's understanding of hell, though I will also discuss other eschatological issues.

Kelly taught about the afterlife, including hell and judgment, both in a focused way in some of his works and in a more tangential way in others. In 1867, Andrew Jukes (1815–1901) published *The Second Death and the Restitution of All Things* in which he denied eternal punishment.[2] Jukes had joined the Brethren after seceding from the Church of England in 1844 and wrote several theological works which were widely used by the Brethren, but he later returned to his post as an Anglican clergyman. Kelly condemned him in his letters, writing "Jukes is a universalist, reliable in nothing," but he also added that universalism was an error which had been in vogue since the second century.[3] In two letters which are separated by many years, Kelly criticized those who took a more liberal view on the subject of eternal punishment, and so showed the consistency of his views on this subject.[4]

Kelly considered facets of the afterlife in several works. His short but full article arguing against mortalism (the belief that there was no afterlife) was not dated, but he took the trouble to argue explicitly against G. Cox, whom he considered to be heterodox in his beliefs about the afterlife.[5] In his collection of Tracts published in 1854, he explored the significance of punishment in contemporary society and how this whole topic impinged upon the appropriateness of belief in hell in Victorian society.[6] In the early issues of *The Bible Treasury* between 1856 and 1857 he wrote a series about the afterlife, in answer to some of the arguments made by David Brown (1803–1897), minister of the St. James Free Church, Glasgow and Professor of Theology at the Free Church College, University of Aberdeen,

---

2. Jukes, *The Second Death and the Restitution of all Things*.

3. Kelly, *Letters*, 4 October, 1897.

4. Ibid., 3 February, 1875 ("My dear brother"—possibly Darby) and 7 January, 1902 (unaddressed).

5. Kelly, *Brief Notice*, 2.

6. Kelly, "The Powers That Be," in *Tracts*, 4–10.

and Thomas Rawson Birks (1810–1883), Anglican vicar of Kelshall and Knightsbridge Professor of Philosophy at the University of Cambridge, in their books about eschatology.[7] He also wrote a tract entitled, "On the immortality of the soul," published in 1865.[8] His commentary on Matthew, in which questions of the afterlife are dealt with, was published in 1868. After this there was a long gap before he dealt with the subject of the afterlife again, in a series of lectures entitled *The Second Coming and Kingdom of the Lord and Savior Jesus Christ*, in 1895.[9] All eight lectures in the volume dealt with future prophecy and life after death, but the one which was particularly relevant to the subject of punishment was "The Judgment and the Eternal State." One tract in a collected volume published in 1905 was entitled "The soul neither mortal nor to sleep," in which he again attacked the doctrine of mortalism.[10] He wrote articles in *The Bible Treasury* on these subjects between 1884 and 1904, and several parts of his exegeses on biblical books were particularly pertinent to this subject. Therefore in this chapter I will also be referring to his publications on John's Gospel, Luke's Gospel, 2 Thessalonians, 1 and 2 Peter and Revelation, which were all published between 1898 and 1905. In 1902 and 1905, he seemed concerned to tackle the meaning of eternal life and this concern was particularly provoked by the heterodox teaching of F. E. Raven amongst the Exclusive Brethren.[11] Kelly was more critical of Raven than of those from other denominations, because he thought that, being associated with the Brethren, he should have known better.[12]

In this chapter I intend to show that what made Kelly's contribution to the understanding of this subject noteworthy was the combination of the breadth of his intellectual understanding, his exposition of the distinctions of language in the Scriptural texts and his eclectic mixture of references to contemporary and historic writers on the subject of the afterlife. If, as I

---

7. Kelly, "Hope of Christ's Coming Again," 44–45; 2, "Relation of Christ's Coming to Time," 57–61; 3, "Pre-millenarianism," 75–79; 4, "The Pre-millennium Advent," 92–94; 5, "The Kingdom," 122–26; 6, "The First Resurrection," 79–81; 7, "The Judgment and the Eternal State," 185–87. Brown, *Christ's Second Coming:*. Trotter, *Simples Essais*.

8. Kelly, "On the Immortality of the Soul," in *Tracts*.

9. Kelly, *Lectures on the Second Coming and Kingdom*.

10. Kelly, "The Soul neither Mortal nor to Sleep," *Tracts*.

11. Grass, *Gathering to His Name*, 199, 205. Raven regarded Christ as God in person as well as man in condition. He did not regard eternal life as a present experience for all Christians.

12. Kelly, "Life Eternal Denied," 23.

have contended in my introductory chapter, Kelly's teaching had a wider reference to Victorian Christianity than we might expect from a Moderate Exclusive Brethren Bible teacher, then it is worth examining Kelly's teaching on the afterlife which included such topics as universalism (all humanity will be saved for heaven no matter what their belief), annihilation (those who are not saved will cease to exist) and mortalism. I intend to examine his teaching on some key texts in the Gospels. In this chapter I also place Kelly's teaching within the context of some major debates about the nature of the afterlife and the controversy about hell in particular. Some wider foundations of conviction, both theological and ethical, were also in question in Victorian society. Nineteenth-century views on the nature of progress, the questioning of evangelism and more secular theories about punishment and its purpose necessarily impacted the dialog about the afterlife and made the subject of hell a contentious issue. I will show that Kelly made reference to these issues in his works, but I start by looking at the contemporary context of Kelly's writing as I outline some major public debates about hell and notorious publications of his day as I believe they must have affected his own interest in the subject.

THE MAJOR PUBLIC DEBATES ABOUT THE NATURE OF HELL

Major debates on the subject of hell were in the forefront of public awareness, and so the possible arguments attempting to prove and disprove hell, affirming different aspects of the doctrine, and challenging the notion of eternal punishment, were all known to the Victorians, especially between the years 1830 and 1880, when the major debates took place.[13]

In 1839 in Liverpool there were three public debates between evangelical Anglican clergy, who defended the more traditional views of hell as a place of eternal punishment for all those who were not Christians, and three Unitarian ministers—Henry Giles, James Martineau and J.H. Thom. In debate the Unitarians stressed the influence of Augustine on this topic, rather than the teaching of Scripture, and they also suggested that through the modern day evangelical movement, individual decision and thus progress to heaven or hell had become more important than attachment to a

---

13. Rowell, *Hell and the Victorian*, 16. Rowell explains that the discussion related to the changing views about penal theory—Ibid., 13. It was also connected with the changing views on the nature of the Bible as "the word of God."

Christian community. The Unitarian argument was that belief in hell was influenced by historical and sociological factors rather than being a true reading of the Bible.[14]

In 1853, F.D. Maurice was removed from his post as Professor of King's College, London University, because of his views on hell which were perceived as heterodox. In fact, Maurice, in many ways an orthodox Christian, did believe in hell and rejected the "universalist" position of salvation. However, he thought that the concept of eternity as being chronologically never-ending had been unduly influenced by the teaching of the enlightenment philosopher Locke in his *Essay concerning Human Understanding* rather than being a result of biblical teaching.[15] John Locke (1632–1704) believed that the only way humans could grasp the concept of eternity was by thinking about the idea of succession and numeracy and this came about through reflection and sensation, rather than through an externally planted idea.[16] Therefore the question Maurice posed was whether eternal punishment necessarily implied never-ending torment.[17] As he was at this time an Anglican clergyman but had been formerly a Unitarian and a prominent Cambridge academic, his views were widely discussed among Christians of all denominations.

Colenso, who saw Maurice as his mentor, tackled the question first in *Village Sermons* (1853), and then, while a bishop in Natal, in his *Commentary on Romans* (1861). As he also produced challenging ideas about the Pentateuch and the nature of biblical inspiration, it was no surprise that his views on hell were controversial.[18] In his *Commentary on Romans*, he went further than Maurice in questioning traditional views on hell and highlighted what he believed to be Paul's universalist passages, saw the threat of hell producing a negative response to missionary preaching, believed in the infinite gradations of good and evil in this life and the next, and clung to the law of human progress in civilization.[19] His views expressed as an Anglican and well-known bishop inevitably caused surprise.

---

14. Ibid., 49.
15. Maurice, "Eternal Life and Eternal Death," *Theological Essays*, 450, 464.
16. Locke, *An Essay concerning Human Understanding*, Book 2, 175, 185–86.
17. Maurice, "Eternal Life," 406.
18. Cf. a fuller exposition of these subjects in my sections on Colenso in chapters 2 and 3.
19. Colenso, *St. Paul's Epistle to the Romans*, 116.

In 1860 *Essays and Reviews* was published. H.B. Wilson's essay on hell caused consternation on the part of traditionalists, and Wilson was the only contributor who was officially judged because of his work. Although the text was really about the crisis of relationship between church and state—hence the title, "Séances historiques de Genève—the National Church"—the existence of hell was called into question.[20] Wilson coined the word "multitudinism," from Arnold's idea that "the multitude" of believers should be an inclusive Christian community based on Christian morals.[21] Once the inclusive Christian community was seen as a majority of society, the "judgment" of hell seemed less relevant and more distasteful, because it was not the sort of judgment which people were prepared to make against other members of a "Christian society." It was in following "multitudinism" that the Broad Church rejected the idea of hell. Wilson believed that even the apostolic churches of the New Testament "were thus multitudinist and early tended to become National Churches."[22] Generally he thought that "there was a much more fluid state of Christian opinion in the first century after Christ."[23] Therefore, he argued that Christianity should preach salvation for all and the preaching of hell was not necessary.[24] Wilson's understanding of the nature of the early church influenced his rejection of a traditional "hell." In 1862, in the Court of Arches, Stephen Lushington condemned Wilson because of his rejection of the damnatory clauses of the Athanasian Creed which were supposed to be accepted by all Anglican clergy.[25] The prominence of this debate and the reaction to it amongst clerics, particularly those of a more conservative belief, showed what a vital subject it was for the Victorians. However, in February 1864, Lord Chancellor Westbury allowed Wilson's appeal. It showed that views were changing and that the Church of England no longer had the authoritative stance it had once had on the subject. The upholders of traditional

---

20. *Essays and Reviews*, 74.
21. Ibid., 79.
22. Wilson, "Séances historiques de Genève," 286.
23. Ibid., 287.
24. Ibid., 82.

25. Kelly held up to criticism the desire to get rid of the Athanasian Creed by the Anglican Church, which he saw as an important symbol of orthodox teaching in the established church, even though he did not agree with the use of a recited creed in worship. Cf. Kelly, *John*, 109.

orthodoxy within the state church, especially the Tractarians, were shocked by this decision.[26]

Through this debacle the damnatory clauses of the Athanasian Creed came to the forefront of Christian awareness. In 1867 a Royal Commission was appointed to "enquire (*sic*) into the rubrics and rituals of the Church of England."[27] The Athanasian Creed suggested that even those who had never heard the Gospel were condemned to hell.[28] Pusey and Liddon, leader of the Tractarians and conservative Dean of St. Paul's Cathedral respectively, threatened to retire from the ministry if the Athanasian Creed was scrapped.[29] At convocation, Archbishop Tait instigated a discussion about religious language and literalism, and by 1890 he could assert that the damnatory clauses were no longer believed literally in the Church of England.[30] His conclusion suggested that conservative theologians, who were concerned about maintaining Christian standards of traditional orthodoxy, would feel bound to give full backing to the doctrine of hell. In seeing themselves as upholders of orthodox belief, the Brethren taught the doctrine of hell.

The last example of expository writing on the subject of hell which I wish to refer to is the work of F.W. Farrar, Archdeacon of Westminster and Dean of Canterbury Cathedral. In *Eternal Hope* (1878) and *Mercy and Judgment* (1881) Farrar defended belief in hell but also proposed the doctrine of universal reconciliation (the belief that God would finally reconcile all rebellion and all opposition to Himself in eternity). He was an evangelical theologian, much criticized by Kelly, who wished to defend orthodox belief but at the same time admit the scholarly work of biblical criticism. As an evangelical theologian who was questioning the traditional understanding of hell, Kelly felt that Farrar was giving in to the liberal wing of the Broad Church. However, measured and sympathetic appeal against the horrors of unending physical torment won Farrar much support in Victorian society. Farrar was keen to understand Christ's teachings on hell within "their historical significance, not in that sense which makes them connote to you a thousand notions which did not originally belong to them."[31] He also made

---

26. Rowell, *Hell and the Victorians*, 119.
27. Wheeler, *Death and the Future Life*, 192.
28. Ibid., 193.
29. Ibid.
30. Ibid., 178.
31. Farrar, *Eternal Hope: 5 Sermons*, 77.

an admiring comment about "Mr. Jukes's excellent book, *The Restitution of all things*," which, we have already noted, Kelly rejected.[32]

KELLY'S TEACHING FROM THE KEY TEXTS OF THE GOSPELS ABOUT THE AFTERLIFE

The Gospels were the key texts which were used by theologians to discuss the afterlife and so, before looking at some of the ideas and doctrines which Kelly taught throughout his work, I now look at his teaching about Christ's parables in Luke's Gospel and Matthew's Gospel, which were particularly pertinent to this subject. Kelly discussed in detail the parable of Dives and Lazarus in Luke chapter 16, a passage which was nearly always at the center of Victorian discussions about the afterlife. This was because it was not clearly shown in the biblical text whether it was an illustrative story or whether it referred to the reality of hell, and also because the incident purported to take place immediately after death and so brought forward the idea of judgment. There were several principles at work here which were frequently present in all Kelly's teaching about the afterlife. Firstly he used the text to assert that there was torment in Hades, the destination of unbelievers before Christ's return, as well as in Gehenna, which was translated as "hell."[33] Despite Kelly's literalist stance on their existence, typology and symbolism were acknowledged to be present in the text, showing that the literalism of the description of hell was not important to him, only the fact of its existence and misery.[34] Symbolism within the whole biblical text was acknowledged, for example, when he explained that Abraham's bosom was always a place of special blessedness in Jewish literature.[35]

Kelly was always rigorous in examining a particular text within its context. Rather than looking at Luke chapter 16 as a proof text of hell, he was interested in the purpose of the teaching of this parable which he did not see primarily as the assertion of the afterlife. He saw it as showing that the Jew in Christ's era was easily satisfied with the earthly life, rather than looking at the consequences of his present life for eternity.[36] The rich man feeling the need for mercy was about the false values of his immediate life

32. Ibid., 68.
33. Kelly, *Luke*, 276.
34. Ibid.
35. Ibid., 275.
36. Ibid.

and the point of damnation was to show the obtuseness of the Jew in first of all not believing in Moses and therefore not believing in Jesus.[37] In his commentary on Luke 16, Kelly touched on the knowledge of heaven from within hell and vice versa which preoccupied Bickersteth.[38] However Kelly was far more circumspect in his comments than Bickersteth was, as when he commented, "Whether the lost can know about the saved and about what it means to have a distance between them, it is not for us to pronounce on."[39] Kelly also used this passage to teach about the development of the meaning of Gehenna within the New Testament. Farrar had suggested that using the term Gehenna was merely an extension of a local illustration of the burning refuse outside Jerusalem.[40] Kelly acknowledged that the name was originally used in the books of Kings and Chronicles and was connected with the Valley of Hinnom where the bodies of children who had been sacrificed were disposed. A question from *The Bible Treasury* specifically asked him to elucidate his views on this, compared with those of Joseph Barber Lightfoot (1828–1889), Edward Hayes Plumtre (1821–1891) and Farrar.[41] In his answer, while refusing to criticize Bishop Lightfoot, Kelly spoke against Farrar, and maintained his own idea of doctrinal development in the Bible. He explained that "the New Testament and especially the Lord Himself deepened its usage and so Gehenna should be understood in the New Testament as meaning endless punishment."[42] Such a reference to doctrinal development showed that his periodical, as well as his longer biblical exegeses, was used to extend his teaching on subjects of contemporary theological interest. Kelly's interest in theological debate on this subject is also shown in his notes on Luke's Gospel, which were added by his editor after his death, based on his original notes and verbal directives, discussing the views of Lightfoot and Julius Welhausen (1844–1918).[43]

Kelly used his commentaries on Matthew chapters 24 and 25 to teach about eschatology in general, especially in its dispensational guise, and to

---

37. Ibid., 279.

38. Edward Bickersteth (1786–1850), Anglican priest and secretary of the Church Missionary Society.

39. Ibid., 276.

40. Farrar, *Eternal Hope*, Sermon 3, 80.

41. Lightfoot and Plumtre were eminent Anglican divines of the evangelical school who were part of the team of translators engaged with the Revised Version of the Bible.

42. Kelly, "Scripture Queries and Answers," 63.

43. Kelly, *Luke*, 471.

clear up some of what he regarded as mistaken ideas about the afterlife and especially judgment. His series of articles in *The Bible Treasury* (1856–1857) was about answering the arguments of those, such as Brown and Birks, who did not share his pre-millennial view of prophecy. Kelly believed that the judgment described in Matthew chapter 24 was the judgment of the nations, which was to take place at the end of the millennium, rather than the judgment of individuals after death.[44] The parable of the sheep and goats which was often used by the Broad Church to show the importance of humanitarian works irrespective of belief was interpreted by Kelly to show how the nations would receive the Jewish messengers, whom he believed would be preaching about Christ as the Messiah during the millennium. Thus Kelly's eschatological interpretation of Matthew chapter 24, which was different from the Broad church interpretation of judgment of all according to differentiation between good and bad works, avoided a contradiction with the Pauline message of salvation through faith alone.[45] As so often in his exegesis, he used precise linguistic analysis to back up his theological schema: he stressed that verse 34 uses the phrase "from the foundation of the world" but according to Ephesians the saints were destined for glory "from before the foundation of the world." Therefore the recipients of this reward would be living on the earth in the millennium.[46] In his exegesis of Matthew he also went some way in his theodicy to exonerate God from any desire to send people to hell. Since theodicy was an unusual aspect of his teaching his desire to justify the need for hell suggests that he was aware of the controversial nature of the subject among his contemporaries. In commenting on Matthew 25:41—"the eternal fire prepared for the devil and his angels"—Kelly observed that hell was not prepared for guilty man unless he chose it—thus making the decision to go to hell a conscious one on the part of human beings rather than one of damnation from a higher power.[47] There was no sadistic enjoyment of hell in Kelly's teaching and there was every desire to show God as being loving and righteous. Kelly's writing also showed how important the idea of judgment was but also the necessity of differentiating between different types of judgment—"it is a grand error

---

44. Thomas Rawson Birks (1810–1883), Knightsbridge Professor of Philosophy at Cambridge University and evangelical Anglican priest. For 21 years he was honorary secretary of the Evangelical Alliance.

45. Kelly, *Matthew*, 379.

46. Ibid., 381.

47. Ibid., 385.

to suppose that all the judgments in the word of God mean one and the same thing. We must leave room for differences here as elsewhere. In what indeed do we find absolute sameness of God's ways?"[48] I suggest that judgment was a far more important facet of the afterlife than the details of hell for Kelly, and indeed that variety of judgment—self-judgment, the judgment of the church as well as the judgment of God—was a major concern for the Brethren in their attempt to create an ideal and purist Christian community; this emphasis on judgment may have mirrored the need for judgment in the Victorian concern for appropriate criminal punishment.[49]

I will deal briefly in this chapter with other doctrines which impinged on the theology of the afterlife, but in his teaching from Matthew's Gospel Kelly's focus on his eschatological interpretation, rather than a description of the horrors of hell, is made clear. In the parable of the wedding guest in Matthew, what concerned Kelly was not the understanding of the nature of "outer darkness" where the wedding guest was cast, but the Jewish rejection of the perfection of Christ—"it is about God the Father providing the wedding garment, which is the righteousness of Christ."[50] Understanding about judgment, heaven and hell, was always subject to Kelly's high Christology and also his veneration of Scripture as "the word of God" which would reveal the will of God, an issue which was more important than wishful thinking, admiration of "good people," or reason.[51] This attitude was apparent throughout his teaching on the subject of the afterlife and was also emphasized in his commentary on the story of Dives and Lazarus.[52]

Rather than dwelling on the gloom of hell, Kelly always concentrated on the blessedness of "the rapture" for the Christian believer and the language connected with it was important for the Brethren. He taught, "The greater the power of the Spirit in the soul, the more ardently does the Bride say "come." This is about anticipation and excitement."[53] Kelly dealt with the afterlife as being a very solemn subject, but his positive anticipation of heaven was also made explicit in his article "Our Joy in Heaven," when

---

48. Ibid., 379.

49. Brethren concern for self-judgment of various kinds is dealt with in detail in chapter 7.

50. Ibid., 330.

51. Ibid., 130.

52. Kelly, *Luke*, 279.

53. Kelly, *Matthew*, 363.

he taught about the Transfiguration.[54] The experience of communion with Christ in the earthly life was merely a foretaste of heaven.

KELLY'S AFFIRMATION OF HELL AND HIS REJECTION OF MORTALISM, THE GENERAL RESURRECTION, ANNIHILATION AND PURGATORY

When he taught about the afterlife, Kelly intentionally reverted to what he believed was the position of Paul and the early apostles. This can be contrasted with the reformed Protestant tradition, which tended to rely on Augustine's interpretation of the Bible, and the Tractarians, who supported the interpretation of the early Church Fathers. Against the Broad Church teaching about the possibility of future redemption for those who had died without repentance, Kelly stated, "There is no hope of any change in their condition."[55] If Kelly thought that the Bible taught this, then that would suffice, but he was also careful not to elaborate on the subject unnecessarily—"We have no claim to ask what He has not told us."[56] As a result he did not dwell on the horrors of hell in his teachings and also readily acknowledged the presence of believers amongst those of different religious views from himself. Thus the Brethren did not take the same view on an exclusive mediation of salvation and ultimate authority as did the Roman Catholic Church of that period. The Brethren were exclusive in stressing the necessity of evangelical conversion, but not in churchmanship or adherence to a particular denomination. Kelly pointed to the words of Luke 21:8 which warned against false Messiahs and wrong teaching. To dwell on love only was "an infidel thought." He continued, "It as much appertains to God to be holy as to be gracious; and the same portion of His word teaches us both these truths . . . the portion of the wicked is in the lake burning with fire and brimstone."[57]

---

54. Kelly, "Our Joy in Heaven," 188.

55. Kelly, "Judgment," 319. Kelly justifies this view by pointing out the way that verse 14 of Revelation chapter 22 with its promise of eternal blessedness is juxtaposed to verse 15 which promises an equally certain future for those who are excluded.

56. Ibid., 314.

57. Kelly, *Luke*, 470. This refers also to Luke 21: 8. "And he said, Take heed that ye be not deceived: for many shall come in my name, saying, I am Christ; and the time draweth near: go ye not therefore after them."(KJV).

We need to ask why the existence of hell was so vehemently asserted by Kelly and also why it was not elaborated on unnecessarily. One of the reasons for this was his view on mercy. Kelly taught that God's mercy could not be shown in the eternal judgment because it had already been shown through Christ. However, he believed that it was because mankind had a spiritual nature, that "he was capable of eternal misery if he persist in refusing God revealed in Christ."[58] He also had particular views about the right time to hear about judgment and its consequences. He wrote the following in his commentary on Matthew—"a great principle of God—that He never opens out the future of judgments on the rebellious, and of deliverance for His own people till sin has so developed itself as to manifest total ruin."[59] Kelly justified this view by pointing out that the deliverance of Israel in the Exodus took place in the context of faith and obedience, rather than in the people's full understanding of what was happening. In the same way, Christians were called upon to affirm their belief in hell, even when they could not fully explain it because complete understanding would only be possible in eternity. However, faith and trust in the Bible and in God could be rewarded in the present. This teaching also linked with the theology of the sinfulness of man, because it was impossible for human beings to ask God for His salvation unless they fully appreciated their unworthiness. Also he believed that it was an important principle that in eternity evil would not be extinguished but separated from good.[60] Kelly recognized times of social change and political uncertainty in the nineteenth century and not only addressed contemporary question in his magazine, *The Bible Treasury*, but was also worried that church leaders wanted to reinterpret Scriptural passages, such as the parable of the sheep and goats, "partly to escape what they dread, and partly in order to gather comfort for their troubled souls."[61] Kelly also categorically denied the need for esoteric and exoteric teaching about this subject. Farrar agreed that detailed teaching about the nature of hell had little effect on the beliefs of the working class.[62]

58. Kelly, *Brief Notice*, 5.

59. Kelly, *Matthew*, 340.

60. Kelly, *Brief Notice*, 7. This idea is connected with his belief in the immortality of the soul, either for good or evil.

61. Ibid., 375.

62. Rowell, *Hell and the Victorians*, 148. Also letters from Westcott and A.R. Symonds, a former missionary in India, vicar of Walmer and author of *The Ultimate Reconciliation and Subjection of All Souls to God*, supported Farrar's view. Cf. Rowell, *Hell and the Victorians*, 147.

Kelly believed that universalism was a "dream" and "more to do with the slighting of sin and loving it."[63] Any denial of eternal punishment led to the "emboldening of sinners." Therefore he believed that preaching about hell made people cautious about crime and sin. Kelly believed that it was easy for society to fall back on heathen conclusions again when seeking the truth about the afterlife. When teaching about 2 Peter chapter 3, he said that Peter denied "the notion that there is perpetuity in the state of things around us." Kelly also wanted his readers to be on guard against those who scoffed at the idea of Christ coming again and the start of eternity.[64]

The subject of purgatory was discussed in the Victorian church and Kelly had his own view on it. The problem of the intermediate state between death and the final judgment and the delay in the second coming of Christ had led to the development of the doctrine of purgatory in the twelfth century.[65] In Victorian times the doctrine of purgatory was justified, not only by the Roman Catholic Church, but by Newman as first leader of the Tractarian movement and then, later as convert to the Roman Catholic Church.[66] Newman taught that development of Christian doctrine, such as the doctrine of purgatory which was taught after the completion of the Canon of Scripture, was acceptable. He argued that any deduction from Scripture necessarily implied development, whether in the Protestant or Catholic tradition.[67] Newman's work on this subject, published at the end of 1845, was written just before his acceptance into the Roman Catholic Church.[68] Newman went back to the early Church Fathers' views on purgatory which differed considerably from medieval Catholic views. He claimed that Clement thought that if penance had not been shown in life, especially for sins after baptism, it had to be continued after death. He called this a discriminating, rather than a destructive fire, which would not be associated with the fires of hell.[69] According to Newman, the doctrines of infant

---

63. Kelly, *Brief Notice*, 6.

64. William Kelly, *The Second Epistle of* Peter, 163.

65. Almond, *Heaven and Hell in Enlightenment England*, 68. Cf. Almond's references to le Goff, *The Birth of Purgatory* (1981), which deals with the growth of the doctrine of purgatory in medieval times in much greater detail.

66. Newman had already discussed the subject of prayers for the dead with Pusey in 1826 and his tracts LXXIX and LXXXX also dealt with the subject of purgatory and the afterlife. Cf. Rowell, *Hell and the Victorians*, 99.

67. Newman, *Christian Doctrine*, 58.

68. Reardon, *Coleridge to Gore*, 145.

69. Newman, *Christian Doctrine*, 388.

baptism and purgatory had developed together.[70] He also believed that purgatory was the only possible alternative to the sleep of the soul between death and Resurrection.[71] Newman claimed that St. Cyprian had preached this doctrine and that it had been necessary in the later years of the early Church to counteract the loss of initial pure love and faithful discipline of the first Christians.[72] Newman justified purgatory by explaining that logical sequence was an important test of truth and also explaining that the doctrine of belief in the soul without the body—a state which had come to be recognized as existing between physical death and the last judgment—had been developed as an exclusive corollary to purgatory.[73] Newman's work on the subject was also parallel to theories of historical and cultural development in the nineteenth century. Some Victorian Protestants wanted more hope for the afterlife than the prospect of hell and therefore found that the doctrine of purgatory was attractive, because it suggested the possibility of personal development.

In this area of cultural development, Broad Church theologians were influenced by the works of Renaissance thinkers, such as Erasmus and Pico, who were affected by Origen's denial of hell and also by the acceptance of non-Christian ways to God. Education and progress were key ideas for the Victorians through the influence of Arnold, Hare and Temple. As one of the key essayists in *Essays and Reviews* and later a bishop and Archbishop, Temple had an enormous influence on Victorian theologians and was denounced by Kelly. Temple believed that human reason would develop even without divine revelation.[74] H.B. Wilson too, who wrote about hell in the same collection of essays, believed that man was a progressive being.[75] In his Bampton lectures of 1851 which were later published as *The Communion of Saints*, Wilson showed that the church had an influence for good over all people in society.[76] Jowett, another essayist, also believed that all religions were steps in the education of the humanity. Such beliefs in prog-

---

70. Ibid., 390

71. Ibid., 63.

72. Ibid., 390.

73. Ibid., 63. By exclusive corollary, Newman meant that the separation of body and soul was clearly necessary for a belief in the state of purgatory, which would precede the resurrection of the body in heaven.

74. Temple, "The Education of the World," 137.

75. Wilson, "Séances Historiques," 288.

76. Wilson, "Lecture V: Galatians 1.3, 4," 175.

ress, had an effect on belief in syncretism and therefore on the implausibility of hell. Jowett also wrote in *The Interpretation of Scripture and Other Essays*, "We feel that God cannot have given us capacities and affections, that they should find no other fulfillment than they attain here."[77] Here the argument about human progress was inevitably linked with the potential of progress after death and therefore the pointlessness of hell. The idea of progress for the essayists also meant development of theological thought and interpretation based on reason, and this was particularly shown in Mark Pattison's essay, "Tendencies of Religious Thought in England."[78] Maurice too thought that the Bible was the record of God's education of humanity, not just doctrinal propositions, and he believed that God wanted to bless the whole of humanity.[79] Maurice's views on the Bible as a record of religious views (following de Wette and other German critics as noted in chapter 2) differed significantly from the literalist view of the Bible as the Word of God. This difference in understanding inevitably affected the Broad Church belief or otherwise in the doctrine of hell.

Kelly did have some views on the idea of developmental theology but not the same as those of the Broad Church. He believed that the world, either in the contemporary sense or amongst unbelievers in the world of the Bible, could understand God as Jehovah El-Elyon "the most High God," revealed in Genesis, but not as a Savior. Therefore his idea of development was that of progressive revelation to an elite who could understand the deeper nature of God. This was true of those who were believers in the Bible as well as those such as the Brethren who showed spiritual understanding through "the new birth."[80] Popular contemporary literature aided sentimental belief in a general resurrection and the continuation of an ideal human life after death. Kelly rejected this idea and said "popular as it may be, it is wholly without foundation—nay, contrary to all Scripture." He thought that even though some passages from Scripture might suggest it, it was "a fundamental error, which will be found to obscure and weaken salvation by grace."[81] It was only the saved who were resurrected to eternal life because only they were indwelt by the Holy Spirit and therefore had the same power

---

77. Jowett, *The Interpretation of Scripture*, 98, as quoted in Wheeler, 227.
78. Pattison, "Tendencies of Religious Thought in England," 396.
79. Morris, *F.D. Maurice and the Crisis of Christian Authority*, 181.
80. Kelly, "The Separate State and the Resurrection," 239.
81. Kelly, "Judgment," 295.

of resurrection as Jesus.[82] He rejected Victorian sentimentality such as the widespread belief that people could become angels after death, although his belief in personal identity after death gave some comfort to the bereaved.[83]

Kelly made clear that he thought that the denial of the soul's immortality was dangerous and not biblically justified.[84] He believed strongly in the immortality of the soul and argued against those who believed in annihilation. He also believed that conscious punishment would occur immediately after death for those who did not believe. He wrote, "The notion of possible mercy in the intermediate condition is absolutely excluded by Scripture."[85] In the May 1900 edition of *The Bible Treasury*, he answered the argument put forward in the book *The Life of the Waiting Soul* (1896) by R.E. Sanderson (1828-1910).[86] Sanderson denied a fixed state at death and, in so doing, went back to what Kelly considered to be a pre-Reformation error. According to Kelly, the High Church movement of the Church of England had taken up this argument for itself in Victorian times.[87] Kelly did not try to argue against those who claimed it would be impossible for the soul to be tormented without the body: he merely stated that it would be so, even though it might not consist of the full punishment. In commenting on Luke 16:22-25, the story of Dives and Lazarus, he affirmed the torment of Hades.[88] In his exposition of Matthew's Gospel he explained that we do not acquire our immortality of soul from Christ, as was argued by Drummond in *Natural Law in the Spiritual World* (1890), but from our inheritance in Adam.[89] Kelly was sure that Gnosticism, whose adherents denied the resurrection of the body, and agnosticism, whose followers believed that the afterlife was unlikely, came together to combat Christian belief, though for different reasons. Rather than saying, as Farrar did, that we do not know what the state of the wicked will be, Kelly asserted that

82. Ibid., 297.

83. Kelly, *Brief Notice*, 7.

84. Ibid., 6.

85. Kelly, *Luke*, 278.

86. Sanderson held various posts in the Church of England including Canon of Chichester Cathedral in 1889.

87. Kelly, "The Intermediate State," 80.

88. Kelly, *Luke*, 275.

89. Kelly, *Matthew*, 276. Henry Drummond (1851-1897) was a Christian academic and explorer who wrote about Christian apologetics for the layman. He was Professor of Natural Science at the College of the Free Church of Scotland. The book which Kelly refers to here is Drummond, *Natural Law in the Spiritual World*..

annihilation does not exist in the Bible. "The notion of sleep, still more of extinction, for the soul, is a baseless and wicked fable."[90] The "lost" were, according to Kelly, "destroyed" but this was true for this life as well, and could not be interpreted as future annihilation.[91] He taught that destruction of the soul never means annihilation but rather "an existence of utter ruin and misery in separation from God."[92] Kelly specifically condemned Farrar's writings; he also denied the doctrine of conditional immortality (only the soul of someone who is a believer is immortal).[93] Rowell has shown that conditional immortality was the only possible alternative to eternal hell for Victorians who followed the tradition of Augustine and Calvin.[94] In *The Bible Treasury*, in the section entitled "Scripture Queries and Answers," Kelly explained why conditional immortality was unacceptable, because it "destroys the true nature and place God gave man as his offspring, in contradistinction from all other animated beings on earth. We have a responsibility as creatures to obey God."[95]

Therefore Kelly taught that every human soul was immortal and that it was made so by the will of God at creation.[96] He believed in Christ being the savior of the body and the soul, so that, in this earthly life, the soul was saved, but in the future life, both body and soul would be saved.[97] When Christ commended his spirit to the Father on the cross, He demonstrated that death had not touched it.[98] Kelly was extremely concerned that Victorian Christian leaders were questioning the immortality of the soul, and he believed that this would have serious consequences.[99] In his argument against what he saw as a false trend, he explained that, although 1 Timothy 6:16 talked about the unique immortality of God, this was about "essential, not conferred, being," and did not negate the truth of the soul's immortality.[100]

90. Kelly, "The Soul Neither Mortal nor to Sleep," 16.
91. Ibid., 18.
92. Kelly, *Brief Notice*, 4.
93. Kelly, "Eternal Life," 61.
94. Rowell, *Hell and the Victorians*, 205.
95. Kelly, "Scripture Queries and Answers," 63.
96. Kelly, *Brief Notice*, 1.
97. Ibid., 3.
98. Ibid.
99. Kelly, "The Soul," 3.
100. Ibid., 16.

THE NATURE OF PUNISHMENT AND OF JUDGMENT AND KELLY'S CONDEMNATION OF THE ANGLICAN CHURCH'S BELIEF IN CHILD BAPTISM AS A WAY OF AVOIDING PUNISHMENT

Many English theologians in previous centuries had already considered the appropriateness or otherwise of punishment in hell. In 1690 John Tillotson, preaching to the Queen about Matthew 25:46, had considered whether God was bound to honor threats as much as promises, the problem of temporary crimes being punished eternally, the possible meanings of "eternal," and theories of annihilation and universalism.[101] In *The Reasonableness of Christianity* (1695), John Locke claimed that Adam's fall did not condemn posterity and wrote against the idea that "everyone descended of him deserved endless torment, in hell fire."[102] The Victorians were particularly interested in the question of how appropriate punishment in hell might be. Birks, in his book *Victory of Divine Goodness* (1867) argued that the fall of Adam was not an inevitable human inheritance, but was rather a precedent for human beings.[103] It is clear that key theological issues, such as the fall of man and natural law, were interrelated with questions about justice and the purpose of punishment.

In 1854 Kelly wrote a tract about the obligation of government to punish wrongdoing.[104] Although his major concern in writing this was to delineate the Christian position in relation to secular government, he did write about the importance of punishment, which is interesting when we consider how concerned the Victorians were about this subject. He believed in the rightness of capital punishment because it was "the requirement of God, grounded upon the fact that *He* made man in *His* image."[105] He asserted that capital punishment was part of God's revelation and that God had not changed his plan. Just because people might be saved in mercy for eternity, it did not mean that a worldly ruler should show mercy to

---

101. Tillotson, "Of the Eternity of Hell Torments," vol. 3, 84, 77, 79, 86–87.
102. Locke, *The Reasonableness of Christianity as delivered in the Scriptures*, 6.
103. Rowell, *Hell and the Victorians*, 123.
104. Kelly, "The Powers That Be."
105. Ibid., 4.

criminals.[106] Kelly was more interested in the reason for punishment than in its effect.[107]

In contrast to Kelly's ideas, key thinking about contemporary penal theory questioned the usefulness of retributive justice. There needed to be a possible reformation for the offender and the deterrent element of punishment should ensure moral conduct on earth.[108] According to Bentham, who was a significant influence on the topic, we must understand the intentions and background of the offender.[109] Therefore hell as an end in itself became obsolete. Michael Wheeler has shown that some Victorians thought hell was pointless because it did not act as a promoter of moral standards or protect against crime.[110] For reformists and social activists, prison was increasingly seen not as a place to inflict further punishment, but as a punishment itself.[111] Dr John Pye-Smith (1774–1851), a progressive Congregationalist theologian, argued that man should dread sin, not the penal consequences of sin.[112] According to such progressive Victorian views, suffering should have a purpose and this was more likely to be brought out in the Platonic view of successive lives or in the theory of purgatory than in the orthodox view of hell for eternity.[113]

Kelly did not believe that Christians had to submit to the same divine judgment as others. He linked this with his own translation of 2 Corinthians 5:10. Everyone should "appear" before the judgment seat of Christ but believers would not be judged there.[114] He also referred to John 5:21 where Jesus asserted that he would be coming again as judge and also in human form. Kelly also contested the translation of the Greek word *crisis* in John's Gospel by asserting that its true meaning was "judgment," not "condemnation," and he applauded the Roman Catholic translation in this instance as being faithful to the Greek original and the Latin Vulgate version.[115] The

---

106. Ibid., 9.
107. Ibid.
108. Rowell, *Hell and the Victorians*, 13.
109. Ibid., 13.
110. Wheeler, *Death and the Future Life*, 184.
111. Almond, *Heaven and Hell*, 100.
112. Ibid., 184.
113. Almond, *Heaven and Hell*, 23.
114. W. Kelly, "Judgment," 281. Kelly examines 2 Corinthians 5:10: "We must all appear before the judgment seat of Christ," (KJV).
115. Ibid., 289–90. John 5:24 (KJV): "He that heareth my word and believeth on him

reason that believers would not come into judgment was that Christ had already been judged on the cross for them, thus closely linking his teaching on the atonement and the future life.[116] This also affirmed the nature of grace, rather than just mercy.

Kelly believed that the Christian would be rewarded for the fruit of his work in Christ and would be judged for his disobedience, but that this was not the same as damnation or purgatory. The saints would also be sitting on the thrones meting out judgment—his interpretation of Revelation 20:4—but this was part of the millennium, not part of eternity. Although there would be judgment of evil works for the Christian, the main thrust of this teaching was to point out that a Christian should be pre-occupied with self-judgment, leading to repentance and, if this did not occur, there should be Brethren assembly judgment and, if both of these failed, then there would eventually be God's judgment. Therefore the judgment of Brethren assemblies was not only doctrinally authoritative but finally helpful in mitigating the need for judgment in the future.[117]

Kelly's distinction between the Kingdom of heaven and the Kingdom of God had considerable effect on his views on judgment. This was different from the teaching of Arnold of the Broad Church about the nature of the Kingdom of heaven (in his lecture to the clergy in Sion College, 22 February, 1876), and the way this was taken up by Maurice and the Christian Socialist Movement.[118] They believed that the Kingdom of heaven could be a natural extension of human society in the present. Kelly taught about the parable of the good and bad seed and the collection of the tares at the end of the age in Matthew's gospel.[119] He allowed that the task of the servants was to watch the good seed and it was the angels who acted judicially.[120] Evil done in the name of Christ, through the Anglican or Catholic Church, could only be rooted out at the end of the age. With this in mind, what Kelly considered to be the dangerously wrong teaching of such churches was likely to remain. Kelly's paradigm of the field meaning the world of Christendom had important implications. It enabled him to condemn or-

---

that sent me, hath everlasting life, and shall not come into condemnation: but is passed from death unto life."

116. Ibid.
117. Kelly, *Matthew*, 361.
118. Chadwick, *Victorian Church*, part 2, 272.
119. Matthew 13:24–30 (KJV).
120. Kelly, *The Coming of the Day of the Lord*, 10.

thodox Christianity in the Anglican and Roman Catholic churches and so justify the need for Brethren teaching. As a justification for his position as a Bible teacher it was very significant. It also helped to explain why there was no point in ameliorating the bad seed. Such interpretation clarified the need for evangelical conversion and for separation from the national church. This is an example of his reading of the parables about the end of the age which affected his views on prophecy and allowed him to read the text as a literalist, a dispensationalist and a thoughtful conservative evangelical.[121] The "ruin of the church" was not just an important fact but had been prophesied by Jesus.[122] It was both a matter of divine revelation but also verified by church history. While the Christian might receive reward according to his works, when his righteousness was based on that of Christ, the unbeliever's works were always evil because they were performed only through the position of Adam.[123] Therefore the literal, fundamentalist understanding of The Fall in Genesis chapter 3 was extremely important for this reading of the Gospels.

The Brethren always emphasized the opportunity to escape judgment in the future by experiencing conversion and change now. Therefore the question of the injustice of hell was not really relevant as there was always an escape from it. Kelly also believed that it was only the conviction of the Holy Spirit who helped an individual to understand the awfulness of hell: otherwise it was a subject for mockery. Punishment was about justice and truth, not about the opportunity to improve. Kelly argued that there must be a distinction made between the resurrection "of the dead" for the believer and "from the dead" for the unbeliever. "Of the dead" meant that this was the start of a resurrection life in heaven; "from the dead" meant only a temporary resurrection before judgment. If there was not this distinction, Kelly argued, there would be "a cloud over the gospel of God's grace and a tendency at last to put the Christian on common ground with the unbeliever."[124] The "rapture," with its accompanying benefits for the be-

---

121. He read this parable as a literalist because he believed that this division between the good and bad was going to happen in the future; he read it as a dispensationalist because he saw it as something which would take place at the end of the millennium; he read it as a thoughtful conservative evangelical because he saw the necessity of "evangelical conversion" in order to be part of the good harvest but he also based his reading on his more extensive understanding of eschatological texts.

122. Ibid., 11.

123. Kelly, *Luke*, 456.

124. Kelly, "Judgment," 300.

liever, was therefore more of an incentive for change than the threat of hell against which a human being had no natural defenses.[125]

In rejecting the Anglican doctrine of regeneration through child baptism, Kelly had to consider the problems of the afterlife for those who had not experienced an "evangelical conversion." While being constant about his belief in the existence of an eternal hell, he assured his readers that "by Christ's death all infants will be saved through redemption." Kelly was adamant about this matter, even asserting in *The Bible Treasury*, "It is wholly unscriptural, that God punishes babies if they are not christened . . . He does not bless little children on earth to send them dying to hell."[126] Although this belief could not be explicitly proved from Scripture, but only deduced, Kelly insisted on it, partly because of his belief in the love of God, and partly because he rejected the idea that God needed infant baptism to provide salvation for children. The first may have been part of his sentimental concern as a Victorian gentleman living at a time of high infant mortality; the latter may have been a result of his distaste for the Anglican custom of infant baptism. This was very different from the type of teaching given by evangelicals and the Catholic writer, Joseph Furniss (1809–1865), who in 1861 published *The Sight of Hell*, in which he propounded the view that even one sin deserved eternal pains in hell.[127]

KELLY'S ESCHATOLOGICAL TEACHING AND BELIEF IN THE AFTERLIFE

As I suggested in the introduction to this chapter, Kelly made numerous distinctions in his teaching about the afterlife, both linguistic distinctions and distinctions in his eschatological reading of the Scriptures. Kelly's teaching on the dispensations of the ages had an effect on his teaching on the afterlife because he was able to distinguish between Christ's teaching to the Church and to the Jews about the subject of judgment and therefore the final outcome of judgment. His views on what was symbolic language and what was literal were also tied in with dispensationalism, because the Old Testament language of realism was connected with the Jews, whereas the New Testament symbolic language was connected with the other-worldly destination of hell or heaven. Kelly constantly asserted the literal truth of

---

125. Ibid., 341.
126. Kelly, "The Word of God," 119.
127. Wheeler, *Death and the Future Life*, 182, referring to Furniss, *The Sight of Hell*.

hell while interpreting the New Testament language symbolically. Unlike other writers such as F. D. Maurice, he did not let contemporary arguments about justice and punishment impinge on his assertion of the truth of "eternal hell." Such a conviction was very much in keeping with his belief in the righteousness and holiness of God, which he continually taught in his various books about the Pentateuch. In this he had much in common with evangelical preachers such as Edward Bickersteth (1786–1850), who strongly asserted God's righteousness so that, in his epic poem, *Yesterday, Today and Forever*, even Satan finally proclaims, "The Lord, is righteous; I and mine have sinn'd."[128] Kelly's strong belief in the utter depravity of man also explains why hell had to be part of truth and reality. Therefore, however insistent he was on his pre-millennial views, he focused far more on his teaching about the Christian life in his work. Unlike some mystics who saw death as taking them nearer to complete preoccupation with God, Kelly did not idealize death.[129] In stating, "death is not, and ought not to be, the object of his (i.e. the Christian's) affections," he also rejected the maudlin sentimental views on death by Victorian writers or even the fascination with the subject as shown by the admirers of Tennyson's *In Memoriam* (1859).[130] He explained that it was very necessary to understand the intended audience in the Gospels so that we might know whether a particular teaching relevant to believers today.[131] He also compared different passages in the New Testament to see whether they were contradictory or whether they had a different context. For example he explained that "In Matthew 25, not a single dead man is spoken of; in Revelation 20, not a single living man."[132] This refers to the two different scenes in these passages—Matthew chapter 25 contains stories about the judgment of the nations, which should take place, according to Kelly, at the end of the millennium. Revelation 20:12 presents the dead standing before the throne of judgment and therefore must, according to Kelly, be after earthly human existence has ended. Thus he explained the apparent contradictions between the two

---

128. Bickersteth, *Yesterday, Today and Forever*, Book 11, lines 41–42, 232. Bickersteth was an evangelical Anglican priest and secretary of the Church Missionary Society.

129. This is clear in the work of Julian of Norwich, an anchorite, who deliberately limited herself to a small building next to the church, as her tomb.

130. Kelly, "The Separate State and the Resurrection," 239. This article is unsigned and is therefore most probably the work of Kelly himself. "In Memoriam" was written in memory of Arthur Henry Hallam, who died in 1833. Tennyson, *In Memoriam*, 39.

131. Ibid.

132. Kelly, *Matthew*, 379.

judgment scenes.[133] Accurate translation was paramount, and therefore his knowledge of the original languages was well used. He translated Matthew 24:3 as "the end of the age" not "the end of the world" (as given in the King James Version), thus carefully distinguishing between the millennium and the final judgment.[134] In the same passage he noted that "generation" had a moral rather than a chronological force, (meaning that it referred to a certain quality of people rather than people from a particular time frame) thus saving students of prophecy from wrong expectations.

KELLY'S UNDERSTANDING OF LANGUAGE WITHIN THE DEBATE ABOUT THE AFTERLIFE AND HIS FAR-REACHING REFERENCES TO CLASSICAL WRITERS

In Kelly's understanding of language there were two principles at work—understanding of symbolic language and a distinction between future earthly (millennial) and heavenly (eternal) events. Within the dispensationalist system the place of the Jewish nation in the future was assured and therefore, because that was for Kelly an indisputable fact, language had to be interpreted figuratively where necessary. In his paradigm of pre-millennial teaching, Kelly interpreted language accordingly. For example he said that Daniel 12:2 and Isaiah chapter 26 and Ezekiel chapter 27 should be interpreted figuratively because here the resurrection was all about the deliverance of the Jews at the end of the age.[135] Numbers were generally read figuratively, as in the 1000-year period of the millennium.[136] He saw this future era as comparable to the experience of the transfiguration in the Gospels and parallel to the Christian's appreciation of God's presence in worship. Careful reading of the Gospel also became important in the distinction he made between the Kingdom of God and the Kingdom of heaven.[137] This allowed him to distinguish between the general world of

---

133. Ibid., 379.

134. Ibid., 343, referring to Matt 24:3: "What shall be the sign of thy coming and of the end of the world?" (KJV).

135. Kelly, "Judgment," 294.

136. Ibid. Kelly explained that he believed 1000 could be a literal number but he thought it more likely to be figurative.

137. Contrast this with the viewpoint of Maurice, whose book *The Kingdom of Christ* showed that God's kingdom was essentially about the rule of justice and goodness established here on earth in the present dispensation. This linked Maurice with the Christian Socialist movement.

Christendom and the world of the true believer, especially in the eternal state.[138] As, according to Kelly, the rapture of the saints would take place well before the rise of "the beast" and the tribulation, he had no need to speculate on the possible identity of "the beast" or his political context.[139] Even within the book of Revelation, Kelly distinguished between different referents. Thus he believed that the events of chapter 21 should be interpreted differently from those of chapter 20 and that different scenes in the history of Jerusalem were referred to in verses 2 and 10 even within chapter 21. Therefore we see that in his eschatology and in his teaching about judgment, Kelly understood the necessity for detailed differentiation.

As far as Kelly was concerned, the blessedness of the future was more important for the believer than the punishment of hell and Kelly's main task was to instruct believers. It would seem that Kelly was in this respect more in line with Broad Church writers such as F.D. Maurice than evangelical preachers who concentrated on the fear of hell. Unlike Joseph Furniss, he took no pleasure in imagining its details. However, he did not feel free to offer comfort to his Victorian audience as Farrar had done. Farrar claimed, "It is expressly because I do not wish to be 'wise above what is written' that I refuse to attach to the word 'hell' shades of meaning indefinitely more dark and terrible than those which it originally possessed."[140] Farrar used numerous references from both Testaments to posit a restitution of all things.[141] Kelly would not have agreed with Farrar's conclusion that "God judges that He might teach; He never teaches that He may judge."[142] In other words Farrar thought that if God judges in eternity, it must be with the purpose of change and the finality of hell does not suggest that purpose. Similarly, for him the purpose of God's teaching must always be to effect change rather than judgment of human beings.

Kelly was careful to assign the right promises in different passages of the Bible to particular events of the afterlife. The promise of 2 Peter 3:13, "Nevertheless we, according to his promise, look for new heavens and a new earth, wherein dwelleth righteousness" (KJV) he saw as belonging to heaven, because it used the phrase "where righteousness dwelleth" whereas in the millennium he believed that righteousness would govern humanity,

138. Kelly, *Matthew*, 234.
139. Kelly, *Coming of the Day*, 54.
140. Farrar, *Eternal Hope*, preface, xiii.
141. Ibid., 87.
142. Ibid., 97.

who would still not be perfect.[143] The language used about Dives and Lazarus in Luke's gospel was for him clearly about the intermediate state—what would be experienced between death and the second coming of Christ—not about the future resurrection.[144] These precise distinctions of language were important to Kelly: he constructed his whole paradigm of eschatology on them. If physical torment in hell existed and if only the resurrected body could suffer physical torment, then the division between those being punished and those not had to take place between the intermediate state and the start of eternity after the Day of Judgment. Therefore the accurate understanding of biblical language and how it affected eschatological interpretation became very important for the Victorians, and it was a major concern of the millenarians, including Kelly.[145]

Kelly was also interested in the linguistic debate, initiated by Maurice and Farrar, on the meaning of "eternal." He believed that the nineteenth-century concerns about its meaning were linked to the teaching of the early Church Fathers, which he considered to be false. He made a point of stressing that hell meant "never-ending doom" adding, "nor does a word intimate that its horrors will ever come to an end."[146] He looked at a similar use of the word in Plato's *Timaeus* and Aristotle's *De Coelo* and said that it meant the opposite of transitory, as it did it in 2 Corinthians 4:18, where the temporal and eternal were set against each other.[147] He asserted his belief in the word "eternal" meaning "never-ending" in the following criticism—"Can any sober person doubt that the denial of Farrar, Jukes etc (*sic*) is inexcusable?"[148] Kelly never denied the use of imagery in the biblical text and was able to interpret it, but he never moved away from the reality of hell. Also, for him as for Maurice, separation from God was the most terrible fate of all, whatever language was used to describe it. Although he argued against Maurice's theology in general, he showed a remarkably similar understanding to Maurice in his interpretation of St. John's language. Maurice wrote, "eternal punishment is the punishment of being without

---

143. Ibid.

144. Kelly, *The Soul Neither Mortal nor to Sleep*, 14.

145. Almond, *Heaven and Hell*, 94.

146. Ibid.

147. 2 Cor 4:18: "'the things which are seen are temporal; but the things which are not seen are eternal.'" (KJV).

148. Kelly, "Eternal Life: Notes on a Lecture," 63. In this article Kelly is referring to Farrar, *Eternal Hope*.

the knowledge of God, who is love, and of Jesus Christ who has manifested it, even as eternal life is declared to be the having the knowledge of God and of Jesus Christ."[149] "Eternity," claimed Maurice, "has nothing to do with time or duration."[150] Kelly also believed that the phrase "eternal life" was relevant to the Christian in the present life, because eternal life had to do with the knowledge of God and of His Son.[151]

In his commentary on Revelation chapters 20 and 21, Kelly referred to John 5:21—"He that hath the Son hath eternal life" (KJV). It was the verse which Maurice was to use to consider the meaning of "eternal" as pertaining to a unique spiritual dimension rather than "never-ending" in a chronological sense. Kelly did not deny the chronological sense but he did look to the word "eternal" as being the unique quality of life in Christ and saw it as starting at the moment of conversion. Therefore his understanding of the word "eternal" came very near to Maurice's and indeed there are some unexpected parallels between Maurice and Kelly's teaching. However Kelly was also adamant that hell meant "the eternal ruin and torment of those that despise Him."[152]

Distinctions between uses of language were part of Kelly's teaching style. This is particularly evident in his teaching about the differences in meaning between "the day of the Lord," meaning the final judgment, "the rapture," meaning the secret consummation of the believers with Christ in heaven, and the "coming or appearing of Christ," meaning the appearance of Christ with the church in order to govern the earth during the millennium. In his detailed analysis of such phrases, Kelly anticipated the study of eschatological terms in modern theological and linguistic studies.[153] His ability to make fine distinctions in the biblical text was backed by his far-reaching references to similar language in other ancient texts and his ability to approve or disapprove of the textual translations of those with whom he had little theological sympathy.

---

149. Maurice, *Theological Essays*, 450.

150. Ibid.

151. Kelly, "Life and Death," 28. Article signed "L. L." but contents are in line with Kelly's thought.

152. Kelly, "Judgment," 319.

153. Caird, *The Language and Imagery of the Bible*. Caird (1917–1984), Dean Ireland's Professor of the Exegesis of Holy Scripture, Oxford University, was particularly concerned with the interpretation of the phrase, "The Day of the Lord," as indeed was Kelly.

Nowhere in his writings is this more evident than in his short book entitled *The Coming and the Day of the Lord, 2 Thessalonians II. 1, 2* published in 1903, towards the end of his life.[154] Here Kelly made wide-ranging references to the church fathers, including Origen (185–254), the seventeenth-century Platonists, and contemporary writers such as Newman, Maurice, Jowett, Farrar and Bickersteth. His detailed linguistic work is shown in the distinction he made between Christ's coming for Christian believers in "the rapture" and His coming for judgment of the world after the millennium. In looking at the order of events in his scheme of eschatology, he argued for a different translation of 2 Thessalonians 2:2, "the day of the Lord is present," instead of the commonly accepted "the day of the Lord is at hand," which implied a future event.[155] In affirming the Revised Version translation instead of the King James Version, Kelly first of all supported what he considered to be the correct translation of Hugo Grotius (1583–1645) even though he considered Grotius too "worldly-minded" to make effective and spiritual conclusions about the implication of this translation.[156] Kelly then justified the refined translation by referring to Aristophanes's *Clouds* for a parallel use of the phrase in classical Greek, which was used in the context of clothes being worn in the present, as well as to the comments of the Congregationalist, John Howe (1630–1705), which agreed with his own translation.[157] With a mixture of censure and admiration Kelly added, "No Puritan was instructed in these truths more than Greeks, Romanists, Anglicans, Lutherans or others, and his adoption of independency injured his intelligence of the Church, as it must all Congregationalists in particular. But he was beyond comparison, the most spiritual and profound of his class." Kelly was broad-minded enough to make this plaudit, although he acknowledged that Howe was a Platonist and followed "the Cambridge school of philosophic divines, such as Cudworth and Henry More."[158]

In the same exposition Kelly disagreed with William Paley (1743–1805), who had claimed that Paul's words about the Lord being "at hand" had been merely a soothing phrase used with the intention of reducing the alarm felt by the Thessalonians after receiving Paul's first letter. Kelly

---

154. Kelly, *The Coming and the Day of the Lord*.

155. Kelly, *The Coming*, 20. This refers to an exposition of the verse, 2 Thess 2:2, "The day of the Lord is at hand."(KJV).

156. Ibid., 21.

157. Howe, *Works*, vol. 5, 252.

158. Kelly, *The Coming*, 28.

called Paley's views "an oversight" and made clear that he thought that the phrase "at hand" intentionally suggested an immediate expectation of "the rapture" on the part of the Thessalonian Christians.[159] Kelly claimed to discern the false impression given by Liddell and Scott's 7th edition of the Greek Lexicon in giving examples from classical Greek which would mean "pending" or "instant," adding that what they really meant was "actually begun or present."[160] Kelly showed here that he had read those who were skeptical about the second coming as a "secret rapture." He himself believed in the precise nature of the original language of Scripture and maintained that there was a difference between the *parousia* and Christ's appearance in judgment on the day of the Lord, and that 2 Thessalonians 2:1 and 8 referred to different events from those given in verse 2.[161] He added, "It is well to leave it to the late Professor Jowett and the incredulous school to teach that the apostle wrote loosely and reasoned ill."[162] Later in the same work he referred to the writings of J. A. Froude (1818-1894), showing his breadth of knowledge of an agnostic novelist with a Tractarian background as well as of the Broad Churchmen.[163] He was able both to appreciate Chrysostom as a great teacher and yet argue against his interpretation of the day of the Lord. He commented, "Chrysostom had not his equal among the Greek fathers as an expositor, yet he (if the first in time) was so dark as to count death the Lord's coming to the saint! Were it so, how many thousands of times He must have come!"[164] Thus we see in this short exposition of two verses in 2 Thessalonians a tendency, which was apparent in his other works on the afterlife, to demonstrate clear eschatological insights and scrupulous attention to textual translation as well as deploying a wide range of references to the works of theologians who thought differently.

---

159. Ibid., 29. Kelly is referring to William Paley, *Horae Paulinae*, vol. 5, 281.

160. Kelly, *The Coming*, 23.

161. Ibid., 60, 32; 2 Thess 2:1 and 8. (KJV).

162. Ibid., 61.

163. Ibid., 69. In his novel *The Nemesis of Fate* (1849) Froude had written with particularly vehement loathing of the idea of hell as an unending physical punishment for the majority. Froude, a historian, used his novels to disseminate his doubts and questions about the Christian faith.

164. Ibid., 34.

SOME CONCLUSIONS ABOUT KELLY'S PLACE IN THE ARGUMENT ABOUT THE AFTERLIFE AND HIS UNDERSTANDING OF BIBLICAL LANGUAGE

For Kelly, writing about the afterlife, language not only revealed truth but a right understanding of language made truth more awesome. Understanding the use of language concerned with the truth about hell was particularly significant. Pusey and Farrar had agreed by the late 1870s that a considerable amount of imagery was used when talking about hell, and they concentrated on the idea of separation from God.[165] Kelly agreed with them and never disputed the use of imagery in the biblical texts when talking about hell, but, even as he understood this imagery, he showed that it revealed the underlying reality which made the truth about hell more sobering, not less so—the reality of being cut off from the God who was Love. However, for Kelly the story of Dives and Lazarus had the character of a parable "as it seems to me."[166] He went on to explain the importance of symbolism: "Figures no doubt are employed but this is founded on that which would be most intelligible to us. It is through the body that we feel the world. From this the Lord takes figures in order to be understood by those who He addresses in presenting according to His own wisdom the case of the unseen world." He went on to explain that "suffering in this flame" means suffering in a way we can understand but that "figures are employed."[167] In interpreting Luke chapter 16, Kelly showed his audience that Christ's teaching was about how we should live now, rather than physical assertions about the nature of the future world.

As the non-literal meaning of the biblical doctrine of hell became more acceptable, for the Victorians mental anguish seemed a better way of explaining hell, because it would be seen as the direct result of sin rather than as punitive action on God's part.[168] Kelly's teaching on hell, while literalist in its acceptance of the reality, showed him to be far more in touch with the idea of mental anguish and soul-anxiety than the threat of fire and brimstone. In the nineteenth century the traditional "*poenus sensus*" (physical punishment) was not dwelt on, because the banishment from God's presence was terrible enough. In this Kelly had much in common

---

165. Rowell, *Hell and the Victorians*, 145.
166. Kelly, *Luke*, 275.
167. Ibid, 276.
168. Walker, *The Decline of Hell*, 69.

with Maurice, even though he took a different position from Maurice about those who were likely to enter heaven. The mental, emotional and spiritual facets of life had far more significance for him than the merely physical. Perhaps this was part of his identity as a Victorian, with a focus on purpose rather than on a material view of the afterlife. In the same teaching Kelly also observed that the subject was often discussed among his contemporaries and he suggested that the reason was that people wanted assurance, especially when so many religious certainties were being discarded. In this he agreed with Farrar, whose aim in his book, *Eternal Hope* (1877), was to give what the title suggested. Kelly acknowledged too that Christians could be prey to psychological worry and wanted to give assurance about eternity to those he considered to be true believers. In this we see Kelly in touch with the concerns of his generation. In his theological interpretation of the afterlife, I have shown Kelly to be a firmly literalist teacher; in his understanding of language, I believe he had a far more nuanced approach.

CHAPTER 5

William Kelly as a Biblical Literalist
The Atonement

INTRODUCTION

Kelly believed that a "right" understanding of the Atonement was essential to Christian belief and he concentrated on this subject throughout his teaching. He was particularly concerned that the idea of "penal substitution" (the belief that Christ was punished to satisfy divine justice) was becoming less acceptable amongst members of the Broad Church and sought to defend it and to give what he considered to be a rounded view of the subject. The scope of Kelly's articles on the topic, his editing of Darby's articles and his frequent references to the subject in many of his books all show that he thought it was of paramount importance. In defending it, Kelly can be seen as a literalist theologian who wanted to affirm what he saw as the "fundamentals" of the Christian faith.

In this chapter I will be referring to Kelly's exegesis of particular biblical books, notably the Pentateuch, Galatians and Hebrews, but also to his articles in *The Bible Treasury*. Kelly wrote the majority of the articles on the book of Leviticus published in *The Bible Treasury*, which he used in order to focus primarily on the Atonement, although his own writing was supplemented by Darby's articles on the offerings. Also, C.E. Stuart (1823–1903), who later diverged from orthodox teaching on the subject, wrote an article on propitiation (the appeasement of God's righteousness) which Kelly felt able to publish in 1886. I refer to Darby's articles in this chapter because I think it is significant that Kelly, in editing the magazine and Darby's work, reprinted five articles between the years 1878 and 1907 on the subject of propitiation, even though Darby had by that time died. Kelly wrote 16 articles on the subject between 1886 and 1903, including one arguing against the interpretation of this doctrine by the Catholic Apostolic Church in 1890. J.G. Bellett's article, "The Atonement," was written in 1883, and is worth studying because Kelly later edited Bellett's writings and Kelly clearly endorsed his views. When looking at the dates of the articles about the Atonement, both those written by Kelly and those of different authorship which Kelly chose to print in *The Bible Treasury*, it seems that the earlier ones, up to 1890, were particularly relevant to the debates about the Atonement in the wider church, while the later ones, from 1890 onwards, were more relevant to the debates about the Atonement which were taking place within the Brethren movement. It is worth noting that details of the "how" and "when" of Christ's act of Atonement became a matter of division primarily within the Exclusive wing of the Brethren, even though they regarded themselves as the guardians of orthodox doctrine. We can also see that Kelly's teaching on the Atonement was linked to his detailed teaching on the book of Leviticus, demonstrating again how in so many ways the Brethren interpretation of the Pentateuch was crucial to their wider theological position. Also in his series of articles written in 1890 which attacked the Catholic Apostolic Church, founded by Irving in 1830, Kelly devoted one particular article to his criticism of Irving's views on the Atonement, although Irving had died in 1834. He clearly felt this doctrine was axiomatic to the heterodoxy of Irving's legacy. However, it was not until August 1902 that Kelly wrote a detailed overview of the topic, criticizing contemporary theological views on the Atonement. I suggest that the reason for this late date is that Kelly was writing both in response to Brethren arguments about the subject and also because of the effect that more liberal evangelical teaching was having on the wider church by the early twentieth century. Kelly wanted to guard against what he regarded as "looser" theological teaching in the Brethren movement and to warn the wider evangelical church of its dangers.

In articles written between August 1886 and August 1902, Kelly examined a wide range of translations and viewpoints. For example, in considering the possible translation of the word "scapegoat" and in determining its gender, he discussed and referred to the Vulgate, the Authorised and the

Revised Versions of the Bible, and quoted from Luther, Gesenius, Friedrich August Tholuck (1799–1877) and Hengstenberg as well as a range of ancient writers and modern translators.[1] Kelly's thorough and scholarly research into his subject and his ability to consider the theological point of view of those of different denominations lent scholarly weight to his interpretation of the subject.[2] In this chapter I will be examining Kelly's consideration of historical formulations of the doctrine of Atonement, but I will also show that Kelly engaged with the views of his contemporaries and gave a sharply focused analysis of their views in "Modern Views Subversive of the Atonement."[3] In this article he particularly criticized those Broad Church theologians who critiqued penal substitution and he analyzed the views of F.D. Maurice in *The Doctrine of Sacrifice* (1854); John McLeod Campbell (1800–1872) in *The Nature of the Atonement* (1869), F.W. Robertson (1816–1853) in *Expository Lectures on the Epistles to the Corinthians* (1859), John Young (1805–1881) in *Light and Life of Men* (1866), Horace Bushnell (1802–1876) in *Vicarious Sacrifice* (1866) and Benjamin Jowett in *Epistles of St. Paul to the Galatians, Thessalonians and Romans*, vol. 2 (1859). Thus we see the scope of Kelly's reading and intelligent engagement and his concern to argue for the doctrine of penal substitution against these viewpoints.

Kelly fiercely defended traditional interpretations of the Atonement against the Brethren teachers, whom he considered to be heterodox. The Exclusive writer, Napoleon Noel, writing in 1928, criticized Newton for

---

1. Kelly, "Appendix 1," 114. These ancient authorities include Symmachus (d. 514 A.D.), an early Pope, Theodoret (393–457), a Christian bishop of Cyrrhus in Syria who wrote a large number of biblical exegeses, Aquila of Sinope, a Jewish authority who made a literal translation from the Hebrew text of the Old Testament into Greek in 130 A.D. and whose work was approved by Jerome and Origen and Cyril of Alexandria (376–444 A.D.), a Patriarch of Alexandria, who was involved in the Christological controversies of the 4th and 5th centuries. Authorities from the early modern period to whom he makes reference are Samuel Bochart (1599–1667), a French Protestant biblical scholar, Georg Benedikt Winer, (1789–1858), a German theologian and translator, Herman Witsius (1636–1708), a Dutch Protestant pastor and professor of systematic theology at the University of Leiden, who was particularly concerned with arguing against the theory of Atonement of Grotius. A nineteenth-century Bible translator whom Kelly surprisingly referred to was Charles Thompson (1814–1895) from Philadelphia, who was connected with a schism of the Mormon Church.

2. For example, Dr. Kay's contribution in *The Speaker's Commentary*, , as quoted in William Kelly, *Isaiah*, v.

3. Kelly, "Appendix ii," 116–19.

following Irving in setting aside the Atonement.[4] Kelly in a letter entitled "God's principle of unity" asserted that supporting Newton in this controversy meant becoming a partaker in the evil deed, because anything relating to Christology and Atonement was theologically crucial.[5] He also opposed Clarence Stuart's theology of Atonement (from 1885) "that Christ made propitiation by presenting his blood in heaven after his death."[6] He later wrote articles arguing against the Christology and Atonement theories of the Exclusive teacher, F.E. Raven, whose particular teaching can be dated from 1890.[7] Thus we see that defending what he saw as orthodox theology of the Atonement was important to Kelly.

In the rest of this chapter I will first look at some definitions of terms which were used about this subject and summarize some of the nineteenth-century views of the Atonement which Kelly saw as inadequate. I will also explore Kelly's own exposition of penal substitution. Then I will give a detailed analysis of his article, "Views Subversive of the Atonement." Finally I will investigate whether Kelly's theology and its implications for Brethren practice have anything to contribute to Boyd Hilton's conclusions about the effect of the Atonement on Victorian society.

DEFINITION OF TERMS AND SOME NINETEENTH-CENTURY VIEWS OF THE ATONEMENT

I now briefly explain some of the key terms which will be used throughout this chapter. Piacular theories connect the atonement of Christ to ancient ideas of sacrifice particularly in the Old Testament, while lustral theories are about the need for purification, washing and spiritual absolution. Propitiation is about appeasing a holy and unbending deity and expiation is

---

4. Noel, *The History of the Brethren*, vol. 1, 152–62. According to Noel, Newton said that Christ dreaded Gethsemane more than the Cross. Christ did not experience the full wrath of God. Although Noel collected most of his material in 1928, it was edited after his death in 1936, and used source material from both Darby and Kelly's works.

5. Ibid., 221. Noel clearly thought that Kelly's letter was a significant testimony to the wrongness of Bethesda's action in receiving those who came from Newton's assembly in Plymouth. Cf. Willliam Kelly, *God's Principle of Unity*.

6. Grass, *Gathering to His Name*, 204. Brethren criticism of Stuart's theology can also be found in William F. Knapp, *A Summary of Mr. C.E. Stuart's Twenty-five Errors*.

7. William Kelly, "F. E. R. Heterodox on the Person of Christ," 78. Ibid., "Life Eternal Denied by F. E. R.," 73–77. Raven's views seem to have been more heterodox as to the person of Christ, and only as a consequence, affecting his views on the Atonement.

about paying the penalty and making amends for sin on behalf of humanity. Fictional imputation through the Atonement is the idea that human beings cannot really be made righteous but are counted to be righteous by virtue of Christ's sacrifice. Real imputation suggests that through the Cross humanity can actually become righteous.

Some of the key theories of Atonement considered throughout the history of the church can be briefly defined in the following ways. The government theory of Atonement was also known as the moral government theory or the moral theory of Atonement and became increasingly popular in the nineteenth century. Supporters of this theory, while believing that Christ's death was a substitute for the punishment people deserve, did not believe that it was an exact punishment, but rather a means of God extending forgiveness while maintaining divine order. They also believed that the effect of Christ's death was not for individuals but for the Church as a corporate entity. The Ransom Theory, a patristic and early medieval theory particularly expounded by Gregory of Nyssa and Augustine, saw the Atonement as God ransoming the soul from the devil, to whom Jesus paid the ultimate price. Universalism was the belief that the Atonement was such a cataclysmic event that all of humanity had been redeemed through the Cross of Christ. Penal substitution was the theory that mankind deserves to be punished for sin and that the only way this could be remedied was if Jesus Christ, who was without sin, could be punished in their place. Calvin believed in limited Atonement—Christ's death was efficacious for those predestined to be saved.[8]

I now come to nineteenth-century views about the moral theory of Atonement, which Kelly opposed. Contemporary writers McLeod Campbell and R.C. Moberley (1845–1903) upheld the moral worth of Christ's sacrifice. Campbell argued that we can see what Christ felt, and how, as a result of his experience of sin, he can draw us into a personal relationship.[9] Moberley saw Christ's experience as one of a perfect penitent and that Atonement could actually produce the forgiving love of God within us.[10] The moral theory of the Atonement evolved quite naturally from the Protestant idea of Christ being prophet, priest and king, with McLeod Campbell particularly seeing Christ's work as prophet and priest culminating in his

---

8. Quinna, "The Atonement," 51–52.
9. Campbell, *The Nature of the* Atonement, 136.
10. White, *Atonement and Incarnation*, 10.

sacrifice on the cross.[11] This writer also moved to the idea that Christ's sorrow was the essence of the atoning sacrifice.[12] The "redemption by sample" idea that if Christ was a representative man, then what he achieved in being accepted by God can be applied to all other human beings after him was upheld by Irving and Arthur Samuel Peake (1865–1929) both of whom showed that on the cross Christ held down the rebellious impulses of the flesh. Therefore, according to these theologians the internal conflict shown in Romans chapter 7 was first experienced by Christ before us and was not just an example of inadequate Christian experience, as it was for Kelly.[13] Patrick Fairbairn (1805–1874) of the Free Church of Scotland in his articles in the *Expositor* (October and December 1876) also demonstrated his belief in Christ's redeeming penitence, his victimization and his developing consciousness of the blackness of sin. B.F. Westcott (1825–1901) in 1888 used the book of Hebrews to explain Christ's human experience as progressive training in the life of holiness and love.[14] F.W. Robertson believed that the sufferings of the innocent Christ were the culmination of his fellowship with human brethren.[15] Benjamin Jowett thought that sacrificial language did not justify a doctrine and John Young in *The Life and Light of Men* saw Christ as only a medium whereby God gave a saving moral influence on men.[16] Horace Bushnell emphasized the lustral power of sacrifice rather than its aspect of punishment and Young wrote about the Fatherhood of God for all mankind. With these emphases, their attitude to the seriousness of sin was very different to that of the literalists.[17] Kelly disagreed with the above views because he did not consider that they came seriously to terms with the purpose of Atonement, or acknowledge the guilt of humanity. He also considered that they lowered the high position of Christ's divinity and saw moral progress in "unconverted" humanity. At the same time, while

11. Mackintosh, *Historic Theories of Atonement with comments*, 168.

12. Ibid., 227.

13. Ibid., 233. In Romans chapter 7 Paul seems to suggest that there is internal conflict in the experience of mankind in living for God. This has been variously interpreted as either conflict in humans before Christian conversion when they try to do what is right or conflict within the converted person who is still living according to "fleshly" principles and not relying on God for the fulfillment of his or her Christian life.

14. Ibid., 258, 260.

15. Ibid., 303.

16. Hodge, *The Atonement*, 149–50. Hodge quotes Young, *The Life and Light of Men*, 27; Jowett, *The Epistles of St. Paul*, vol. 2.

17. Bushnell, *Vicarious Sacrifice*, 404. Young, *The Life and Light of Men*, 48.

Kelly rejected the moral influence theory, it did not make him ignore or belittle the moral perfection that he found in the life of Jesus.[18]

During the nineteenth century, piacular views on the Atonement were gradually replaced by more abstract theories, and there was generally a humanization and rationalization of the doctrine. The move towards the primacy of the incarnation affected the Victorian understanding of the Atonement. Vernon White has shown how there came to be an emphasis on inter-personal rather than human/divine penitence and that Christ's example came to mean merely the demonstration of a perfect human response to suffering.[19] There was also a strong emphasis on salvation being brought about by divine action rather than through conscious knowledge of that action, thus allowing for the salvation of those who had never heard of Christ. As the rise of biblical criticism took place, unique revelation gave way to the idea of Christ's self-giving.[20] While conservative theologians such as Hodge and Kelly pointed to the use of blood sacrifices, which were thought necessary as atonement for sin amongst primitive tribes, Jowett, Maurice, Young, Campbell and Bushnell rejected this and argued that the only purpose of sacrifice was to express the repentance and spiritual aspirations of the worshipper, not as an act of propitiation.[21] William Thompson (1819–1890), the future Archbishop of York also observed that piacular sacrifices were only relevant to crude civilizations.[22] F. D. Maurice maintained that the Old Testament sacrifices were symbolic expressions of the worshipper's attitude and that any heathen interpretation of the word "*hilasmos*" (the Greek word for propitiation or sacrifice) must be rejected.[23] Kelly agreed that they were symbolic but also asserted that they revealed real truth. There were some points of similarity to Kelly's views amongst theologians with wider views. Fairburn noted that the sin offering was most typical of Christ's atonement and also stressed the importance of the sprinkling of blood on the mercy seat—a view which Kelly also taught.[24] Jowett too admitted that the Old Testament was hidden in the New and vice versa.[25] For Darby and Kelly the

---

18. Kelly, *Isaiah*, 417.
19. White, *Atonement and Incarnation*, 60.
20 MacKintosh, *Historic Theories*, 308.
21. Campbell, *The Nature of the Atonement*, 20. Bushnell, *Vicarious Sacrifice*, 11.
22. Hodge, *The Atonement*, 126. Thomson, *The Atoning Work of Christ*, 48, 206.
23. Maurice, *Doctrine of Sacrifice*, 72, 154, as quoted in Hodge, *The Atonement*, 128.
24. Fairburn, *Typology*, vol. 2, 321, as quoted in Hodge, *The Atonement*, 131.
25. Jowett, *The Epistles of Paul*, vol. 2, 476, as quoted in Hodge, *The Atonement*, 148.

sacrifices of the Old Testament were not primitive rituals but showed God in his immutable and holy purposes and were a perfect preparation for the Atonement. Their view of the sacrifices of Leviticus prepared the way for their high view of the sacrifice of the Atonement.[26]

Although in his views on the Atonement Kelly can be defined clearly as a literalist, I would also like to point out the differences between Kelly and the reformed theologians. We can see the differences by comparing his view with that of Hodge. Hodge was a reformed theologian and the son of a Princeton fundamentalist but there are clear contrasts between his approach and Kelly's. While Kelly always wrote on the subject of Atonement through biblical exegesis, most notably when he wrote about Leviticus, Hodge wrote a theological treatise on the subject. Thus we see Kelly's approach to doctrine as being integral to an understanding of the whole text, whereas Hodge had a more analytical concern with doctrine per se. As Ralph G. Turnbull pointed out in the introduction to a later preface to Hodge's work, Hodge regarded the Westminster Confession of Faith (1646) as "a standard of belief and practice next only to the supreme authority of the Bible," thus showing that historic formularies of doctrine were extremely important to him in undergirding his theological beliefs.[27]

Kelly also moved in a different direction to those evangelical Anglicans who wanted to accept the new biblical criticism and the Broad Church views on the Atonement. Kelly was a solid authority for those evangelicals who wanted to stay with a literalist point of view, both within the Brethren movement and the Church of England.[28] His work contrasted with that of the broader-based evangelicals, such as F. W. Farrar who wrote in 1857 *The Christian Doctrine of Atonement not inconsistent with the justice and goodness of God* and who showed that he understood the moral objections to orthodox beliefs about this subject.[29] T. R. Birks upheld the Atonement but said that sin was a disease which needed personal healing and a debt which needed paying for everyone.[30] This was important because, instead of considering penal substitution in its severer aspects, Birks humanized it,

---

26. Darby, "A Few Words on Propitiation or Atonement," 98.

27. Hodge, *The Atonement*, preface.

28. For example, Rigg, *Modern Anglican Theology*, 387, 391. Rigg wrote critically of Anglican neology and defended the doctrine of substitutive expiation very explicitly.

29. Hodge, *The Atonement*, 274.

30. Ibid., 370.

used metaphor to make it less stark, and made it potentially applicable to every human being, rather than to just an select few.

KELLY'S TEACHING ON THE ATONEMENT

When Kelly explained the meaning of the Atonement, he defined language carefully both with regard to the Hebrew of the Old Testament and the Greek of the New. In his editorship of *The Bible Treasury*, he used Darby's analysis of some of the terminology as a basis for his own teaching. Darby had pointed out that the word "atonement" was often used vaguely and that it was not appropriate to use it in New Testament scholarship, as it was frequently used inaccurately in modern English translations.[31] Following other great theologians such as Anselm, the reformed theologian Hodge preferred the word "satisfaction" as a translation, but his interpretation of the word was different from either Darby's or Kelly's.[32] Hodge focused on its application to human destiny (the need for forgiveness resulting in acceptance by God), while the Brethren emphasized its divine perspective (the need for God's righteousness and justice to be vindicated). This focus was important for Brethren theology and gave Kelly a particular viewpoint on the meaning of the Atonement.

Kelly's views on the Atonement encompassed a number of different aspects but in his teaching he was most concerned to defend the doctrine of penal substitution which he believed was being denigrated by the more liberal nineteenth-century theologians.[33] Therefore in much of his teaching about the subject he actively defended the doctrine of penal substitution, while acknowledging that there were other, legitimate ways of reading the Atonement, as long as the central truth was not lost. He also understood that, over the centuries, different theories of the Atonement were relevant to particular cultures. When examining the key chapter, Isaiah 53, he observed that, in the Old Testament the Holy Spirit presented the Atonement in a number of different ways from God to man and from man to God and so he considered all the permutations of the relationship between God and human beings.[34] All of Kelly's teaching was in the context of his understand-

---

31 Darby, "Atonement, Propitiation, Substitution," 335. Darby was happier to use the word "propitiation" in the context of the New Testament.

32. Hodge, *The Atonement*, 33

33. Kelly, *Romans*, 153.

34. Kelly, *Isaiah*, 421.

ing, demonstrated in his biblical exegesis, of the great historical theories of the Atonement. He criticized universalism.[35] He was aware of the Ransom Theory.[36] He attacked the Socinians with their more humanist interpretation of the Atonement.[37] He considered the Governmental Theory of both Grotius of Holland and of Calvin to be inadequate.[38]

Kelly's understanding of the Atonement rested on his understanding of the nature of God. His belief in the immutable justice of God could only be met by the act of penal substitution. Kelly was pleased to quote Darby in the latter's assertion that this was not about any change in God's attitude to guilt.[39] The Brethren emphasized the nature of God, not man's need of forgiveness in the Atonement. As Darby expressed it, "the divine glory and nature are in question."[40] The Brethren applied the symbols of "sweet savor," "incense," "rest" and "mercy seat" to Christ's propitiatory sacrifice on the cross, rather than to any Church rituals as the Tractarians customarily did.[41] They focused on the idea of propitiation rather than expiation because defending God's holiness was more important to them than allowing human beings to be forgiven outside exacting parameters.[42] Kelly supported the doctrine of "propitiation, which indeed is the strongest possible proof of His love, while it equally proves His holiness and necessary judgment of

---

35. Kelly's views on this are examined later on in this chapter, as we look at his answers to nineteenth-century theologians. Note that they have already been referred to in chapter 4 on the subject of "hell."

36. Kelly, "Azazel ," 327.

37. The Socinians were named after Faustus Socinus (1539–1604), who was noted for his tolerance and willingness to learn. He was part of the Minor Reformed Church of Poland which from 1565 became the first non-Trinitarian denomination (although the non-Trinitarian Arian had originally opposed the Athanasian doctrine at the Council of Nicene). Socinians emphasized the doctrine of Christ's humanity and were thought of as free-thinkers and the description was often used to represent movements of free thought within other churches. This was also important because of the strength of Unitarianism in nineteenth-century Britain. Clearly Kelly uses the word in a general way to describe theologians whose free thought with regard to the Trinity he disapproves of, as shown in his opposition to Samuel Davidson as shown in chapter 3. Alistair Mason, "Unitarianism," 731.

38. Kelly, "Azazel," 327.

39. Darby, "Propitiation or Atonement," 97–98.

40. Darby, "The Atonement," 228.

41. Darby, "Propitiation or Atonement," 97.

42. Ibid. Cf. earlier in this chapter for a definition of propitiation and expiation.

our sins."[43] The Brethren were in agreement with the Church of England scholar-bishops, F. J. A. Hort (1828–1892) and B. F. Westcott, in their emphasis on God's justice rather than God's wrath, and also in their focus on the debt of human nature rather than the individual's sin.[44] In this Kelly agreed with Hodge, who proposed that the Atonement cannot be unjust if Christ, who is God, voluntarily took on our punishment.[45] Darby and Kelly emphasized the idea of the two scapegoats and the holiness of God, and this distinguished them from Anglican evangelicals, who highlighted the importance of forgiveness of sins.[46] Kelly applied the same emphasis when he wrote about Azazel, the scapegoat on the Day of Atonement, where God's judgment of sin was always connected with death. He argued that if Christians did not get the question of God's satisfaction and purity sorted out in the Atonement, and thus honoring the all-encompassing nature of God's righteousness, they would probably make "a ruinous mistake" theologically, because "the primary aspect of atonement is towards God."[47]

Darby and Kelly tackled the vexed question of "the wrath of God." They claimed that wrath and love were compatible, and that, as God had always loved mankind, the action of the Cross did not need to confer that favor. Kelly wrote in his footnote to Darby's article that in the New Testament there was no mention of wrath.[48] In the two men's extensive writing on the subject, the Atonement was connected not only with God's love for humanity but also with the love within the Trinity.[49] Darby saw the emphasis on God the Judge as a defect of the Reformation, but he also thought that the Broad Church was responsible for downgrading the importance of the Atonement.[50] Kelly maintained too that poor understanding of the Atonement led to lack of assurance for the individual believer and too

---

43. Kelly, *Isaiah*, 360.

44. Hilton, *The Age of Atonement*, 294, referring to *Life and Letters of Fenton John Anthony Hort*, vol. i. 314–16 and 426–29.

45. Hodge, *The Atonement*, 199.

46. Darby, "Letter," 97–98. In Darby's explanation of the Day of Atonement in Leviticus, one scapegoat stood for God's holiness being justified while the other (which escaped into the wilderness) stood for human beings being rid of their sins. Kelly followed Darby's paradigm in this teaching.

47. Kelly, " Azazel," 325.

48. Darby, "Letter," 97.

49. Kelly, "Azazel," 323.

50. Darby, "The Atonement," 227.

much emphasis on mere forgiveness of sins.[51] For the love of God to be fully grasped, a complete understanding of the Atonement based on what Kelly saw as adequate theological premises was necessary.[52] A right understanding of the Day of Atonement and the contents of the Holy of Holies in the Tabernacle would lead to an acknowledgement of Christ as the true center of the Pentateuch narrative.[53] I will explore this idea further in chapter 7.

Brethren belief in The Fall led to the belief in the just punishment of sin and the clear distinction made between sin and sins. Sin described the inherited evil state of human beings; sins were the wrong actions and thoughts which individuals chose. Darby explained clearly that birth in sin is only mentioned once in the Old Testament in Psalm 51:5. He said that the Old Testament assumed it but did not state it. That was why the Day of Atonement was for sins committed and that the tabernacle was sprinkled with blood because of defilement from a sinful world. The state of sin would only be put away after death.[54] This was why an exalted view of the Atonement was so important for Kelly and the Brethren. Kelly held that it was important to see that God the Father hid His face from Jesus in divine abandonment on the Cross.[55] Christ's death was not simply a result of man's wickedness but was also expiatory to satisfy God.[56] According to Kelly, Christians should believe that the scapegoat prefigured Jesus lifting the burden of sin.[57] The Brethren view of the Atonement was holistic—even disease in the Old Testament had to do with sin. There were no secondary causes.[58] Kelly summed the view up by saying, "If Atonement gets its value, so does God's love and sin withal."[59]

The doctrines of Incarnation and Atonement had implications for each other. Kelly stressed that "the work of atonement was solely in His death"; therefore the Atonement as merely an extension of Christ's Incarnation was not acceptable to him. He argued that both the rationalist and the ritualist could talk about the Incarnation, "for it is the alleged ground of

---

51. Kelly, *Romans*, 107.
52. Kelly, "The Day of Atonement," 228.
53. Ibid., 276. Kelly, *Hebrews*, 159.
54. Darby, "Letter," 335.
55. Kelly, *Isaiah*, 419.
56. Ibid., 418.
57. Kelly, "Life Eternal Denied," 6.
58. Kelly, "Atonement for Flux," 82.
59. Ibid.

blessing without Christ's sacrifice ... but it is His death which Scripture reveals as the true groundwork of redemption." He asserted that a doctrine which did not center on the correct understanding of Christ's death erroneously made light of sin and judgment.[60]

KELLY'S ARGUMENT WITH CONTEMPORARY THEOLOGIANS ON THE SUBJECT OF THE ATONEMENT.

In his exegetical works Kelly often referred to alleged false understandings of the Atonement and in particular issues of *The Bible Treasury* he intentionally answered various arguments made by contemporary theologians. Kelly pointed out the inadequacies of the Broad Church and Evangelical writers on this subject. He called them all "virtual Socinians," because, according to him, they all saw Christ's death as being primarily an example of love and martyrdom.[61]

In his major article on the subject Kelly highlighted F.D. Maurice's *The Doctrine of Sacrifice* (1854), which Kelly claimed treated Christ's sufferings as merely an extension of his life.[62] Maurice had commented on how much he admired Irving's Scottish inheritance.[63] He had also made clear the difference between his own understanding of the Fall of man and that of reformed theologians.[64] Maurice observed that in Knox's *Confession*, the Fall comes as the second article, while in the Anglican 39 Articles, the second article is on Christ, the ninth is on The Fall, and, while the Church of England spoke of its consequences, it did not refer to it as an historical event. Maurice added perspicaciously, "the importance of this diversity could scarcely be overrated."[65] Maurice could not see the Fall as an essential

---

60. Kelly, *Hebrews*, 164.

61. Kelly, "Modern Views Subversive of the Atonement," 116–19. Socinian views on the Atonement were partially answered by the popular governmental theory of Grotius of Holland (1583–1645). Because of their connection with early Unitarian theology, Kelly sought to denigrate the authors he was criticising, by associating them, even loosely, with the Socinians.

62. Maurice, *The Doctrine of Sacrifice*.

63. Ibid., Introduction, xiv. By "Scottish inheritance" Maurice meant the gradual liberalising of Scottish Presbyterian divines in the nineteenth century. Scottish theologians of the time were renowned for their intellectual acumen and their openness to German higher criticism.

64. Ibid., xxiii.

65. Ibid.

part of the law under which humanity exists.[66] Clearly Maurice understood that a different theological emphasis on the Fall would have a crucial consequence for other doctrines. Kelly accused Maurice of philosophizing on Christ, rather than taking the power of Christ to answer for the Fall because Maurice's argument "obliterates the guilt and ruin of fallen man" and as a result it "accounts in no true sense or divine way for the sufferings of Christ at the hand of God."[67] In this way we can see that divergent views on the Fall led to divergent views on the Atonement.

Although Kelly allowed for the spiritual union of believers with Christ, he had no time for Maurice's advocacy of a general union of mankind with Christ. Therefore we see that the consequences of the doctrine of Atonement for Kelly and Maurice were far reaching. Kelly claimed that Maurice's theology destroyed truth and holiness, because, according to Maurice, mankind in general was touched by God, whereas, according to Kelly, there was no evidence of this in human experience.[68] For Maurice the doctrine of Atonement resulted in the view that God was our heavenly Father and that Christ was in every man.[69] In his Sermon X on Romans 3:20-27, he showed that Christ had already made peace on the cross, and, using a verse from 1 John, that Christ had made atonement for the whole world.[70] While Kelly in his exegesis of Galatians focused on the problem of Christians returning to the law through the Church of England, and also the necessity of understanding the curse of the law before coming to an evangelical conversion experience, Maurice argued that we do not need to experience the curse of the law with its terrors before understanding the covenant and that we should concentrate on its blessings.[71]

The next contemporary theologian to come under Kelly's attack was the Presbyterian, John McLeod Campbell (1800-1872). Campbell's interpretation of the Atonement came as a result of his parish work in Scotland, where he found that his parishioners had little joy in their religion, and so he had a desire to change their views. Campbell has later been characterized by a more appreciative assessor than Kelly as a creative reformed

66. Ibid., 294.
67. Kelly, "Modern Views," 116.
68. Ibid.
69. Maurice, *The Doctrine of Sacrifice*, xxiv.
70. Ibid., 154-55, 162.
71. Ibid., 140.

theologian and a revisionist dogmatic theologian.[72] Interestingly, it was while Campbell was reading the early Church Fathers and the Reformed confessions on Atonement that he was made to think about the Puritan Jonathan Edwards's question about whether God was satisfied with Christ's repentance on behalf of humanity, and whether the death of Christ had been necessary for forgiveness and atonement to occur.[73] This is significant because it shows that Campbell could take up a question from an orthodox Puritan writer and take it much further, out of the line of orthodoxy. That same question had the potential to deflect the emphasis from the death to the incarnation of Christ, because if Christ repented on behalf of humanity before his death, then it was logical to argue that such repentance could have been more significant than the death itself. This was a line of argument which Kelly constantly resisted. It also shows how a probing mind from any theologically orthodox position could open up problems of the exact timing and nature of the Atonement and this questioning occurred in the most orthodox Brethren circles. Campbell's seemingly heterodox position had links with the theology of Luther and the Reformers, because Campbell pointed out that the Reformers too speculated at what point in Christ's passion the Atonement might have started to be effective.[74] Campbell did not deny penal substitution but he saw it as only one aspect of the Atonement and that breadth of view eventually took his views beyond what the Brethren regarded as orthodox belief.[75] Thus, Campbell started to consider the possible "vicarious penitence of Christ."[76]

In his book, *The Nature of the Atonement*, Campbell speculated on the nature of human progress, approaching the subject through Reformed theology rather than through the Broad Church views of Arnold and Hare. He believed that "the Redemption for the whole world" meant that "man was raised to a level higher than that on which he stood at first."[77] By this he meant that through the cataclysmic event of the Atonement, progress in human civilization could be made—a completely opposite view to that of the Brethren on the ruin of the world. Again, in the writings of Campbell an incarnational emphasis on theology also contributed to the idea of prog-

72. Jenkins, "John McLeod Campbell," 838–39.
73. Ibid., 838.
74. Ibid., 839.
75. Kelly, "Modern Views," 116.
76. *Oxford Dictionary of National Biography*, 839.
77. Campbell, *The Nature of the Atonement*, xxiii.

ress.[78] I have just shown that Maurice saw the law as already superseded by the new covenant in man's experience. Campbell saw "the reign of law" as referring to the laws of the universe and he therefore was a proponent of "natural law." In the nineteenth century there was a significant division between those who supported natural law and those who did not, with the more liberal evangelicals turning towards it and the more conservative against it.[79] It was not just the theology itself but the implications of the theology which were unacceptable to extreme evangelicals, including the Brethren. Taking John 1:5 as his basis, Campbell argued that while the "'darkness comprehended it not,' the darkness was modified by the light."[80] This much wider view of the Atonement led to more positive views about universal salvation.

However, there was a line of argument in Campbell which was curiously similar to the beliefs of the Brethren and which we might therefore judge to be unexpected. Campbell argued that if God provided atonement, then forgiveness must have preceded atonement because the love of God was the cause of the Atonement, not the other way round. Darby said that it was the fault of the Reformers that God was seen only as an unbending judge, but he also said that Christ must be lifted up and acknowledged in individual lives in order to find forgiveness.[81] He pointed out that it was not God's love which saves us because God has always loved human beings. The Cross was first of all about glorifying God, rather than only about love to mankind.[82] Campbell agreed with Darby and Kelly that the love of God was the cause, not the effect of the Atonement.[83] Campbell also believed that the Atonement was not just a fictional imputation but a real imputation and in this Darby and Kelly were in agreement and strayed away from Calvinist doctrine.[84] Kelly and Darby also pointed out that there was no talk of the wrath of God when Christ was on the cross. The reason for penal substitution, which in its full form Campbell found abhorrent, was because of the

---

78. Ibid., xxiv.

79. Bebbington, *Evangelicalism*, 90.

80. Campbell, *The Nature of the Atonement*, 17. The verse quoted is John 1:5 "And the light shineth in darkness: and the darkness comprehended it not." (KJV).

81. Kelly, "The Atonement," 227. Kelly, "Azazel or the People's Lot," 342.

82. Darby, "A Few Words on Propitiation or Atonement," 97.

83. Campbell, *The Nature of the Atonement*, 20.

84. Ibid., 102. However Darby and Kelly stressed God's righteousness being vindicated, while Campbell believed in the imputation of Christ's righteousness.

holiness of God, a concept which was of paramount importance for the Brethren.[85] Thus, while Kelly was able to agree with Campbell on the supreme motivation of love in the Atonement, he disapproved of Campbell's abandonment of the concept of vicarious suffering through the crucifixion and his looking instead at the purpose of the whole Passion experience. Kelly called it "the swamping of necessary truth," and accused Campbell of being unable to accept the full suffering of Christ when forsaken by the Father.[86]

In his detailed and combative article Kelly went on to criticize the theology of F. W. Robertson (1816–1853), a popular preacher both in Brighton, where he was a Church of England vicar at Holy Trinity church from 1847 until his death, and also in London. Like Campbell in Scotland, Robertson had a successful pastoral ministry, particularly amongst the poor. However, theologically he was an isolated figure, even though he was considered to be a conservative preacher and not part of the Broad Church movement, as he had given up his earlier evangelicalism to accept a broader theological position.[87] Such a position affected his theology of Atonement. Kelly particularly attacked Robertson's *Expository Lectures on the Epistles to the Corinthians* (1859) and accused him of saying that Christ suffered only from the actions of sinners rather than bearing the sins themselves. Robertson wrote, "Christ simply came into collision with the world's evil and bare (*sic*) the penalty of that daring."[88] Kelly was outraged that the judgment of God had been left out of Robertson's system. Robertson's theology was, according to Kelly, more "about a victim being overcome with evil."[89] Robertson's theories, like Maurice's, were based on interpretations of the Incarnation, and he saw humanity as being united by Christ's work on the cross. Again we can see Brethren outrage at this perceived inclusive nature of Christianity, in place of an exclusive, purist view. Kelly rejected Robertson's hope for human nature, because it was based on the example of Jesus.[90]

John Young's book *The Life and Light of Men* (1866) also attracted criticism from Kelly.[91] Young had deliberately distanced himself from what

---

85. Campbell, *The Nature of the Atonement*, 20 and Darby "A Few Words," 97.
86. Kelly, "Modern Views," 116.
87. *Oxford Dictionary of National Biography*, 225–26.
88. Robertson, *Sermons*, Series V, 93.
89. Kelly, "Modern Views," 116.
90. Robertson, "The Sinlessness of Christ," 69–70.
91. Young, *The Life and Light of Men*. Young's book also received considerable

he saw as narrower evangelical views on the Atonement, although he still classified himself as an evangelical within the tradition of the United Presbyterian Church in Scotland.[92] He criticized those who minutely dissected the Old Testament sacrificial system when teaching about the Atonement.[93] He clearly rejected the reformed view of the Atonement as "satisfaction."[94] Like other liberally minded theologians, he believed in "the Fatherhood of God and the childship (sic) of all souls."[95] Most important for Young was not the idea of penal substitution but the sympathetic and self-sacrificial nature of divine love which was capable of changing people and rooting out sin and its effects.[96] Such an interpretation of the Atonement was inadequate as far as Kelly was concerned. In his article Kelly asserted the importance of sacrifice throughout the Bible and argued against Young's ideas about salvation—"Dr. Young is false to say 'a true salvation is not escape from the cause of sin, present and remote.'"[97] Young denied the need for expiation and propitiation, but in *The Bible Treasury* we see Kelly continually expounding these themes.[98]

Next, Kelly turned his attention to the work of Horace Bushnell (1802-1876), an American Congregationalist, sometimes called the father of American liberalism, whose book, *Vicarious Sacrifice*, Kelly criticized.[99] Kelly summed up Bushnell's work by saying, "His is another variety of atonement by moral power," and he criticized Bushnell for denying atonement to be penal substitution.[100] By "moral power" Kelly meant that for Bushnell the crucifixion had such a beneficial effect on mankind in general that it gave humanity the power to rise morally and conquer a depraved human nature. While it is true that Bushnell taught that vicarious punishment would be unjust, he also explained that Christians have to be careful

---

criticism from Archibald Hodge in his book, *Atonement*. Kelly was writing this criticism of Young's work in 1902.

92. Ibid., vii.
93. Ibid., 259.
94. Ibid., 302.
95. Ibid., 481.
96. Ibid., 144, 302.
97. Kelly, "Modern Views," 118.
98. Darby's 5 articles on the subject of propitiation were used in Kelly's magazine between the years 1878 and 1907, and Kelly wrote 8 articles based on the Levitical sacrifices between 1886 and 1903.
99. Encyclopaedia Britannica and Bushnell, *Vicarious Sacrifice*.
100. Kelly, "Modern Views," 116.

neither to understate or overstate this doctrine; rather, we should see that "Christ simply engages, at the expense of great suffering and even of death itself, to bring us out of our sins themselves and so out of their penalties."[101] Love, said Bushnell, was essentially a vicarious principle, but it had more to do with sympathy than punishment.[102] Thus, in avoiding the concept of vicarious sacrifice and emphasizing Christ's moral power through growth and process, Bushnell moved away from Kelly's position of high Christology. His emphasis on moral power, rather than attribute power, made him question the perfection of Christ and the evil of man.[103]

Kelly and Bushnell interpreted Isaiah chapter 53 and its link with Matthew 8:17 differently. Bushnell argued that the phrase "bare our sicknesses" meant that Christ "took them on his feeling."[104] He saw this emotional identification with sickness rather than becoming sick himself as a parallel to Christ's identification with sin in the Atonement. Kelly noted that Matthew 8:17 applied the first part of Isaiah 53:4 to Jesus healing the afflictions of the Jews, but felt that it was better to use 1 Peter 2:24–25 when considering how Isaiah 53:5 applied to Christ's work on the cross.[105] Kelly also argued against F.D. Maurice who had said that according to 1 Peter 3:18 atonement was never connected to Christ's sufferings.[106]

Bushnell also reacted against the theological dogmatism which he perceived in literalist theologians. He pointed out that Christ's words, "Why have you forsaken me?," were a cry of passion rather than a logical question.[107] Kelly agreed that Christ had shown passion in his question but he thought that the words were deliberately included by the Gospel writer to make a theological statement—Christ was separated from God the Father on the Cross. Like Campbell, Bushnell found inspiration in the attitude of Jonathan Edwards (1703–1758), who had suggested that Christ might have shown sympathy towards sinners rather than being a substitute for them.[108] Conversely, Kelly insisted on starting afresh with the biblical text rather than reverting to Reformation theology. Kelly also strongly resisted

---

101. Bushnell, *Vicarious Sacrifice*, 7.
102. Ibid., 11.
103. Ibid., 141–43.
104. Ibid., 7.
105. Kelly, *Isaiah*, 417.
106. Ibid., 420.
107. Bushnell, *Vicarious Sacrifice*, 130.
108. Ibid., 255, quoting Edwards, *Miscellaneous Observations*, 5.

Bushnell's suggestion that Christ came into a corporate state of evil with mankind—"under all the corporate liabilities of the race."[109] Like Jowett, Bushnell refuted the idea that we can read back into the sacrifices of the Old Testament to find the sacrifice of Christ.[110] Although Bushnell thought that the physical was a type of the spiritual, he did not think that the Levitical sacrifices were a prophetic form of the gospel and he rejected the detailed Old Testament symbolism of the Atonement.[111] He emphasized the lustral rather than the piacular power of sacrifice.[112] The Incarnation was a more important for him than for Kelly.[113]

In response to Benjamin Jowett's work, Kelly accused him of undermining divine authority with regard to the Atonement.[114] Kelly quoted Jowett at length and opposed Jowett's view that parts of the Bible contradicted themselves.[115] Jowett had warned that mystical allusion was not enough to create authority with regard to the Atonement, which is partly what the Brethren were doing with regard to the Levitical sacrifices, which they allowed to be pointers to their own doctrine of biblical development. In contrast, Jowett said that Christ had hardly ever referred to his own death in terms of sacrifice. However, Kelly quoted Matthew 20:28 and 26:28 to argue against him.[116] Jowett claimed that Homeric rites could be seen in exactly the same way as Jewish traditions, but Kelly claimed a unique role for the work of the Holy Spirit in Scripture.[117] Kelly was concerned to point out that the Holy Spirit used the prophets to make the death of Christ real and argued that Jesus himself suggested the significance of his death.[118] Jowett was critical of any "uniform system" being built into biblical interpretation but Kelly rejoiced in the integrity of the whole text.[119] Jowett linked attitudes to the Atonement to attitudes to inspiration of Scripture

---

109. Bushnell, *Vicarious Sacrifice*, 327.
110. Ibid., 388.
111. Ibid., 388–90.
112. Ibid., 408.
113. Ibid., 457.
114. Kelly makes particular references to Jowett, *Epistles of St. Paul*, vol. 2.
115. Ibid., 549.
116. Ibid., 556. Kelly, "Modern Views," 117.
117. Jowett, *Epistles of St. Paul*, 553.
118. Kelly, "Modern Views," 118.
119. Jowett, *Epistles of St. Paul*, 564.

and particularly criticized the idea of analogy.[120] He believed that those who supposed a narrow view of the Atonement as meaning penal substitution were likely to be literalist in their views on biblical inspiration. Thus he felt that the tendency to analogy amongst theologians was too restrictive. He also felt that the understanding of the doctrine of the Atonement in the nineteenth century had been too influenced by the German Romantic movement and that philosophical viewpoint necessarily affected theological interpretation.[121] He warned that "when we multiply words we do not multiply ideas; we are still within the circle of our own minds."[122] Ironically, Kelly would have agreed, believing that dynamic spirituality, rather than wordy argument, resulted in accurate Scriptural interpretation.

THE BRETHREN CONTRIBUTION TO "THE AGE OF ATONEMENT"

Boyd Hilton has shown that the theology of the Atonement had an influence on the wider values of Victorian society and that, conversely, Victorian social values influenced understanding of the theology of the Atonement.[123] He showed that Atonement was a crucial doctrine affecting morality and economics and that the more liberal evangelicals had a greater influence on their society than did the stricter, more "unworldly" evangelicals. Hilton quotes Thomas Archer (1806–1864) and William Thompson as supporters of a forensic view of the Atonement, but there is no mention of the Brethren.[124] What is noteworthy is that Kelly taught about the Atonement throughout his life, both in the period covered by Hilton's book up to 1865 and until 1906.

In contrast to Hilton, Martin Spence has examined the development of Victorian Evangelicalism from the 1820s until the turn of the century. Spence has supplied analysis of the Brethren position as futurist millennarianians in answer to Hilton's omission. However, he has only written

---

120. Ibid., 58. Hilton shows that Butler's theory of analogy was gradually seen as outdated in the nineteenth century and that as a text it was withdrawn from university matriculation exams.

121. Ibid., 571.

122. Ibid., 594.

123. Hilton, *The Age of the Atonement*.

124. Ibid., 288–89 referring to Thomas Archer, "Philosophy of the Atonement," and Thompson, *The Atoning Work of Christ*.

about Darby as the architect of "dispensationalism" and has only done so as demonstrating a contrast to the position of historicist millenarians about which his book is concerned.[125] While I do not consider this division of theological views to be as clearly defined as Spence would suggest, I affirm some of his basic arguments. We should not stereotype evangelical beliefs as being "action based" rather than "idea based."[126] This book shows that Kelly was an "idea based" Christian. The assumption often made by church historians that there were only intellectuals in the Anglo–Catholic and Broad Church wings of the church is a false one.[127] Kelly, with his measured view of the value of prophecy, had much in common with scholars from Trinity College, Dublin earlier in the century, who discredited overly detailed prophetic speculation, and with historicists who were discerning critics.[128] Kelly was interested in challenging the foremost defender of historicist premillennarianism, Edward Bishop Elliott (1793–1875) on interpretive and linguistic grounds.[129] Ralph Brown also argues against any "simple categorization" of mid nineteenth-century Evangelicalism as being "liberal" or "conservative."[130] However, Brown does equate futurism exclusively with Irvingism and states that it had largely been discredited by the 1830s. The popularity of Kelly's work shows that this was not the case.

As early as 1856, Kelly warned about the dangers of abandoning the penal substitution theory of Atonement which was then being questioned by many Christians. He wrote, "Without the doctrine of Atonement (such is the deceit of the heart) admiration of the person of Christ and of His life, may, in fact, be the admiration of oneself."[131] Kelly's work certainly demonstrated what Hilton called "an amalgam of enlightenment rationalism and evangelical eschatology," which Hilton saw as characteristic of evangelicals in the first half of the century.[132] More interesting is why Kelly continued to champion the doctrine of the Atonement so purposefully later in his life. He always opposed any teaching which suggested social optimism and belief in human progress; thus in 1883, on the publication of Henry Drum-

---

125. Spence, *Heaven on Earth*, 118–24.

126. Ibid., 26.

127. Ibid.

128. Ibid., 49, 84.

129. Kelly, *Revelation*,

130. Brown, "Evangelical Social Thought," 126.

131. Kelly, "Notes of the month," 70.

132. Hilton, *The Age of the Atonement*, 3.

mond's *Natural Law and the Spiritual World*, he published a critical review. Later he saw that doubts about Mosaic authorship could lead to lack of confidence in the rituals of the Pentateuch as a prototype of the Atonement. That was why he also thought it important to edit articles which criticized *Lux Mundi*, as I have shown in chapter 3. Kelly argued particularly against the non-conformist retreat from a traditional Atonement theology and found himself up against the influence of F.D. Maurice. Even though Kelly's spirituality often had surprising parallels with that of Maurice, he was unflinchingly opposed to Maurice's view that orthodox theories of the Atonement "outrage the conscience."[133] However, in looking at Kelly's views on the afterlife in chapter 4, we have noted some surprising links with F. D. Maurice, whom we would normally associate with Broad Church soteriology, and which Martin Spence convincingly shows to be a more accepted part of the historicist premillennarian position.[134] I have already shown that Kelly was influenced by Romanticism and had his intellectual roots firmly in the Enlightenment. According to Bone, there is no sharp contrast between these two cultural movements but a development of ideas and Kelly's work mirrors that development.[135] Even though Kelly opposed Broad Church views on universalism as I have shown in chapter 4, he did admit to the biblical basis for different methods of salvation, as shown in his exposition of the future salvation of the Jews. That is just a step away from admitting the possibility of different salvation plans for different peoples, even though Kelly's dispensationalism presented chronological boundaries for opportunities of salvation.[136] However, later in the century, when penal substitution was criticized by non-conformists such as Campbell, Kelly felt it important to refute them. I suggest that Kelly's focus on the theology of the Atonement in his own writing and in his editorship of other Brethren work might allow us to characterize the Brethren as a small but vigorous, radical movement of the nineteenth century. Their position was different to that of both the religious establishment and the non-conformist churches.

Changing beliefs about other doctrines and secular issues also affected understanding of the Atonement. Views on natural theology were pivotal to teaching on the Atonement during the nineteenth century.[137] Hilton has

---

133. Hilton, *The Atonement*, 289, quoting Maurice, *Theological Essays*, 137–41.
134. Spence, *Heaven on Earth*, 51.
135. Bone, "The Question of a European Romanticism," 123–32.
136. Spence, *Heaven on Earth*, 203.
137. Hodge, *The Atonement*, 67–68.

shown that Chalmers' work transferred belief in natural theology from the physical to the mental and that Broad Church belief in natural theology made way for their seeing the Atonement as a symbolic rather than a historical event.[138] Kelly's opposed both these interpretations. Views on money and international events had a greater effect on evangelical Anglicans than they did on the Brethren. Their teaching on moral seriousness and on separation from the "world"—including the "religious world"—made the Brethren less vulnerable to social and financial crisis. Kelly, with his ability to clarify and teach theological argument and engage with major disputes of the day, provided a well articulated defense of the doctrine of penal substitution for conservative evangelicals.

Hilton has noted the influence of Irving and the Catholic Apostolic Church on Victorian religious society.[139] He has also shown that there was a split between the moderate evangelicals (mainly Anglican) and the extreme evangelicals (mainly non-conformist), using those terms with regard to their expectation of the Rapture and withdrawal from worldliness. Kelly's contribution was to compose a series of articles on the Catholic Apostolic Church and to criticize Irving's views on the Atonement as being inimical to a balanced biblical understanding.[140] However, Kelly's teaching did not follow the simple division between the moderates and extremists on the issue of joy and suffering. He taught a deeper spiritual experience which naturally emanated from his interpretation of the Atonement—penal, individual, once for all, a verifiable transaction leading to further spiritual experiences which emanated from the truth of this doctrine.[141] Kelly also taught the validation of humanity as the result of the Atonement. "In truth," Kelly asserted,

> Scripture knows no such thing as trusting in the working of the Spirit in us as distinguished from trusting in ourselves or in our works. For what the Spirit enables us as God's children to do is ever counted as our own, and will be remembered and rewarded accordingly when God proves Himself not unrighteous to forget our work and the love shewn to His name.[142]

---

138. Hilton, *The Atonement*, 186.
139. Ibid., 10.
140. Kelly, "The Catholic Apostolic Body or Irvingites," 93, 94.
141. Kelly, *Romans*, 102, 113.
142. Ibid., 127–28.

This emphasis on humanity is unexpected, different from the idea of "transaction for guilt" which Hilton has defined as being basic to the views of extreme evangelicals. It also runs counter to Spence's argument that it was the historicist premillennialists alone who had a strong sense of the humanity of Christ and who had moved away from the traditional division between flesh and spirit.[143] Spence's challenge to Hilton's idea that all premillennialists were world-denying and "pessimistic" is a valid one, but I would also like to support that challenge on behalf of Kelly too.[144]

It was also a particular characteristic of Kelly's teaching and editorship that it was cerebral. This side of the Brethren has often been ignored by the historians of theology. In an article published in *The Bible Treasury*, J.G. Bellett emphasized the imagery of the court and justice because it showed the ability of Christians to rely on fact even if their experience was cold.[145] Kelly's detailed intellectual analysis of the Atonement was worked out through his exegesis of the Tabernacle and Day of Atonement narratives and the book of Hebrews. Kelly was a leader of a movement which was part of the intellectual tradition of Evangelicalism and it is inaccurate to define him merely as a biblical literalist. Spence has categorized incipient fundamentalists of the nineteenth century as being interested only in the inductive and scientific hermeneutic of the Bible.[146] However Kelly was far more interested in the interpretation of language and particularly symbolism, a subject which I explore in more depth in chapter 7. His work certainly does not fulfill Spence's description of a typical futurist premillennarian biblical interpretation as being "arcane and wooden."[147] While we might rightly link Kelly with the spiritual passion and "quest for personal sanctity" of the proto-Pentecostal movement, the foundation of his spirituality was intellectual rather than emotional.[148] Thus he was a precursor of the conservative intellectual stream of twentieth-century evangelicalism. Revival meetings in the late nineteenth century tended to emphasize re-consecration and therefore give the Brethren an opportunity to influence those who had already been converted but wanted a deeper commitment.[149] Cerebral Brethren Bible

143. Spence, *Heaven on Earth*, 6.
144. Ibid., 6, 61.
145. Bellett, "The Atonement Money," 273.
146. Spence, *Heaven on Earth*, 80–81.
147. Ibid., 85.
148. Ibid., 254.
149. Ibid.

exegesis met that need. While being in step with the holiness movement and therefore influenced by Romanticism, the Brethren represented a more intellectual and radical evangelical movement than that found within the Church of England.

In examining the effect of the Atonement on Victorian society, Hilton claimed that evangelicalism in the 1830s became more morose as the penal substitution theory advanced.[150] However, even though Kelly's understanding of the Atonement was based on the doctrine of penal substitution and continued to be held by him from the 1850s up until the early twentieth century, when it was less popular, it actually had the effect of confirming well-being rather than inducing a paralyzing sense of guilt because it led to complete forgiveness and reliance on Christ's continual and exclusive work of mediation.[151] Although mediating a seriousness in worship, Kelly's view of the Atonement promoted an intrinsic joyfulness, which was at odds with the prevailing atmosphere of the established Church.[152] While being concerned with "righteous living," they did not endorse a stultifying social respectability. Kelly noted that Paul was much more critical of the Galatians than he was of the Corinthians, even though the latter were blatantly immoral.[153] As religious error was more serious for them than sexual sins (though neither were these overlooked), the Brethren did not easily fit into any stereotype of Victorian respectability or hypocrisy.

Hilton has also claimed that the Victorian understanding of the Atonement affected the development of nineteenth-century capitalism.[154] In Brethren history, we can see a tension between capitalist values and spirituality. Despite their rejection of the religious establishment and hierarchy, Brethren leaders were generally upper-middle class with the addition of some aristocratic families, who would have been natural supporters of individual capitalism and paternalism. Ralph Brown has noticed the potential for paternalism amongst Anglican evangelicals, but, amongst the Brethren, as a movement which had no formal hierarchy, there was not only scope for paternalism but also organic social development.[155] While there was a strong understanding of financial discourse, at the same time

---

150. Hilton, *The Atonement*, 212.
151. Kelly, "Azazel," 325–26.
152. Kelly, *Galatians*, 184–85.
153. Ibid., 5.
154. Hilton, *The Atonement*, 6.
155. Brown, "Victorian Anglican Evangelicalism," 675–704.

there was a rejection of individual materialistic attitudes. This is shown in J. G. Bellett's article on "The Atonement Money," where the money brought to the priests on the Day of Atonement was shown to involve a financial transaction for the purpose of spiritual cleansing. Bellett showed that financial language is predominant in the explanation of the Atonement, but also the warning that numbering is a symbol of appropriation and therefore dangerous.[156] The Brethren had divergent views about riches. On the one hand, they often gave up all that they had and lived in a sacrificial way.[157] On the other hand, they often came from an upper-class Victorian background or were part of the emerging entrepreneurial classes.[158] They both rejected middle-class capitalism and were the products of it. In some ways the Brethren were natural Tories, but most of them abstained from voting. Unlike their Anglican counterparts, they were not interested in Erastianism or their national identity. This gave the Brethren far more potential to be the international movement which it became. They believed in individual responsibility towards God, a view which was reflected in their belief in the Atonement and conversion, and in their theodicy they upheld the right of God to act according to his own principles. It would be interesting to find out to what extent social principles influenced the foundation of the Brethren movement.[159] While Hilton characterizes the extreme evangelicals as being consumed with guilt and not contributing to the economic prosperity of Victorian society, Kelly's teaching shows us the Brethren ability to deal with guilt. In their material success, which was often a result of their hard work, and in their lack of interest in social revolution, the Brethren contributed to Victorian prosperity and social harmony.

In Ralph Brown's challenge to Boyd Hilton's central thesis, I agree with his assertion that "mid-nineteenth century evangelicalism defies simple categorization and the polarization of views between moderate and extreme evangelicals suggested by Hilton."[160] He also argues against the "morose" ac-

---

156. Bellett, "The Atonement Money," 157.

157. This can be seen both in the example of Groves and Hudson Taylor as a missionaries and in the testimony of the simple living of the most wealthy amongst the early Brethren. Cf. Grass, *Gathering to His Name*, 39.

158. Grass, *Gathering to His Name*, 84. Grass refers particularly to the early leadership of the Brethren.

159. It is beyond the scope of this book to further the argument with regard to the Brethren but I am arguing that we should not ignore the place of the Brethren—both Exclusive and Open—in this process.

160. Brown, "Evangelical Social Thought," 126.

cusations of Hilton against the pre-millennialists.[161] However, Spence also says that such accusations may be true of the Brethren.[162] While defending the "material" theology of the historicist pre-millennarians, Spence does not consider the human/mystic tension of a writer such as Kelly, which I will explore in more detail in chapter 7.[163] Spence also implies that the futurists did not need to argue intellectually for or against the school of higher criticism.[164] Kelly's opus proves that to be untrue. Against Hilton, Brown and Spence, I maintain that Kelly, a Brethren theologian, despite being a futurist pre-millennialist, did have a positive view of the body, was not predominantly morose or ascetic, was involved in intellectual debate, and cannot be considered in the same way as the Irvingites.[165]

In this chapter I have shown the importance of the Atonement, especially its traditional interpretation as penal substitution, in the teaching of William Kelly. As a well known biblical exegete and magazine editor of the nineteenth century, Kelly's defense of the Atonement in all its facets, and his stand against more liberal interpretations of this doctrine, make his teaching of great significance. In the area of this particular doctrine, we can see him as a literalist, ready to argue with all those who posited different interpretations and differing from the champions of the Reformed Church in the way he used his teaching of Leviticus in *The Bible Treasury* and his exegesis of particular biblical books such as Romans, Galatians and Isaiah. Therefore in Kelly we have a literalist whose teaching on the doctrine of Atonement was not confined to a Protestant creed, but was rooted in his integral understanding of the biblical text.

---

161. Hilton, *Age of Atonement*, 212.
162. Spence, *Heaven on Earth*, 61.
163. Ibid, 39.
164. Ibid, 258, 260.
165. Brown, "Evangelical Social Thought," 136.

Chapter 6

William Kelly and Mystic Spirituality

INTRODUCTION

In this chapter I will be looking at Kelly's mystic spirituality—his views on baptism, his promotion of the doctrine of the Trinity (especially his high Christology) and his teaching about the Ascension—in addition to his being a "conservative intellectual" and "literalist" as I have demonstrated in the previous five chapters. I will also be discussing his advocacy of the Epistle to the Ephesians as the high point of the Canon of Scripture, and the way his spirituality resulted in both individual and corporate worship amongst the Moderate Exclusive Brethren groups. As an introduction to my analysis of these strands of his theology, I look at how Kelly measures up to the characteristics of the Christian "mystic" tradition and, at the same time, his own reservations about that tradition.

First I discuss whether Christian mysticism can be defined and whether a recognized canon of mysticism exists. In the article written by Denys Turner, formerly Norris Hulse Professor of Divinity at Cambridge University, for *The Oxford Companion of Christian Thought*, we can see that the meaning of the word "mystic" is closely associated with the word "mystery" and *The Oxford English Dictionary's* definition of these words is important for an understanding of how the term "mystic" applies to Kelly's writings.[1]

---

1. *The Concise Oxford English Dictionary of Current English*, 798: Mystery: "hidden or inexplicable matter . . . religious truth divinely revealed, esp. one beyond human reason." Mystic: 1. Spiritually allegorical, of hidden meaning. 2. One who seeks by contemplation

Ewert Cousins brings out the significance of mystery meaning "hidden" or "secret" not "rapture or ecstasy" and he explains that this definition was relevant to the Ancient Greek mystery religions as well as to Christian mystics of the medieval period.[2] This sense of "hidden" is particularly appropriate to Kelly's spirituality, as I will show later in this chapter. According to Turner, mysticism relates to what is "pre-linguistic" and is "above cultural condition."[3] However, it is clear that while the experience itself might seem to be ineffable, it can only be mediated to others by language. Professor Turner denied an intentional tradition of mysticism and affirmed that mysticism as a school of theology was not acknowledged before the nineteenth century.[4] He also defined mysticism as a revolt against ecclesiastical authority. This is significant in the light of my comments in the first chapter of this book about Brethren attitudes to the nineteenth-century established Church and their revolt against ecclesiastical norms of the day. As Turner goes on to define the concept of mysticism, we can see how Kelly fits in to this tradition. He underwent a deep spiritual experience through his conversion and his reading of the Bible, and he expressed his adoration of God not only in his weekly worship with the Brethren but also in the hymns he wrote. In his biblical exegesis too there was an awareness of transcendence. Turner proposed that the language of mysticism involved exalted language and particularly metaphorical language. Later I will argue that this is true of Kelly's language too. Although mysticism has traditionally used exalted language, Christian mystics have always insisted that their spirituality is the way of ordinary Christians.[5] Likewise Kelly, in his deep experience of God, always said that his teaching was one of utter simplicity and available to the most uneducated Christian.[6] I also affirm the relevance of Katz's link of mysticism with the Scriptures in Kelly's work as I suggested in the first chapter of this book. Evelyn Underhill (1875–1941), whose life overlapped with Kelly's, both described and analyzed the mystic experience and some of the mystics' most important writings, and, in defining mysticism, she

---

and self-surrender to obtain union with or absorption into the Deity, or who believes in spiritual apprehension of truths beyond the understanding.

2. Cousins, "The Fourfold Sense of Scripture," 121.
3. Turner, "Mysticism," 460.
4. Ibid.
5. Ibid., 462.
6. Kelly, *Ephesians*, 12.

contrasted this with a vaguer and looser use of the term.[7] She claimed both an historical and psychological definition of the term—"the direct intuition and experience of God."[8] This first-hand experience of God, which had to be experimentally known, was what characterized the early Brethren. Underhill noted that the words "love" and "union" were particularly significant for mystics and Kelly used them prominently in his study of Ephesians.[9] The prophetic element of mysticism to which Underhill drew attention was also present in Brethren writings and their sense of the corporate life, and in how they encouraged deeper communion and prayer amongst themselves.[10] Understanding prophecy properly was part of unlocking the "sealed book" and led to the power of unlocking the "mystery," and was the reason why Kelly believed that the Brethren had an important theological role to play.[11] By distinguishing between the future millennium on earth and eternity spent in the presence of Christ, Kelly was able to unite his existential mystical experience with his vision of the future.[12] Underhill distinguished between natural, dogmatic, and mystical theology and felt that the third illuminated the other two; this certainly makes her analysis of mysticism relevant to what we find in Kelly's teaching.[13] Kelly's mystical theology influenced his biblical exegesis (in Underhill's terms, "dogmatic theology") and his view of the nature of mankind in the world (what Underhill called "natural theology").

In her analysis, Underhill also saw mystics as being narrow-minded, intense and intolerant, and she believed that they needed to be surrounded by others of the same persuasion.[14] Such people were naturally creative and gathered disciples to themselves.[15] Among the influential group of early Brethren leaders such as Darby, Wigram and Kelly, we can perceive this dynamic to be true. They demonstrated "a peculiarly contagious character

---

7. Underhill, *The Mystics of the Church*, 9.
8. Ibid.
9. Cf. later in this chapter when I look at his commentary on Ephesians in more detail.
10. Underhill, *The Mystics of the Church*, 12–13.
11. Kelly, *Isaiah*, 35.
12. Ibid., 33 and 34.
13. Underhill, *The Mystics of the Church*, 15.
14. Ibid., 16, 20.
15. Ibid., 21.

of Christian joy and holiness."[16] As in the case of other mystics, their deep spiritual experiences energized their prodigious work schedules. This was clearly true of Kelly, who worked—writing, editing, teaching and counselling—for long hours until only one month before his death at the age of eighty-five.[17] Underhill also noted that mystics displayed strong self-discipline and underwent intense spiritual experiences, and that their message was appreciated by others.[18] There was always an audience for Kelly's teaching, written and oral both within all strands of the Brethren movement and outside in the wider church.[19]

A near-contemporary of Kelly, William James (1842–1910), was a psychologist with a particular interest in the religious experience. In lectures XVI and XVII of his seminal Gifford Lectures 1901–1902, James defined mysticism in the following ways. He observed that mysticism is a direct and ineffable experience; it has a noetic quality; allows for significant experience and hence authority in the Christian community, and leaves a legacy of written work; the mystic also has his own self in abeyance and is subject to a higher will.[20] All these definitions were relevant to Kelly's religious experience, and to his leadership role in the Brethren movement. It is interesting that James argued that evangelical Protestantism, whose theology we would normally associate with Kelly, had abandoned the methodical mystic discipline.[21] While not using a set liturgy, the Brethren nevertheless taught and demonstrated contemplative methods in their "breaking of bread" meetings, and these formed clear patterns and taught personal meditation of Scripture at a high level. While in their theology they concentrated on God reaching down to them rather than their own reaching up to God, they received teaching on how to study and contemplate the Bible. James also pointed out that joy in suffering was a typical mystical attitude and Kelly stressed the inevitable course of trials in this world for a committed Christian.[22]

---

16. Ibid., 37.
17. Cross, *The Irish Saint and Scholar*, 151–52.
18. Ibid., 54, 57.
19. Cross, *The Irish Saint and Scholar*, 56.
20. James, *The Varieties of Religious Experience*, 371–72.
21. Ibid., 397.
22. Ibid., 415.

Kelly's extant library reveals "the catholicity of the collection" and suggests his careful reading of the Church Fathers and Greek mystics.[23] It also reveals his knowledge of German mysticism through the writings of Heinrich Suso (1295–1366) and Gerhard Tersteegen (1697–1769).[24] Nonetheless, Kelly was critical of some of the traditions of mysticism and saw their dangers.[25] He followed Darby in his cautious attitude to the traditional writings of mysticism. Darby claimed that the mystical tradition was more about desire than love and had a tendency to exalt the feelings and imagination too much. In contrast, he believed that Christianity should put us "in full possession of the love of God."[26] Nevertheless, in wanting to be preoccupied with God alone, Darby and Kelly were following the path of the greatest mystics. Darby acknowledged that the first epistle of John "touches the borders of mysticism but with the finger of God."[27] In this article, which Kelly thought worthy of publication, Darby was answering an enquiry about the value of the writings of Madame Krugener (1764–1824), a Baltic German religious mystic and author. While criticizing some aspects of her work, he expressed admiration of her devotion and was well enough versed in mysticism to recognize the influence of other mystics in her work.[28] Throughout his exegetical writing, Kelly was critical of the Greek tradition of philosophy which had such a strong effect on the work of the Church Fathers and he endorsed Paul's criticisms of the Gnostics

---

23. Cross, *The Irish Saint and Scholar*, 144. This quotation is from an extract of the Librarian's report on William Kelly's library to the Free Library and Museum Committee 11th October 1904, in the minutes of proceedings of the Middlesbrough Town Council, 1903–04. Kelly's library contents must always count as incidental evidence for his reading and it is his written works which must be counted as stronger evidence for his knowledge.

24. Suso was "one of the chief German mystics and leaders of the Friends of God, a circle of devout ascetic Rhinelanders who opposed contemporary evils and aimed for a close association with God." (*Britannica Online Encyclopaedia*). Tersteegen was a German Reformed religious writer who had a great influence on radical Pietism, and who translated the French mystics and Julian of Norwich. His influence led later to the founding of the Moravian Church by Count von Zinzendorf in 1727. They preached strongly in favor of the new birth and against worldly amusements. The Moravians had a great influence on John Wesley and on the 19th-century Brethren movement.

25. Kelly, *Ephesians*, 75.

26. Darby, "Letter 1," 312.

27. Ibid., 314.

28. Ibid., 316.

in the biblical epistles.[29] Many of the later mystics also warned against the theology of some of the Church Fathers and Kelly was clearly concerned about the influence of pagan philosophy on their Christianity. His library suggests his extensive reading of Plato, Plotinus and Philo.[30] It is clear from other non-Brethren writers that Greek pagan philosophers such as Plotinus did have an enormous influence on the early mystics.[31] Kelly was critical of the influence of "the lofty aspirings of Plato," and "the high and noble sentiments as Philo represents" with regard to a right understanding of the Incarnation.[32] He warned against Origen's allegorization of the Scriptures and his understanding of the incarnation, as a step towards a platonic unification with God.[33] In this we again see Kelly's concern with an orthodox understanding of the Incarnation and the way his high Christology separated him from other writers.

Kelly sometimes used the word "mysticism" in a critical way. He was suspicious of too much "unfocused" waiting on God, which he believed was the hall mark of some mystical traditions. In one of his letters, he warned that "mysticism unsettles as to Christ, eternal life and God's righteousness, and many tracts fly about."[34] He criticized "oriental" mysticism and warned about the dangers of prying into the unseen.[35] He claimed that this sort of mysticism had only an appearance of humility which was deceptive and dangerous. It was an early error of the Church Fathers, he felt, to mix philosophy with Christianity, and Kelly asserted that this had continued to be so in his own day.[36] He was wary of any mystic teaching which failed to distinguish between the experience of believer and unbeliever.[37] He was also critical of any doctrine of perfectionism, which he connected in one instance to the seven of churches mentioned in the book of Revelation, and which he perceived to be a "form of Pelagianism." He concluded that

---

29. The Gnostics' preoccupation with the soul, divorced from the body and ecstatic utterances in the "mystery religions" was always considered to be a source of danger to the early Church. Cf. Colossians 2. 8. and 18.

30. In his library, Kelly had all the major works of Plato and of Philo, including separately *In Libros Mosis* and Plotinus, *Enneades*.

31. Underhill, *The Mystics of the Church*, 61.

32. Kelly, *Colossians*, 43.

33. Kelly, *Romans*, 230. Louth, *The Origins of the Christian Mystical Tradition*, 65.

34. Kelly, *Letters to Herman Wreyford*.

35. Kelly, *Colossians*, 60.

36. Kelly, *Philippians*, 43.

37. Kelly, *Colossians*, 73.

this doctrine was "not the truth, though there may be truth here and there, mixed up with what is at bottom mysticism."[38] While Brethren teaching presented the truth about dying to the world and to sin, Kelly proposed that many Christians had a tendency to "substitute mysticism for the truth."[39] In other words, in his view, a general mysticism revealed in ecstatic spirituality could be a cover for a lack of real evangelical conversion or a lack of intellectual rigor in analyzing Scripture. While the Brethren enjoyed mystic experience, it certainly had its parameters. Nowhere did it stray too far from an intellectual analysis of the Scriptures, nor did it ever become divorced from practical experience. He followed in the tradition of mystics believing that their Scriptures are "authentic centers of divine, transcendental, ultimate truth. It assumes they are revelations of God."[40] Kelly's place as a conservative intellectual in the evangelical tradition, which I have demonstrated in chapters 2 and 3, is therefore very important as a foundation of his spirituality. Theological orthodoxy is part of the mystic tradition and Kelly was keen to adhere to high standards in his writing and to make sure that the Brethren community interpretation of the Bible was consistent with this.[41] Kelly's mysticism was subservient to his intellectual and evangelical spirituality.

Grass and Stunt have shown that there were connections between the Brethren and the Quakers with their mystical inheritance.[42] Moreover, when attempting to define the spirituality of the Brethren movement, Grass goes beyond the transfer of evangelical Quakers to the early Brethren.[43] He characterizes the trajectory of the Exclusive Brethren in the nineteenth century as "increasing introversion and separation arising from the development of their assembly-orientated mysticism."[44] This suggests the possible mysticism of the Exclusive Brethren tradition and I propose that Kelly contributed to this. As no other Church historian, apart from Grass and Stunt, has so far suggested this link between the Brethren and mysticism, I would like to explore this idea through the teaching of Kelly. The

---

38. Kelly, *Letters*, July 1875, "My Dear Brother."
39. Kelly, *Colossians*, 74.
40. Katz, "Mysticism and Interpretation of Sacred Scripture," 15.
41. Ibid., 19.
42. Stunt, *Early Brethren and the Society of Friends*.
43. Grass, *Gathering to His Name*, 32, 38. Newton and Tregelles were examples of leading Brethren who had been Quakers.
44. Grass, *Gathering to His Name*, 199.

Brethren always put direct experience of God before ecclesiastical tradition but Kelly's strong belief in The Fall and the ruin of mankind meant that he rejected the Quaker belief in the inner divine light in every soul.[45] Usually there is a divide in the mystical tradition between those who were more theocentric and those who were more Christocentric.[46] Kelly had far more in common with the latter though his theology always led him to move from talking about Christ to talking about the Trinity, and he was looking forward to a complete preoccupation with the Trinitarian God in eternity.[47]

How Kelly's spirituality can be defined is interesting and significant. He believed that being "dead even to the best things in the world and alive to the highest things" was something which had already been accomplished, rather than a state to be achieved through effort.[48] This was the "resting" teaching so beloved of Hudson Taylor (1832–1905) and, in the early twentieth century, of Watchman Nee (1903–1972), two men who were strongly influenced by the Brethren.[49] There is also some evidence from his writing that Kelly saw the gift of the Holy Spirit as being "subsequent to conversion even if very near the time," thus making him support a particularly exalted type of spirituality.[50] Kelly contrasted this position favorably with the teaching of traditional mystics whose object was to die and who dwelt only on inward experiences and human effort—"they endeavor to crucify themselves."[51] However, if we look at the sense of revelation and at the spontaneous inward joy of a number of traditional mystic writers, this disparagement is seriously mistaken. As so often, the Brethren regarded their own teaching as superior to that of others. Kelly dismissed traditional mysticism as "the reverse of God's mysteries and the mere mist

---

45. Underhill, *The Mystics of the Church*, 138.

46. Ibid., 25.

47. This is evident in all his work, but particularly in his work on St. John's Gospel and Ephesians.

48. Kelly, *Colossians*, 79.

49. Watchman Nee (original Chinese name—Nee To-Sheng) had a great influence on the twentieth century Chinese church and, through his writings, on the international church. The over 500 churches he founded in China were characterized by lay leadership, intense teaching about conversion and Christian holiness, and teaching about the Rapture. Nee acknowledged the influence of J.N. Darby and Madame Guyon in his theological works.

50. Kelly, *Lectures on the New Testament Doctrine of the Holy Spirit*, 172.

51. Kelly, *Colossians*, 79.

of men's fancies."⁵² Kelly also believed that his teaching was fully accessible to anyone: it was not an esoteric mysticism.⁵³ He recognized that his teaching could be regarded as "mere mysticism," with the word "mysticism" here being interpreted in a derogatory way as something overly esoteric and fully of the imagination.⁵⁴ Kelly insisted that this teaching was not esoteric, but contained the foundations of the biblical doctrine of baptism.

Kelly's spirituality has a particular claim to being part of the mystic tradition, because of his exposition of the word "mystery." While using the word "mystic" pejoratively in his criticism of others, Kelly advocated the mystery of Christ's body (the church) and mystic glory (the church's identification with the ascended Christ).⁵⁵ He taught that, as Christ's glory is not yet seen in the world, the mystic life must be hidden and secret, and those who experienced it would be rejected by the world.⁵⁶ He explained that "the mysteries of Scripture are truths once locked up but now revealed."⁵⁷ Kelly often implied that through Brethren teaching the Church in the nineteenth century could be particularly enlightened on this subject.⁵⁸ Despite there being some negative attitudes towards traditional mysticism, there is clear evidence of the major Christian mystic traditions in Kelly's writings.⁵⁹ Kelly was a great admirer of Paul, the founder of Christocentric mysticism, and saw Paul as the divinely appointed revealer of the "mystery."⁶⁰ For Kelly, what was special about John's Gospel and his epistles was that the apostle "brings out most strikingly the love of God." According to Underhill, mystics have a greater preoccupation with the glory of God than with their personal interests and so Kelly was not restricted by the potential narrowness of Brethren thinking. Character-building and discernment, prayer and discipline, were also the mystic hallmarks of Kelly's life. There is in

---

52. Kelly, *Ephesians*, 75.
53. Kelly, *Colossians*, 53.
54. Ibid., 65.
55. Ibid., 35, referring to Col 1:27.
56. Ibid., 80.
57. Kelly, *Ephesians*, 76.
58. In his letter, 18th March, 1891, Kelly rather patronisingly wrote that Dean L. of the Anglican Church, "though sound in his intention, has become restricted in his theology and not got past justification by faith."
59. For example, love mysticism sees the language of love applied to the relationship between God and Israel, Christ and the individual Christian and the Church, and bridal mysticism concentrates on particular marriage register applied to those topics.
60. Kelly, *Ephesians*, 118.

Kelly's work a sense of freedom and ability to bring spiritual revival to his audience.[61] We see a link between Kelly and the Jewish mystic, Philo, who believed very strongly in the allegory of the Hebrew Scriptures and always followed the Pentateuch to find spiritual understanding of his life with God.[62] Kelly's erudite understanding of the Bible, particularly in his use of patterns of typology for biblical teaching, was very much in the tradition of Origen.[63] Kelly had a particular link with the mystics from the Athanasian heritage, such as Gregory of Nyssa, because of their Trinitarian stance and high Christology, and he always stressed the unknowability of God apart from the Incarnation and the Atonement.[64] Like the desert fathers, Kelly had much to say about fighting against the flesh.[65] Certain biblical books were of particular significance to mystics: Kelly shared with Bernard of Clairvaux (1090–1153)—whose complete works, in a 1609 edition, are in his library—a love of the Song of Solomon. Love mysticism and bridal mysticism were strong features of both Bernard of Clairvaux and thirteenth- and fourteenth-century German mystic writers.

KELLY'S TRINITARIANISM

When we consider Kelly's mystic spirituality we should examine his preoccupation with the glory of the Trinity, as particularly revealed in the glory of Christ. Kelly's emphasis on this doctrine was very much in keeping with the tradition of the Greek Fathers, the medieval writer, Bonaventure (1221–1274), and the tradition of "intellectual or logos mysticism."[66] The passage which has been associated with this theme is Christ's discourse in John's Gospel, chapters 14 to 17, and Kelly's exegesis of these chapters is notably profound. He explained that the whole Gospel of John was much

---

61. Underhill, *The Mystics of the Christian Church*, 119.

62. Louth, *The Origins of the Christian Mystical Tradition*, 27. For example Philo used Leviticus 2.14, the offerings of the first fruit, to analyze the disciplined life with God. Kelly did much the same with other Old Testament passages. Kelly's library reveals his reading of Philo. He had a 4–volume translation by Yonge dating from 1854; his complete works edited between 1828 and 1830; *De Cophini festo et de Colendis parantibus*; *De Animalum proprietate*; and *In Libros Mosis*.

63. Underhill, *The Mystics of the Christian Church*, 64

64. Ibid., 80, 84. Kelly possessed three volumes of Gregory of Nyssa's works, published in 1638.

65. Ibid., 100.

66. Cousins, "Bonaventure's Mysticism of Language," 252.

more about the Son going to the Father than the synoptic Gospels.[67] The first disciples believed that Jesus came from God, but they did not understand the greater truth taught in these chapters that after the Ascension they would be in touch with the Father, and in fact with the whole Trinity.[68] For Kelly, Trinitarian mystic understanding of the Christian position was more important than any understanding of Christ as an earthly Messiah. Kelly believed that the Brethren had "recovered" this truth for the Church in a special way. John's Gospel was important to him because it did not speak primarily of the sorrows of Gethsemane; instead, "it sets forth the glory of His person."[69] While other gospels dwelt on the humanity of Christ, John's was about "God's purposes heavenly and everlasting."[70] In this exegesis Kelly combined theocentric and Christocentric forms of mysticism.

Kelly's mysticism was energized by his special understanding of the Trinity, which he believed had important consequences for the position of the believer. According to him, the Son had to be in the most intimate relationship with the Father, and that was why the Christian had to find his or her primary position in the heavenly places now.[71] This pointed to the identity of Christ in the Godhead.[72] Consequently Christians must enjoy beholding the glory of Christ.[73] It was a special "secret glory" which the initiated could contemplate, and which denoted the very highest possible inward experience.[74] As Kelly considered eternal life as an existential experience of knowing the Father, an understanding of the Trinitarian nature of God was absolutely vital to this experience.[75] The glory of Christ in the Trinity was axiomatic to the Brethren understanding of God and also to their entry into the experience of contemplation.[76] It was why Christ had to be the object of the Christian adoration.[77] It was also why worship should

---

67. Kelly, *John*, 344.
68. Ibid., 345.
69. Ibid., 346.
70. Ibid., 348.
71. Ibid., 284.
72. Ibid., 296.
73. Ibid., 371.
74. Ibid.
75. Ibid., 372.
76. Ibid., 290.
77. Ibid., 305.

be in the present earthly life rather than in some future state.[78] Kelly believed that in John's Gospel the fatherhood of God, rather than His other attributes of such as those embodied in the Jehovah God of the Old Testament, was uniquely revealed through the person of Christ.[79] In his writing about 1 John, Kelly foregrounded the word "communion" for its particular spiritually intimate resonance. He taught that the Christian was not only brought into the presence of God through conversion, but that, as a result, the Christian could have communion with Father and Son, as a reflection of the communion which existed between the persons of the Godhead.[80] Therefore this "communion" was of a very exalted and privileged kind. The apostle John was the unique teacher of this truth within the Scriptures and Kelly's understanding of John's writings, which have always been seen throughout the centuries as having a special mystic quality, was profound.[81] Kelly thought that those outside the Brethren had missed out on this full Trinitarian understanding, because they had under-appreciated not only the heavenly position of Christ but also His infinite nearness to the Father.[82] He asserted, "All (its) blessedness turns on who and what and where Christ is."[83] This understanding of the Trinity also influenced Brethren teaching on prayer, the means of mystic contemplation. Kelly advised that in matters of the Church, Christians should pray to Jesus, but more generally, as a result of the Ascension, to the Father.[84] His reading of John 14:14 ("in my name" being placed at the end of the verse) underlined his theology because any answer to Christian prayer must be the result of Christ's high position as God, not as a mere prayer formula.[85] Consequently the Lord's Prayer was not for the Christian, because it had been given before the Ascension.[86]

Kelly claimed that, while most of the Christian church seemed indifferent to the Ascension, he not only believed it as a fact, but also maintained that it was "full of weighty and fruitful consequences for us."[87] One of the

---

78. Ibid., 337.
79. Ibid., 304.
80. Kelly, *The Advocacy of Christ*, 6.
81. Ibid., 17, 21.
82. Kelly, *John*, 296.
83. Ibid.
84. Ibid., 339.
85. Ibid., 340.
86. Ibid.
87. Ibid., 301.

consequences of this mystic theology of the Trinity was greater power for the first disciples and, consequently, for all other Christians since that time who had access to communion with the full Trinitarian expression of who God was because of Christ's intercession for and oneness with the Christian on earth. This emphasis on the Ascension was also important for Kelly's belief in the humanity of Christ and therefore for the significance of the Christian's humanity.[88] Instead of dwelling on the sufferings of the Cross, Kelly taught that John chapters 14 through to 17, though ostensibly part of the Garden of Gethsemane discourse and so part of the Passion narrative, actually taught primarily about the source of joy for the Christian believer. Clearly, mystical rather than worldly joy was at the heart of Kelly's teaching and Brethren identity.[89] For Kelly, these chapters of John were especially connected with the teachings of the Epistles, which were so important to him.[90] The Trinitarian theology of John tied in with Paul's Trinitarian assumptions in the book of Ephesians. Kelly showed that in chapter 15 particularly, the Holy Spirit acted as a witness to the future ascended Christ and the glory of Christ.[91] For Kelly it was God's grace which revealed the truth of the Trinity. As a corollary to this, persecution of Christians was inevitable because "the world" (meaning for Kelly both the obviously secular and the formal "religious" world) "hated grace."[92] Therefore Kelly felt that it was the completeness of Brethren theology, incorporating both Trinitarian understanding and its exposition of the doctrine of the Ascension, which elicited criticism and persecution from the established Church and contemporary Victorian theologians. In Kelly's own view his theology, literalist, conservative–intellectual and mystic, would inevitably attract opposition.

MYSTICISM AND THE DOCTRINE OF THE ASCENSION

Kelly applied the word "mystic" to the body of Christ in a positive way; for him it was always associated with "union" of the church with Christ after the Resurrection, rather than with the doctrine of incarnation. He wrote, "the mystical body is formed by the Holy Ghost, sent down after He rose from

---

88. Ibid.
89. Ibid., 337.
90. Ibid., 324.
91. Ibid., 323.
92. Ibid.

the dead."[93] While the term "the body of Christ" has, since Paul's Scriptural writings, been regarded as a mystical association of believers attached to the "headship" or leadership of Christ, Kelly's teachings stressed the "union" of the Christians with Christ in his position of glory "at the right hand of God."[94] The "mystery" which was so important to Kelly was the union of Christ and the church, the heavenly and the earthly being combined at this present time.[95] Kelly also implied that what God wanted to teach his followers consisted of "mysteries," and there is in his writing a sense that only those choosing to be taught by him or being part of the Brethren could fully understand them.[96] According to Kelly, Ephesians 3:18, referring to the fullness of Christ's love, was not about the Incarnation or the Passion of Christ but about the mystery of the Church being the body of Christ.[97] However, true mystic spirituality should not imply that the Christian was cut off from life on earth and the body. Such a false mysticism was "the reverse of God's mysteries and the mere mist of men's fancies."[98] The mystery was something which was kept secret, not something which could not be understood.[99] He went on to explain that the mystery concerned the disappearance of Christ in the Ascension, rather than a takeover of the Kingdom, which was what the Jews had expected. Also Kelly taught that the whole universe would eventually be under Christ's authority.[100] At this point his mysticism became theocentric rather than Christocentric and gave him a wider perspective than just the evangelical. The position of the church was also to be important to the whole of society in the millennium. Christ would exert authority over the Jews and unbelieving Gentiles, but not over the Church because He would be sharing His authority with them as equals. Therefore there is a strong sense of the Brethren saints being in charge in the future earthly kingdom. Although Kelly saw the language in Ephesians as symbolic, it was a figure that conveyed an intense degree of

---

93. Kelly, *Philippians*, 22.

94. This phrase occurs several times in the Epistles, notably Eph 1:20, Col 3:2 and Heb 12:2.

95. Kelly, *Ephesians*, 26.

96. Ibid., 25, 76.

97. Ibid., 138. Eph 3:18, "may be able to comprehend with all the saints what is the breadth and length and depth and height" (KJV).

98. Ibid., 75.

99. Ibid., 114.

100. Ibid.

intimacy, "full of the richest comfort and the most exalted hope."[101] This allowed for the intense longing of Brethren mysticism but also for their dignity and sense of significance.

This mystic union was also reflected in Kelly's teaching about adult baptism. According to Kelly, Anglicans confused the baptism of John the Baptist with Christian baptism, and even the Baptist church had little understanding of the Christian identification with Christ's death and life.[102] This hallmark of Kelly's interpretation of baptism was important for his mystic theology because, firstly, baptism meant an intense experience of death to the world. Kelly emphasized that baptism by immersion had to symbolize the experience of death to sin and that this could only take place with the consent of the individual rather than happening as part of the covenant promises to the family as in Reformed Anglicanism or as a sacramental mystery as in Tractarian Anglicanism. For Kelly baptism was a parallel to the Passover event symbolizing death to the old way of life for God's people.[103] He subsumed the Crucifixion into the text of the Passover, and so made the Old Testament text transcend time and anticipate the Christian experience.[104] Death to sin in baptism was also about feeling humiliation and meant that the Christian had no place in the world. This humiliation needed to be entered into because it was the prelude to a higher level of spiritual experience.[105] Kelly accused the Roman Catholics and the Church Fathers of making baptism merely a sign of new spiritual life. Instead, he said, "it teaches that we are buried with Christ."[106] Baptism was not just about having a relationship with God, because the saints in the Old Testament had experienced that without baptism and even without circumcision.[107] Secondly, baptism also stood for resurrection and union with the ascended Christ and manifested a more intense experience than that of Adam's innocence before the Fall.[108] Thus Kelly distanced himself from Platonic thought, that is, that the soul gradually making progress back

---

101. Ibid., 115.

102. Kelly, "Correspondence: Recent Baptismal Agitation," 15.

103. Kelly, "The Feasts of Atonement," 113.

104. According to Simon, page 79, "the Passover text is such a rich one that it can easily act in this way."

105. Kelly, "The Atonement for Flux," 82.

106. Kelly, "The Day of Atonement," 310.

107. Ibid.

108. Kelly, *Romans*, 125.

to a state of higher unification with God, which was characteristic of some mystics, or from the popular Victorian idea that the soul would return to its original state of innocence (made popular through the influence of Romantic poets such as Wordsworth—"trailing clouds of glory do we come," from *Reflections on Early Childhood and Intimations of Immortality*).[109]

Being one with Christ now should lead the Christian to long for the coming of Christ, and for the Christian—in contrast with the Jew—that longing would always be spiritual. For Kelly it was always significant that the Son of God was coming for the Church in person—his understanding of "the rapture"—and so his eschatological view of union with Christ was also significant for his mysticism.[110] According to Kelly, his understanding of union with Christ both in a future event and in the present was beyond human intelligence and needed to be revealed by a higher power.[111] It was a greater blessing to have Christ in heaven than Christ on earth.[112] Therefore for the Brethren, internal, mystic experience was more important than any physical encounter. To have God the Father revealed to them through the Son "was wholly outside and above man."[113] However, this deep spirituality was not about being a special type of person: it was about the integrity of Christian character, so there was in Kelly's teaching a special mixture of exclusivity and inclusivity.[114] Other mystics have acknowledged that their experience was only for a small minority in the church: the Brethren claimed it was for every Christian and was a vital part of their theology. This teaching, based on John's Gospel and the Epistles, "must be really entered into to be understood" and, if it was, Christians could "rest in the Father's love."[115] However, as with so much mystic teaching, there was a battle between good and evil, and the Devil was seen as the particular adversary of God the Son.[116] The Brethren exhorted their followers to cling to the Ideal, personified in Christ. As in any reaching after the Ideal, there was always a straining after more, and inevitably a falling short, so that even if the Brethren rejected the idea of self-effort instead of grace in conversion,

---

109 104 Wordsworth, "Reflections on Early Childhood," 628.

110. Ibid., 284.

111. Ibid., 290, 331.

112. Ibid., 338.

113. Ibid., 352.

114. Ibid., 287.

115. Ibid., 343.

116. Ibid., 287.

they always had aspirations for a greater spirituality. The theology of the Ascension had a huge effect on Brethren affections and "affection" was the basis of Kelly's mystic spirituality.[117] His exegeses cannot be categorized as merely intellectual or theological analysis—their purpose was also to draw his audience into a mystic love relationship with Christ. There was an intimacy revealed in his understanding of John 14:20.[118] Spiritual union was "more real and permanent" than anything physical and it was with the risen Lord on high.[119] He himself thought that Christians who emphasized the importance of the priesthood of Christ or even the Atonement "are apt to be a cold set of people, in danger of becoming formal and dry doctrinally, as well as deficient in sensitiveness of heart and conscience for the glory of God."[120] Thus Kelly placed a premium on his own understanding of the affections which his spirituality drew out. This phenomenon, according to Katz, is in keeping with the mystic tradition in which "highly charged spiritual encounter" is always valued more than intellectual exploration.[121]

Such an inner experience was arguably always more important for Kelly than any concern with justice or good government. Preoccupation with the Beloved or the Giver of blessings was more important than any form of service.[122] This glorious preoccupation with Christ in a transcendent experience gave his writings a different tone to any merely literalist discourse. Kelly stressed that, while believers were looking for and obeying God's commandments, they should also be feeling them deeply.[123] In his commentary on John 14:21, we see Kelly's minute analysis of the Scriptures, as he explored the difference between "hath the commandments" and "keeps the commandments." Kelly concludes, "The desire to do his will finds and knows what it (i.e. the commandment) is."[124] His intellectualism and his mysticism are combined as his language soars above the ordinary, using interconnectedness, abstract vocabulary and Trinitarian register.[125]

---

117. Ibid., 285, 363.

118. Ibid., 296. John 14:20, "At that day ye shall know that I am in my Father, and ye in me, and I in you" (KJV).

119. Ibid., 297, 355.

120. Kelly, *The Advocacy of Christ*, 7.

121. Katz, "Mysticism and the Interpretation of Sacred Scripture," 15.

122. Ibid., 316.

123. Ibid., 298.

124. Ibid.

125. Ibid.

His writing revealed an expression of delicate understanding of the relationship of the persons of the Trinity, for example, "loving Him (i.e. the Son) draws down his Father's love, who honors the Son and will not be exalted at His expense."[126] In addition to the Trinitarian, there is a use of moral and abstract language—"Thus only does Christian practice flow from Christian principle and privilege; and all is of Christ by the Holy Ghost in us." There is a terse use of paradox and exclamation—"How comforting that our duty as Christians supposes our blessedness! How humbling that the gift of the Spirit makes our failure inexcusable!" There is a strong emotional aspiration in his language—"And how cheering to the heart the abiding sense of the presence of the Father and the Son with us as thus walking! Would that we knew it better!"[127] He drew parallels with Colossians 1:9 and 10, thus linking revelation with practical holiness, and stressed that, in the physical absence of Christ, obedience revealed the true state of the heart.[128] The cycle of obedience and affection would result in greater revelation. This cycle was of paramount significance for Brethren experience. Kelly stressed that spirituality was not just a manifestation but "an abode"—a powerful picture of his mystical knowledge of God.[129] The result would be that God's followers would draw from an inexhaustible divine well of peace.[130] Here we see how individuals become part of the whole, but unlike Platonic and eastern mysticism, where the individual no longer counts, the Brethren never lost their sense of the individual. This was partly the result of their strong belief in the humanity of Christ at the Ascension.

Kelly's contemplation of the Ascension thus also had a transformative effect which went above and beyond the idea of an initial forgiveness experienced at "conversion."[131] Following from this, the commissioning and consequent courage of the first disciples and of later believers stemmed from their devotion to the glorified Christ.[132] Christ was not just the object of contemplation but the archetypal role model—"the firstborn among

126. Ibid.
127. Ibid., 300.
128. Col 1:9, 10: "For this cause we also, since the day we heard it, do not cease to pray for you, and to desire that ye might be filled with the knowledge of his will in all wisdom and spiritual understanding. That ye might walk worthy of the Lord unto all pleasing, being fruitful in every good work and increasing in the knowledge of God" (KJV).
129. Kelly, *John*, 300.
130. Ibid., 301.
131. Ibid., 363.
132. Ibid., 357.

many Brethren."[133] "Eternal life" as an existentialist experience became the deepest gift God could give, because Christ Himself was eternal life before the foundation of the world.[134] Again we see Trinitarian theology having a huge impact on Brethren mysticism. Just as Christ had always possessed the glory of the Godhead, so as man he would always have the present and future glory, thus permitting believers as human beings to have the experience of glory now. As Christ's work was complete, human beings were blessed.[135] This was also why humans were joint heirs with Christ, not just inheritors from God.[136] According to Kelly, in the future, the saints as co-inheritors would give testimony to those on earth when Christ came in glory.[137] Again his eschatology, combined with his Trinitarianism, gave a strong foundation to his mysticism. Therefore there is in Kelly's theology a combination of future union in glory and present contemplation of the glory of Christ—"the secret glory which none but His own are permitted to contemplate."[138]

Kelly claimed that his teaching on the subject of the Ascension was unique in the Christian church because the theologians of the Reformation had not fully grasped it. As a result this subject had particular significance for Brethren spirituality. Kelly accused the wider Christian church of not sufficiently promoting and teaching the blessing of the Ascension. Most Victorian Christians thought they could only appreciate the enjoyment of the presence of Christ at their death.[139] In contrast, the Brethren claimed that enjoyment in the present as was clearly demonstrated in their collective worship. As far as Kelly was concerned, earlier Christendom, like the Jews before them, had not been spiritual enough and had been "too engrossed in earthly things."[140] For Kelly, the believer's strength should come through the contemplative experience of Christ glorified. This then accounted for the power of Brethren spirituality.[141] This contemplation was rooted in their theology of man's ruin and incarnation. Since The Fall, humanity had

133. Col chapter 2, quoted in Kelly, *John*, 363.
134. Ibid., 350.
135. Ibid., 351.
136. Ibid., 355.
137. Ibid., 368–69.
138. Ibid., 371.
139. Ibid., 9.
140. Kelly, *Lectures on the Church of God*, 43.
141. Kelly, *Philippians*, 14–15.

always been the agent of dishonor for God, but when Jesus Christ was glorified as man in the Ascension, God the Father could once again delight in mankind. Such teaching drew the Brethren into the intimacy of the Trinity.

THE IMPORTANCE OF THE EPISTLES WITHIN THE CANON OF SCRIPTURE, AND ESPECIALLY EPHESIANS WITH ITS UNIQUE TEACHING ABOUT THE ASCENSION

An important characteristic of Brethren life was a deep search of the Scriptures. Thus, compared with other evangelical groups, it became more of an intellectual movement and an ability to analyze sacred text was combined with mysticism in a powerful way. Kelly noted that none should be satisfied with what they already knew but should search more deeply to make spiritual progress.[142] Brethren worship was therefore always informed by intellectual searching. To the Brethren, Paul was a more important apostle than any other because he taught pre-eminently "the mystery of the church" and completed the word of God.[143] Paul's teaching took the church forward from the experience of the day of Pentecost, which was why the Brethren did not major on the Pentecostal gifts.[144] According to Kelly, if there was such a thing as apostolic succession, it should have been from Paul not Peter.[145] Prophetic Scripture in Romans 16 referred to Paul because he was the one who revealed the mystery.[146] Kelly saw the system of the Epistles as a Canon within the Canon.[147] While Romans and Galatians were about justification, Colossians was about Christ in the heavens and why earthly systems were dangerous and should be rejected. Hebrews was about Christ pleading for humanity in the heavens, but Ephesians was the most important of all because it was about the Christian's privileges in the heavenly

---

142. Kelly, *Philippians*, 20.

143. Ibid., 35, 36. This of course was not because Paul wrote the final book of the New Testament chronologically but because his teaching about the church was considered by the Brethren to be its cumulative teaching.

144. Ibid., 37.

145. Kelly, *Ephesians*, 118.

146. Ibid., 120.

147. Many strong believers in the Canon of Scripture have had their own Canon within the Canon—in other words books of the Bible which they see as being particularly important. Thus Luther gave particular support to the book of Romans as encapsulating his "justification by faith" doctrine and had little time for James, as being of practical rather than theological significance.

places in Christ now.[148] I suggest that Kelly's own translation and exegesis of Ephesians was particularly significant in his own opus and he saw it as the apex of Paul's teachings in his other epistles. In addition, Kelly's studies on the other Pauline epistles contributed to the teaching which culminated in his exegesis on Ephesians. His work on Philippians and Colossians was important because it did much to link the teaching of Galatians, Colossians and Ephesians and to place this teaching in due perspective and order. Philippians stressed the joy of the Christian as he or she understood this teaching—"He would thus make us (sic) more happy."[149] Galatians was concerned with warning people about legalism, which Kelly associated with the established church.[150] Colossians, with much important teaching for his theology, was about "the power of his glory" and showed the necessity of a deepening acquaintance with God as an important adjunct to obedience.[151] The Brethren have often been accused of authoritarianism.[152] However, Kelly's teaching on the Epistles shows that a particular understanding of Church leadership was only part of their collective worship experience—the experience of "the glory of God" was far more significant.

Kelly's teaching about the book of Ephesians was in many ways the pinnacle of his insight and understanding of the Scriptures. The main theme was "union with Christ" and "the privileges of the body."[153] According to Kelly, Ephesians was about Christ's likeness to God in his moral qualities and about the ideal of where the Christian Church ought to be.[154] Ephesians concentrated on the Trinity and on God's intentions before the world began, linking it with Genesis, which was a foundational source for Kelly's teaching.[155] Kelly's writing about Ephesians shows that understanding the nature of God, rather than theodicy or practical teaching, was what was important to him, and explains how he made a significant contribution to nineteenth-century theological teaching.[156] His burning concern with understanding and teaching about the nature of God rather than with apolo-

---

148. Kelly, *Colossians*, 54–55.
149. Kelly, *Philippians*, 15.
150. Kelly, *Colossians*, 2.
151. Ibid., 13.
152. Stunt, "Two Nineteenth-century Movements," 229.
153. Kelly, *Colossians*, 1.
154. Ibid., 88, 51.
155. Kelly, *Ephesians*, 4.
156. Ibid., 5.

getics per se gave his work similarities with that of F.D. Maurice, whose profound grasp of the love of God so inspired the broader Anglican church, but whose theological stance as a "Broad Church liberal" would normally set him far apart from Kelly.[157] Kelly's exegesis of Ephesians showed that for him the "ideal" was accessible in the present experience rather than merely a future hope.[158]

SOME CONCLUSIONS ABOUT THE CONTRIBUTION OF KELLY'S MYSTIC SPIRITUALITY TO THE CHURCH

Kelly believed in the uniqueness of the Scriptural understanding given to the Brethren, and that meant that it should be guarded carefully. He used the word "devotedness" to challenge the second generation of Brethren worshippers who might otherwise have become complacent.[159] Kelly advised that more self-discipline was needed after their separation from the world through an evangelical conversion experience than before, when they might have been part of a worldly church.[160] The standards of personal holiness which he taught were extremely high, because he believed that low standards would lead to "carelessness and self-exaltation."[161] He warned his readers, "he who ceases to walk dependently is morally ruined already" and that godliness is "the spirit of constant reference and subjection to God in things small or great."[162] All mystic writers have stressed the need for discipline and self-denial as part of having a deep experience of Christ.

In promoting Brethren corporate spirituality, Kelly rejected the contributions of other denominations. He warned against new denominations, such as the Catholic Apostolic Church, arguing that good teaching always "supplies missing links, deepens the foundations and enlarges the sphere" of biblical understanding.[163] For Kelly, Brethren promotion of the Ascension was not new teaching but rediscovery of the old, whereas he believed

---

157. Maurice, "Eternal Life and Eternal Death," 476.
158. Kelly, *Ephesians*, 21, 24.
159. Kelly, *Lectures on the Church of God*, 33.
160. Ibid., 35.
161. Kelly, *Letters*, 16 June, 1851, addressed to "My dear Mr. C."
162. Kelly, *The Advocacy of Christ*, 8.
163. Kelly, *Colossians*, 5, 6. Kelly criticized the high church liturgy of the Catholic Apostolic Church, their practice of the charismatic gifts and Irving's Christology and view of Christ's identification with fallen humanity.

that the newly formed Catholic Apostolic Church was promoting the "new" doctrine of ecstatic tongues. He spoke against "worldly" Anglican worship, where merely decent people were considered to be worshippers.[164] Kelly promoted an internal intimate spirituality rather than an external sacramental theology. He submitted that outward failure in the Christian life was always the result of secret failure before God and he taught his followers to be acutely aware of such faults.[165] However, he always kept the goodness of God before his readers and stressed that God did not love believers as the result of their repentance.[166] Thus he believed that Anglicans were too busy calling themselves "miserable sinners" rather than enjoying the rest and peace of salvation; this affected their hymnology which became "the aspirations of anxious souls."[167] He criticized the Church of England for praying for a fresh outpouring of the Holy Spirit in their weekly services, when it was obvious to him that Christians had all they needed already and he was particularly critical of evangelicals within the Church of England.[168] He referred to the "slipshod laxity of evangelicalism," which did not allow its adherents to truly experience the joy of the Lord.

Kelly's promotion of inner spirituality distanced him from the more overtly ecstatic experiences of the incipient Pentecostal movement.[169] True spiritual experience was a deeper experience than the effervescence of any charismatic gifts.[170] Kelly harshly criticized the Catholic Church and spoke of its cruel former persecution of Protestants and other dissenters, which he considered to be worse than that inflicted by the world.[171] Rejection by "worldly" systems of religion was what the Brethren were called on to expect.[172] In his view, even the Reformed Church denominations were guilty of envying those who had more light.[173] It was inevitable that the depth of

---

164. Ibid., 63.
165. Kelly, *The Advocacy of Christ*, 22.
166. Ibid., 24.
167. Kelly, *Ephesians*, 117.
168. Ibid., 293.
169. Kelly, *Lectures on the Church of God*, 55.
170. Kelly, *Ephesians*, 57.
171. Ibid., 319.
172. Ibid., 326.
173. Ibid.

the Brethren experience in worship and contemplation would be envied and criticized.[174]

Self-judgment was an important part of Kelly's spirituality—"how humbling that the gift of the Spirit makes our failure inexcusable."[175] If the Brethren lacked the externally imposed system of discipline of the monastic orders, they experienced harsh self-judgment. Thus the blessedness of transcendent joy and the harshness of ascetic discipline were brought about by an inward, mystical process. Given their strong belief in the Trinity, disobedience meant "absence of love" for Christ and for God the Father.[176] Therefore obedience through understanding the Word of God was a key discipline. Even the water from Christ's side at the Crucifixion was considered to be a symbol of the cleansing effect of the Word of God rather than part of the sacrament.[177]

Kelly's mysticism was, above all, Christocentric; it was more than just a sense of the mystery of the Divine. The love of the Father for the Son should produce in individuals the ability to be involved in love and contemplation. Such contemplation started on earth with our worship and would continue in heaven after death. Kelly talked about a deep inner experience. "We need to have enjoyment of what He is towards our souls."[178] Kelly stressed the value of love even without knowledge—"intuition of divine affection."[179] Like many mystic writers in the past, he used the Gospel story of Mary and the alabaster box of ointment to explore this. Mary, rather than the disciples, expressed this love, "as an example of the power of the Spirit of God acting in a simple, upright, loving heart that feels intensely for the object of its reverence, Christ Himself."[180] This was the expression of an individual, pure and deep love; as such it was at the heart of Kelly's spirituality. Christ was always "the most attractive and precious object before us."[181] Whereas the understanding of truth was important—as was reflected in his vast range of reading—it was love for Christ alone which was of supreme significance.

---

174. Ibid.
175. Ibid., 298.
176. Ibid., 299.
177. Ibid., 305.
178. Kelly, *Philippians*, 34.
179. Ibid., 36.
180. Ibid., 37.
181. Ibid., 69.

Kelly stressed a combination of affection and spiritual wisdom.[182] He called the Lordship of Christ an important and practical truth for both the individual and the Church.[183] This was a truth which the Brethren were called upon to teach and which we have already seen was a high point of controversy in the Victorian church.[184]

Kelly taught that individual and corporate worship were about enjoying the glory of Christ and having a daily, intimate relationship with Him. Appreciating the glory now and anticipating the Christian appearance in glory with Christ were both parts of the Christian experience.[185] Kelly claimed that the world would see the glory of Christ when he came to reign, but would never understand the intimate love.[186] For the Brethren, the experience must start with the individual before finding its corporate expression and for this reason Kelly encouraged the individual believer to experience the fullest communication with God in the here and now since God had promised to dwell with his Church through all eternity.[187] Kelly also taught that, as the Holy Spirit always worked through individuals, it would be wrong to talk about the Church teaching particular doctrines.[188] This led to a very different spirituality than that practiced by the Tractarians. As the individual should be ruled by God, nearness to God in the affections was more important than obeying particular details of teaching.[189] This is interesting as it has often been felt that the Brethren were a highly authoritarian church, which allowed no differences of opinion. Darby's supporters in the Exclusive Brethren followed that kind of ecclesiastical authoritarianism, but Kelly's teaching was free from such narrowness. It was his concentration on his intellectual analysis of Scripture and his encouragement of mystic joy which prevented this problem from arising amongst the Moderate Exclusives, some of whom became known as "the Kelly Brethren." However, his teaching did promote intense introspection and the necessity of intentional concentration on spiritual matters. According to Kelly's teaching, other

---

182. Kelly, *Colossians*, 79.
183. Ibid., 93.
184. Ibid., 108.
185. Kelly, *Ephesians*, 51.
186. Ibid., 52.
187. Ibid., 139, 141.
188. Ibid., 143.
189. Kelly, *Philippians*, 73, 21.

Christians should be valued only in so far as they sought Christ alone.[190] Christ had to be steadily adhered to in order to keep nature at bay, even after conversion.[191] Kelly warned about outward signs which could easily be "vain and empty."[192] Like many Christians who were leaders in the mystic tradition, he encouraged his hearers and readers to aim only for the highest levels of spirituality. That he was successful in his aims is suggested by the high regard in which his teachings and writings were held.

---

190. Kelly, *Colossians*, 84.
191. Ibid.
192. Kelly, *Ephesians*, 213.

CHAPTER 7

William Kelly's Spirituality Revealed in his Typology and Understanding of Language

INTRODUCTION

An important way that Kelly expressed his spirituality was through his response to, and understanding of, typology. Typology looked at Old Testament characters as "types" of Christ and incidents in the Old Testament as precursors of situations in the New Testament or even in the contemporary Church. What was referred to in the New Testament—either Christ or the Church—was known as the "anti-type." While historically, typology has not necessarily been linked to mysticism, it was a paradigm which allowed Kelly's mystic spirituality to flourish because it was based on the text of Scripture but did not primarily involve an academic analysis of that text. Through the study of this genre there was enormous capacity for intense spiritualization of the Old Testament, which was a characteristic of Brethren teaching. In this chapter I shall be looking at the way Kelly placed great emphasis on the Old Testament in general but also at the way typology in the books of the Pentateuch and Genesis in particular was significant for the development of his mysticism. What is also important is that Kelly not only interpreted the biblical text mystically but also succeeded in making his own discourse mystical. Most mystics have written creatively about their spiritual experience. What was unusual about Kelly was that he not only wrote biblical exegeses as an intellectual, but that he transformed the purely intellectual into a spiritual discourse. Frequently he took the words of the biblical text and not only explained them but also transposed biblical language, making it part of his own register and foregrounding it to make it express his personal spiritual experience. He not only inspired others to engage with the text spiritually as well as intellectually on an individual basis but also promoted the Brethren form of corporate mystic spirituality. In this chapter I propose that Kelly was a significant typologist and that he made a substantial contribution to nineteenth-century studies of the Old Testament, not only as a literalist and conservative intellectual, but also in his expression of mystic spirituality.

THE CONTEXT OF VICTORIAN TYPOLOGY

Chris Brooks and George Landow have already established that typology was a significant religious and literary mode for the Victorian church.[1] Landow cited Henry Melvill (1798–1871), evangelical Church of England vicar and principal of the East India Company College, Charles Spurgeon (1834–1892), Baptist minister and preacher, John Keble (1792–1866), Church of England priest and leader of the Oxford Movement and author of *The Christian Year*, J.H. Newman and Patrick Fairbairn as "the better and more influential Victorian typologists," and considered that such writers often contributed to Hebraic studies.[2] As Kelly was particularly interested in critiquing Fairbairn's work, I will now give a brief résumé of Fairbairn's career and his theological stance.

Fairbairn was ordained as a Church of Scotland minister in the Orkney Islands in 1830, but became a staunch supporter of the Free Church of Scotland. In 1853 he was appointed Professor of Theology at the Free Church College in Aberdeen, but in 1856 he moved to Glasgow University, where he became professor and principal. Lionel Ritchie notes his theological alignment—"while his sympathies were liberal, his orthodoxy was never impugned."[3] In his major work on typology, Fairbairn was more supportive of German higher criticism than Kelly and he admired Hengstenberg, de Wette and Baur.[4] He could accept with greater equanimity than Kelly that

1. Brooks, *Signs for the Times*. Landow, *Victorian Types*.
2. Landow, *Victorian Types*, 53.
3. Ritchie, "Patrick Fairbairn."
4. Patrick Fairbairn, *The Typology of Scripture*, 44–45. The second edition, which

the Church Fathers believed that allegorical truth within the text was more significant than literal truth. Fairbairn was much more inclined to justify what he was doing within his own chosen system of biblical interpretation than Kelly. In order to identify a type in the text, he explained, "It must be clear from Scripture that the introduction of the type was done deliberately in the mind of God," by which he meant there was clear justification for a type within the text.[5] He paid more attention than Kelly to the idea of historical development within the Bible, and he thought that the Old Testament writings were only elementary religious principles of the world.[6] In his prophetic views Fairbairn disagreed with Kelly's pre-millenarian and dispensationalist position and was less inclined to refer all types to a highly idealized Christology. However, despite these differences, what strikes the modern reader is how much Fairbairn and Kelly were in agreement on basic evangelical doctrines. It is a sign of the intense interest in typology of the Victorian church and the unique place which the Brethren occupied within the full range of Victorian ecclesiology that Kelly could write seven detailed and closely argued articles broadly acknowledging and even admiring Fairbairn's accuracy of typological interpretation, whilst using strong language to condemn those areas of Fairbairn's typology which revealed an understanding of doctrine different from that taught by the Brethren and which Kelly deemed to be crucial to an understanding of "truth."

Chris Brooks has shown that typology was useful to an evangelical scholar because it allowed "events to be read as simultaneously real and symbolic."[7] This was a helpful aspect of typology for Kelly who, as I have already shown, believed in plenary inspiration as well as being a conservative intellectual. When writing about the servant of Abraham finding a bride for Isaac, Kelly spent little time on the details of the story in terms of trying to justify it as a historic text, but instead, he concentrated on a mystic interpretation of its message.[8] He saw the passage as an allegory about the love of the Trinity for the church. Later in this chapter I will make a detailed study of Kelly's use of typology in this particular story.

Kelly uses for reference, combines the two volumes of the original edition.

5. Ibid., 60.
6. Ibid., 81.
7. Brooks, *Signs for the Times*, 14.
8. Kelly, *Pentateuch*, 88.

Brooks explains that typology also allowed for certainty and authority which, in a changing world, was helpful for a Victorian Christian.[9] It allowed the preacher to resolve any apparent contradictions in the text.[10] Fairbairn believed in progressive revelation and was more in tune with the Broad Church idea of progression than Kelly but, nevertheless, typology, even for a conservative evangelical, had an essentially progressive nature as it looked forward to the future prophetically.[11] Thus, through typology, we are able to place Kelly more clearly within his Victorian context, as he was able to show, for example, that Jesus quoted the Psalms and applied them to himself and that the apostle Peter made it clear that the Old Testament prophets were speaking to the church.[12] At the same time Kelly believed he needed to denounce Broad Church views of typology (which he thought relied too much on historical progress) and High Church views of typology (which relied too much on the Levitical offerings being a type of the Eucharist).[13] Nevertheless, typology allowed all three church traditions to cohere on the reading of the sacred text. Typology could be understood as symbolism and so work in a sacramental way for the High Church, a literary way for the Broad Church and a prophetic way for the Evangelical Church. It allowed Kelly to avoid precision about future events, and so not to be caught up in a simplistic millenarianism. Fairbairn showed that all types "are material embodiments of spiritual ideas."[14] As the types by themselves were inadequate to express spiritual aspiration, typology allowed Kelly to express his high Christology, which was almost impossible to articulate in logical language but could be suggested through this means. It also fitted in with the idealism of the contemporary Romantic Movement and contributed to Kelly's mysticism.

Horne was another theologian whom Victorians admired as a typologist and whose work was familiar to the Brethren. According to Horne, it was important that a type always referred to the future, including the future

9. Brooks, *Signs for the Times*, 96.

10. Landow, *Victorian Types*, 47.

11. Ibid., 11.

12. Kelly, *The First Epistle of Peter*, 52. Kelly quoted 1 Peter 1:12, "Unto whom it was revealed, that not unto themselves, but unto us did they minister the things, which are now reported unto you by them that have preached the gospel unto you with the Holy Ghost sent down from heaven; which things the angels desire to look into" (KJV).

13. Landow, *Victorian Types*, 28. Landow uses Keble, *Sermons 2*, 343 to illustrate his point.

14. Fairbairn, *Typology*, 51, 58.

people of the church.[15] Therefore some of these types actually had fulfillment after Christ's death and resurrection. This allowed recent movements like the Brethren to have significance.[16] There was also a sense in which there could be personal fulfillment in the text.[17] Landow has pointed out that Browning and Rossetti could have imaginative outlet to their spiritual longings through poetry.[18] Belonging to a Christian movement which abjured what it would have seen as "worldly," Kelly had no such outlet, but I suggest that this intensified his religious experience, his own enjoyment of writing about the sacred text, his love of poetry in hymnology and his need to see God's people as despised by the world. I also suggest that it intensified his personal experience of the text, making its referents internal rather than external. Horne had pointed out that typology worked differently to allegory.[19] Allegory and parable ran parallel to the true spiritual meaning and did not purport to be historically true. Horne felt that typological interpretation was very different from the interpretation of allegory and he much preferred the term "symbolic interpretation."[20] In using the system of typology to interpret the Bible, Kelly could defend Scriptural inerrancy while indulging in mystic writing. As Landow has shown, for typology to work as mystic idealism the signifier and the signified had to be equally true, and the literal, historical and narrative levels had to remain believable.[21] It followed that spirit and the ideal were more important than the original narrative, thus raising the exegesis onto a mystic level. In the nineteenth century the pressures of biblical criticism generally moved to change typology into allegory and emblem, because the allegory could be distanced from the historical nature of the text and biblical criticism raised doubts about the historical accuracy of the narrative. Thus for the Broad Church it became easier to see Old Testament narrative as a fictional story which was allegorical.[22] Kelly resisted this movement towards doubting the

---

15. Horne, *An Introduction*, vol. 1, 157–58; vol. 2, 528.
16. Landow, *Victorian Types*, 47.
17. Ibid., 50.
18. Ibid., 51.
19. Horne, *An Introduction*, vol. 2, 258.
20. Ibid., 434. Horne meant that interpretation of allegory implies that the original text can only be read as an imaginative allegory, while "symbolic interpretation" implies that within the historic text elements can also be interpreted symbolically.
21. Landow, *Victorian Types*, 52.
22. Ibid., 57.

authenticity of the text and allowed his understanding of typology to nourish his spirituality. Horne explained that a type was like "a rough draught," "a symbol of something future and distant," and this projection into the future was used by Kelly in his observations about prophecy.[23]

In his analysis of mysticism, Katz has shown that typology is a hermeneutical method which is very attractive for mystics because the way that typology works as repetition and a spiral in history demonstrating that "the future will be like the past and that the past prefigures the future."[24] Typology also affirms not only the historic reliability of the Scriptures but also the "transcendental purpose" of historic events.[25] This sense of purpose and significance was very important for Kelly in his exegeses. The way typology enforces the nature of history works against any "merely" spiritualizing interpretations which are evident in the works of a writer such as Origen.[26] It is also interesting that Jewish mystics use typology when they look to the future.[27] Typology, affirms Katz, is "a form of mystical scriptural exegesis."[28] Its teleological purposes were particularly significant for Kelly, and it allowed him to be caught up into the wonder of his relationship with God as a present experience and a future hope.

Kelly frequently used typology in his biblical exegeses, and, while I will be referring to a number of his works in this chapter, I will be making special use of seven articles from *The Bible Treasury* which were published in 1856–57 under the heading "The Types of Scripture," and in which he gave a detailed critique of the second edition of Fairbairn's *The Typology of Scripture*.[29] After examining Kelly's response to Fairbairn, I will explore his typology as revealed through his understanding of Scriptural text and through his wider exegesis. I will also examine the way typology helped him to explore symbolic language within the biblical text, the way he transposed Old Testament incidents and topography into symbols of the

---

23. Horne, *An Introduction*, vol. 2, 529. Horne saw these as being figures from history which prefigured Christ, such as David; details of the law in the Pentateuch which he saw as prefiguring the atonement and work of Christ; and prophetic references which pointed to eschatology, such as Babylon referenced in the prophets and in Revelation.

24. Katz, "Mysticism and the Interpretation of Sacred Scripture," 37.

25. Ibid., 38.

26. Ibid., 39.

27. Ibid.

28. Ibid., 41.

29. Kelly, "The Types of Scripture," i., 103–07; ii., 119–22; iii., 135–38; iv., 151–55; v., 167–70; vi., 183–85; vii., 197–202.

Christian believer's spiritual experience, and how various kinds of biblical imagery became part of his own text and an expression of his own spiritual longings. I will be making particular reference to Kelly's *Lectures on the Revelation*, a work which is relevant to his understanding of typology, and especially prophetic typology and his own use of language. It is interesting that, according to the Preface, these lectures were taken in shorthand and printed in 1858-9 "in a periodical form."[30] Although they were written so early in his career, they were re-edited in 1860-61, 1869 and 1871. In the 1860 edition they were preceded by a critical edition of the Greek text with a close English translation and this translation won critical acclaim from the German higher critic, Heinrich Ewald.[31] In this work Kelly made interesting observations about his understanding of typology. He maintained that we should be careful with types and parables not to "insist on a technical minuteness of application in order to throw overboard the profound lessons of truth they convey to the circumcised ear."[32] In other words, in his use of typology Kelly was more interested in the whole biblical text than in proving a particular point from typology. This attitude gave his work both a breadth of vision—it is outstanding in its grasp of wide biblical references—and the possibility of confining his understanding of typology within his own paradigm. Kelly's work often swung between these two extremes. Kelly also believed that the book of Revelation had a particular link with the Old Testament, which is why a study of these lectures is particularly enlightening as to Kelly's understanding of typology.[33] I will also be referring to a broader range of Kelly's work including his lectures on the Pentateuch, Isaiah, the Song of Solomon and Hebrews.

KELLY'S RESPONSE TO FAIRBAIRN'S WORK ON TYPOLOGY THROUGH HIS BIBLE TREASURY ARTICLES

Kelly wrote a series of articles monthly between December 1856 and June 1857 and studying them provides a foundation for an understanding of his

---

30. Kelly, *Revelation*, preface.

31. Pickering, *Chief Men among the Brethren*, 106.

32. Kelly, *Revelation*, Introduction, xii. In this phrase Kelly employed metonymy (the ear stands for the listening person) and metaphor (the circumcision is the Old Testament picture of the spiritual Jew which comes to mean the converted Christian believer). Kelly's language here is typically elliptic and dense.

33. Ibid., 6-7.

typology. In the first of his articles written in response to Fairbairn's work and entitled "Historical Glance and General Principles," Kelly explained why the subject of typology was special to him as a Bible teacher. He said that with its insight "comes a fresh and super-added light, which attaches the affections and the mind with immensely increased tenacity to the Word of God."[34] Kelly connected typology with the affections and believed that it also drew the mind of the believer to be pre-occupied with the Bible. In this way typology enhanced the spiritual reading of the text. He drew a parallel with the Gospel story of the feeding of the five thousand, noting that there would always be an abundance in even "the left-overs" through reading the text in this way. Thus Kelly gave hope to those who would persevere with the study of typology and also used "a miraculous story" to take the idea of study beyond exegesis and to give typology a moral quality, which we might see as being more akin to the place of allegory for Medieval Christian writers.[35] In accusing the early Church Fathers of not being concerned enough with typology, Kelly was assigning himself a role in the dissemination of this theological understanding.[36]

Kelly's main objections to Fairbairn's interpretation of typology were that it was too "reformed" in its basis and too interested in seeing obedience to the law as the significant way of living the Christian life. However, Kelly agreed with Fairbairn's positive analysis of Salomo Cocceius (1603–1669), Hermann Witsius (1636–1708), Cotton Mather (1663–1728) and Benjamin Keach (1640–1704) and he also agreed that Augustine had "the greatest light of patristic antiquity."[37] Kelly had some sympathy with Fairbairn's condemnation of anyone who introduced what he considered to be "the most frivolous conceits" when it came to typology.[38] Kelly complained that the chief fault of most typologists was not making Christ "the centre (*sic*) of the Bible," in other words not seeing all the parts of the Old Testament narrative as ultimately pointing to the Christ figure.[39] Kelly agreed with

---

34. Kelly, "The Types of Scripture no. 1," 103.

35. The medieval mystics were particularly keen on taking a biblical story such as the encounter of Mary and Martha in their home and using it to elaborate on their own theology concerned with the superiority of the monastic orders to lay service in the church.

36. Kelly, "The Types of Scripture no. 1": 103.

37. Salomo Glassius—German theologian and biblical critic; Johannes Cocceius—Dutch theologian; Hermann Witsius—Dutch theologian; Cotton Mather—American Puritan leader; Benjamin Keach—Particular Baptist preacher in London.

38. Fairbairn, *The Typology of Scripture*, vol. 1, 30.

39. Kelly, "The Types of Scripture, no. 1," 103.

Fairbairn about distinguishing between what was alleged to be a type (the way Bible teachers might choose to use biblical figures as types without their being any clear textual justification for that use) and what was designed to be a type (the way the New Testament writers deliberately used Old Testament figures as types). However Kelly went further than Fairbairn's more cautious approach to typology because he thought that if the reader demanded too much of a chapter-and-verse proof in the New Testament, it had the effect of unhelpfully limiting the reading of the biblical text. Kelly wanted to go beyond the chapter–and–verse analysis of the text. He accused other denominations of demonstrating "dullness of hearing" as mentioned in Hebrews chapter 5.[40] Kelly also argued with Fairbairn about the practical application of the types.[41] One distinguishing feature of Kelly's articles is that he gave a very detailed analysis of Fairbairn's work, showing his agreements and disagreements. For example, he acknowledged what he considered to be Fairbairn's proper interpretation of the cherubim in the tabernacle, agreed with the connection he made between the Old Testament passage and the energy and judgment in Revelation chapter 15, but disputed Fairbairn's "image of mercy and hope" for the future and rejected the use of "us" in Fairbairn's translation of Revelation 5:9.[42]

Kelly could be extremely critical, at one point denouncing Fairbairn's scheme as "unreasonable and open to objection," but he was pleased whenever Fairbairn criticized German higher criticism.[43] Kelly always quoted at length what he agreed or disagreed with, and felt that Fairbairn's analysis had been far too superficial.[44] Generally, Kelly saw Fairbairn's *Synopsis* as "excellent and instructive," but his typology as having "errors and defects."[45] He also used his articles to comment on Horne's typology, and, while generally agreeing with his stance, he accused Horne of giving a narrow and arbitrary reading. He explained that New Testament understanding of types would give us "samples, some plain, and others more obscure."[46] He

---

40. Ibid., 105. Heb 5:11: "Of whom we have many things to say, and hard to be uttered, seeing ye are dull of hearing" (KJV).

41. Ibid., 107.

42. Kelly, "The Types of Scripture no. ii," 121. Kelly refers to Fairbairn, *Synopsis*, 73 and *The Typology of Scripture*, 236.

43. Ibid., 12.

44. Kelly, "The Types of Scripture, no. iii," 135.

45. Kelly, "The Types of Scripture no. vii," 199.

46. Kelly, "The Types of Scripture, i," 104.

encouraged his readers to be stimulated by the Holy Spirit to see more in Scripture for themselves. However this could lead to an idiosyncratic reading of the Scriptures which could be highly idealistic in its Christology.

While Kelly agreed with Fairbairn that we should exercise caution in overstepping the limitations of Scripture, he used his articles to explain the inferred sanction of Scripture for typology, and this allowed him to claim a certain authority in interpretation. Kelly explained that with regard to typology, Scripture was best read by one who showed "subjection to the Spirit of God." Clearly Kelly was claiming that sort of spiritual authority for himself and for the Brethren movement. When he emphasized "*And* the children of God are not equally spiritual" it was clear that the different levels of understanding amongst Christians were important to him. He went on to explain that all Christians do not have the "single eye" i.e. the spiritual devotion necessary for understanding.[47] For example, Kelly claimed to be better taught than Herbert Marsh (1757–1839), Bishop of Llandaff and Bishop of Peterborough, and promoter of higher criticism in the Church of England. In his interpretation of the extension of Old Testament types, Kelly said that although it was not obvious from Genesis itself that Cain and Abel would work as a type as well as Adam and Eve, by looking at Jude chapter 2 and Hebrews 12:24 he could justify using Cain and Abel in typology. As Cain and Abel represented acceptable and non-acceptable worship somewhat cryptically in the Old Testament story, and worship was very important to the Brethren, it is significant that Kelly took this as a type which was relevant to his contemporaries. He went on to argue that if the deluge was accepted as a type of God's judgment, as indicated in 1 Peter chapter 3, then other details of Noah's story could also be used as types. Using this argument of extended typology, he maintained that all the surrounding circumstances of Melchizedek's story must be important. Therefore the full title of God as given in Genesis must be relevant to the Christian even though only one, "the most High God," was actually quoted in Hebrews chapter 7. It is almost as if Kelly's typology was extending beyond what was taught in the New Testament, thus making space for a much greater mystical interpretation of the text.

Kelly made an important connection between historical fact (which he affirmed) and teaching, which, as in the case of other Brethren writers, operated on an idealistic and authoritative level. For example, in an article published 1 December 1856 he explained that the story of Meribah

47. Ibid.

in Numbers chapter 30 was not "mere historic fact."[48] He wrote about typology as a fertile field to be ploughed, and claimed that the sparseness of New Testament references to the Old Testament did not invalidate the finding of other lessons and analogies. This self-appointed permission to extend the use of analogy in the text placed high value on his own spiritual judgment. Kelly was arguing against Fairbairn's more limited understanding of typology and he expressed his intention of writing more fully on the subject in *The Bible Treasury*.[49] However, rather than simply producing another series with an explicit title, he gave biblical exegesis which was permeated with typological interpretation. Kelly was more satisfied with these interpretations than with those of Fairbairn's.[50] Nonetheless he often showed approval of some of the minutiae of Fairbairn's teaching. For example, he agreed that the choice of seventy palm trees in Exodus was linked to the choice by Jesus of seventy disciples in the Gospels.[51] Kelly showed here that the biblical symbolic number system was part of his literary interpretation.

Therefore we see that Kelly's typological interpretation revealed his spirituality. Kelly made it clear that his theology affected his typology and vice versa. He applauded Fairbairn on his basic evangelical doctrines, about which they were in agreement. When Kelly wrote his article about Leviticus, he was able to agree with Fairbairn about the offerings being parallel with Christ's sufferings.[52] However he disputed Fairbairn's interpretation of the necessity of law under grace. According to Fairbairn, the innermost shrine of the tabernacle demonstrated the types of Christ but the apartment outside the veil showed what the Christian should do in his life. Kelly rejoined that Fairbairn's analysis "limited Christ's place."[53] There is also in Kelly's teaching a special transposition of the means of spiritual growth from the law and self-effort to grace. He believed that anything which would damn by the law became possible under grace because God's standards of perfection had been met by the grace of Christ. He gave Urim and Thummim as

---

48. Kelly, "The Types of Scripture, no. 1" 105.
49. Kelly, "The Types of Scripture, no. iii," 137.
50. Kelly, "The Types of Scripture no. iv," 152.
51. Ibid., 153.
52. Kelly, "The Types of Scripture no. vii," 199.
53. Kelly, "The Types of Scripture no. v," 169. Kelly felt that all the teaching about the Tabernacle should rightly refer to Christ and that, if one part of it suggested the way in which the believer should regulate his behavior, then that detracted from the high Christology which was so important to him.

an example of instruction which under the law was a cause of ruin and but then "becomes by His grace the occasion and means of instruction."⁵⁴

KELLY'S MYSTIC USE OF THE OLD TESTAMENT TYPOLOGY, AND PARTICULARLY THAT OF THE PENTATEUCH, IN HIS NEW TESTAMENT TEACHING

In examining the significance of the Pentateuch for Kelly's typology, I want to concentrate on the story of the marriage of Isaac in Genesis chapter 24. As an old man, Abraham wanted to make sure that his son Isaac married someone from his own family rather than from Canaan where he was living. He sent his servant on a journey to carry out this task. The servant proceeded by first praying and asking God to show him the right girl, and then that she would be the only girl at the well who not only agreed to his request for water but offered in addition to water his camels. In this way Rebekah was chosen and returned with the servant to marry Isaac, bringing many gifts from her family. The narrative makes it clear that Sarah, Isaac's mother, had died just before this event, and that, despite having no part in the choice of bride, Isaac loved Rebekah.

When considering Kelly's typological understanding of this story, we should do so against the background of his contemporaries. Fairbairn too taught that typology must raise the reader's appreciation of the Old Testament.⁵⁵ Landow has explained that for the Victorians typology helped to give a "completely ordered world" and that this was partly what literalists craved.⁵⁶ Shlomo Biderman believes that it is part of the mystic tradition to "preserve and strengthen the authority of Scripture," and Kelly saw this as his calling in the world of nineteenth-century theology.⁵⁷ However, he went further than other Victorian typologists in his appreciation of the significance of the Old Testament. For him, not only did the Old Testament clarify the New but also the New Testament clarified the Old. It was as if they were being written at the same time and for the same purpose. For example Kelly made an explicit link between the death of Sarah in Genesis chapter 23 and the Jewish rejection of the Christian message delivered by Peter in Acts chapter 3. By reading Acts in this way, Kelly claimed that a

54. Kelly, "The Types of Scripture no. vi," 184.
55. Ibid., 177.
56. Landow, *Victorian Types*, 40.
57. Biderman, "Mystical Identity and Scriptural Justification," 79.

Christian could understand the significance of Sarah's death better: "the true key is placed in our hands."[58] Here Kelly's understanding can be seen as mystic because he communicated a sense of God being in control of the whole reading of history. Although he claimed that the key was in the text itself, he believed that an accurate interpretation, demonstrating spiritual understanding, such as his own, was essential. Again he explained that the New interpreted the Old—"It is happy when the truth of Christ illuminates consecutive chapters of the Old Testament."[59]

Understanding Kelly's appreciation of Genesis as a key text helps us to understand his mysticism better. Kelly used the story of Isaac and Rebekah to teach some important spiritual truths, even though it is not obvious to the modern reader that the narrative itself authorizes such typological treatment. When writing about the servant's prayer for the choice of a wife for Isaac in Genesis chapter 24, Kelly commented, "There is more about prayer in this chapter than in any other in Genesis." He also went on to explain that there was much about worshipping too, and about what the Church should be like.[60] According to him, the prayer also explained much about the relationship between the Trinity—"God has let our hearts into His own secret in what He is doing for Christ."[61]

Interpreting Genesis in this way was foundational for Kelly's mystic theology. Particular characters in Genesis were used by Kelly as part of his theological paradigm. For example, Isaac, not normally seen as one of the most outstanding characters in the book of Genesis, had special significance for Kelly. He thought that God had revealed Himself in a special way to Isaac, not as El-Shaddai (the Almighty), nor as Elohim (suggesting abstract majesty), but as Jehovah (which implied a special relationship), and in a way which was different to His relationship with Abraham or Jacob.[62] The reason for Kelly choosing Isaac as a significant character was because Isaac was the Bridegroom, who in New Testament terms symbolized Christ in heaven. Kelly interpreted what he considered to be a very precise use of language in this section of Genesis in order to validate his point. Whereas in the promise of Abraham, the patriarch was told that his descendants would be as many as the stars in heaven and grains of sand, in the Isaac

---

58. Kelly, *Pentateuch*, 83.
59. Ibid., 86.
60. Ibid., 88.
61. Ibid.
62. Ibid., 92–93.

narrative only the former comparison is made because Isaac's future was interpreted as being heavenly. I have already shown in chapter 6 that the Ascension of Christ dominated Kelly's theology; his reading of Genesis was through the lens of this doctrine. Although Kelly was a dispensationalist, and we will see later in this chapter how his eschatology affected his typology, and acknowledged that Abraham represented an earthly as well as a heavenly heritage for the Jews, he thought that Isaac was more important because he represented the heavenly Bridegroom.[63] Sarah too was an important symbol, showing "the passing away of all covenant dealings," which for Kelly meant the end of Judaism.[64] This interpretation justified for Kelly the Brethren accusation that the Church of England in particular demonstrated legalistic tendencies which were incompatible with the true freedom understood by the Brethren. Thus we have two characters, whose historicity Kelly would have loudly defended against Broad Church doubts, being used as symbols and representing New Testament ideas. In assigning these personages a mystic significance Kelly was able to make them part of his theological paradigm.

Two other Old Testament characters whom Kelly used typologically were Noah and Enoch. The distinction which he made between them reveals the high value he placed on the contemplative gifts. If Noah represented human governance, then Enoch represented being caught up with Christ in mystic worship, as the church should be.[65] Kelly believed that if it was impossible for us to see Noah as the one who represents the establishment of justice in the millennium, then it would be impossible for us to appreciate the role of Enoch.[66] Further, Kelly approval of Fairbairn's analysis of Shem, Ham and Japheth, probably fed Victorian understanding of different racial groups. However, when it came to understanding Abraham, the father of faith, Kelly said of Fairbairn, "his method and applications are meager and defective."[67] This was because Kelly did not consider Fairbairn to have a wide enough understanding of the Abrahamic covenant, which had a Jewish as well as a Christian character. Moses was also an important character in typology because he did not stay in Egypt in a position of worldly influence, but chose to identify fully with the despised people

63. Ibid., 93.
64. Ibid., 87.
65. Kelly, "The Types of Scripture no. iii," 135.
66. Ibid.
67. Ibid., 136.

of God.[68] The reader might also be reminded that Moses was rejected by his own people just as Christ was rejected by the Jews. Kelly sometimes criticized Fairbairn for extending typology unnecessarily, but it is clear that he used exactly whatever fitted in with his own scheme. For example, Kelly criticized Fairbairn for emphasizing the hardening of Pharaoh's heart, but then he chose to link Pharaoh with "professing Christendom."[69] Kelly also believed that Fairbairn had not sufficiently understood that the plagues as signs were primarily for Israel rather than for the sake of the Egyptians.[70] Just as the despised people of Israel were at the heart of the Old Testament narrative, the despised people of the Brethren movement were loved by God and in fellowship with Kelly.

Kelly considered that there was much more work to be done on the New Testament in the light of the Old and he wanted to apply himself to this.[71] Such an all-pervading typology permitted a much freer interpretation of the biblical text than a literalist might have accepted and also allowed for a mystic intensification of the text, the possibility of using it as a deeper means of worship, and the emulation of a higher and deeper Christology. Kelly felt able to do this because of the way he interpreted the words of John in 1 John—"the anointing you have received of Him abideth in you and ye need not that any man teach you."[72] As the New Testament specifically allowed for the capacity of teachers to use the text aright, Kelly was able to fill this role. In 1 Corinthians 10:1 the reader is reminded that "all our fathers were under the cloud," but in verse 6 Paul explains that these people are examples or types, figures of us; so Kelly, with what he saw as New Testament permission, expanded on the idea of examples being employed as types.[73] Kelly explained that there might not be a "catalogue raisonnée" of Old Testament figures, but that they were "profusely used."[74] Paul might use Deuteronomy 25:4 in 1 Corinthians 9:9 but the chapter of Deuteronomy could be used in numerous ways and could be made relevant to his contemporaries.[75] This way of reading of the text approaches a fore-

---

68. Kelly, "The Types of Scripture no. iv," 151.
69. Ibid., 152.
70. Ibid.
71. Kelly, "The Types of Scripture no. i," 104.
72. 1 John 2:27 (KJV).
73. 1 Cor 10:1 and 6 (KJV).
74. Kelly, "The Types of Scripture no. i," 104.
75. "Thou shalt not muzzle the ox when he treadeth out the corn." Deut 25:4 (KJV).

grounding of the text in such a way as to create a new text in its own right. The provision for the Levites explained in Numbers chapter 18 was alluded to in 1 Corinthians 9:13 but, according to Kelly, much more could be taken from the same Old Testament chapter to be relevant to the Christian's walk with God. Just as the mercy seat, the candlestick and the altar were taken as typological in Romans chapter 3, Revelation chapter 1 and Hebrews chapter 13, many other details of the Tabernacle could be used to instruct the Christian. There may have been reasons why the Apostle Paul did not draw attention to them at the time but as a Bible teacher Kelly was at full liberty to do that in his teaching.[76]

It seems that his preoccupation with typology became an additional way for Kelly to express what he considered to be a deeper spirituality. Perhaps his was a more intellectually acute way—and one that he would have considered less superficial than approaches associated with charismatic signs as preached by Irving and incipient Pentecostalism, with the holiness movement as encouraged by the Salvation Army and the Keswick Convention, or with moral perfection as taught by the Wesleyans. The whole Levitical system (seen as the apex of typology) revealed more and more to those who "with all ever-increasing fullness as the eye becomes more single to Christ and the ear more attuned by the Spirit to his voice."[77] If Kelly was accusing Fairbairn of squeezing "the types of Scripture into a human system," he himself was making them part of his own mystic structure. Kelly linked this system to the teaching of Ephesians chapter 1—"a new and more glorious era"—so that the future of the church would clearly be linked with the past of the Old Testament, and Ephesians, the embodiment of mystic teaching, would be linked conclusively with the Torah.[78]

KELLY'S UNDERSTANDING OF BIBLICAL IMAGERY

Bridal imagery in Kelly's writing can be placed in two categories—his work on the Pentateuch, particularly connected with the story of Isaac and Rebekah, and his writing on the Song of Solomon. Both were connected with typology; both point out the difference between the place of the church and of Israel and the need to distinguish between the two.

---

76. Kelly, "The Types of Scripture no. i," 106.
77. Ibid.
78. Ibid.

Kelly saw Isaac as the type of Christ and Rebekah as the type of the church, Christ's bride. In his work on the Pentateuch, Kelly wrote about both.[79] Isaac was a type of Christ, because he was the heir who had been almost sacrificed but then rose up from the altar, and also the anti-type of the Lamb that God would provide for a burnt offering—a reference to the Messiah as the Lamb of God.[80] Even within this teaching Kelly pointed out the difference between the Church and Israel, examining God's title given in this story, "the God of heaven and earth." Within the story of the call of Rebekah Kelly discerned the call of the church and connected it with the mystery of the Church in Ephesians chapter 3. He claimed that it was necessary to understand this story in the Pentateuch in order to grasp full biblical teaching about the Church. Isaac had to stay in Canaan, which represented Christ as the head of the Church staying in the heavenly places. The Church was thus called to stay with the ascended Christ and to have the mind of heaven on earth.[81] The bride, as the Church, was being called from the world (Mesopotamia) to join Isaac in the Promised Land (Canaan).[82] As part of Kelly's typology, geographical places had symbolic meaning.

The story of Isaac was extended further through Kelly's typology. Links were made with Hebrews chapter 11 and Galatians chapter 3.[83] As the "revealer" of the mystery of the Church, Paul was called upon to prepare the bride of Christ.[84] The Canaanites typified the world rulers described in Ephesians chapter 6 but Canaan itself typified heaven. While the Bride was being called, the Son was in heaven, just as Isaac was in Canaan while his bride was being found.[85] Isaac's wife, Rebekah, knew obedience and intimate union with her husband, thus using traditional mystic imagery to suggest a love relationship with Christ. This intimate affection was the result of an appropriation of the relationship.[86] As was common in Kelly's typology, every part of the story had its place. Thus the servant who was commissioned to find a wife for Isaac used a prayer which anticipated

---

79. Kelly, *Pentateuch*, 85.
80. Kelly, "The Bride Called for Isaac (Gen. xxiv. 1–9)," 321.
81. Ibid., 322.
82. Ibid., 323.
83. Kelly, "The Call of the Bride," 360.
84. Ibid., 361.
85. Ibid., 362.
86. Ibid., 362–63.

praying in the name of Christ.[87] As often in Kelly's teaching, there was a link with the second coming of Christ. As Isaac came to meet his new bride, so Christ would come to meet the Church in "the rapture."[88]

The nature of love was explored in an interesting way in Kelly's study of the Song of Solomon. Again the emphasis was on present affection, so that "His love is so completely ours that even when we go to heaven it is not that He will love us better, but that we shall enjoy it perfectly."[89] Kelly went back to the Jewish interpretation of the Song of Solomon and saw it as an expression of God's love for the Jews, but he also added the dimension of believing that such a love would be shown again in the Millennium when the Jews would recognize Christ as their Messiah.[90] Kelly also linked the language of this book to the language of Matthew's Gospel, because the apostle alluded to "the bridal relation as the sign or symbol of Christ's special love to His people."[91] Therefore the Song of Solomon became also a book about prophecy and could be linked to Revelation chapter 14. For example, the title of the book referred to the lover who was the King, a biblical character who would be recognized by the Jewish people, not by the Church.[92] Despite this, along with traditional mystics, Kelly believed that the Christian was entitled "to take all the love of it" for himself.[93] In his translation, Kelly replaced the symbol of the rose, so beloved by mystic writers, with the narcissus.[94] He also rejected the Roman Catholic interpretation of seeing the mother and bride as one, and of seeing the Virgin Mary in this.[95] Interestingly, Kelly felt that the language of the Song of Solomon was not intimate enough to describe the love relationship between Christ and the Church. He pointed out that the language used was that of aspiration in love rather than total unity between bride and bridegroom. Not only did this interpretation preserve the purity of the poem but it showed that he thought the language of union was demonstrated more exactly through

---

87. Ibid., 364.
88. Ibid., 365.
89. Kelly, *Two Lectures on the Song of Solomon*, 18. This book was based on sermons delivered in Blackheath, 1877.
90. Ibid., 20, 23.
91. Ibid., 3.
92. Ibid., 28, 36.
93. Ibid., 55.
94. Ibid., 39.
95. Ibid., 49.

baptism and oneness in worship and through the mystic language of John's Gospel and the Epistles.[96]

In accordance with Katz's description of mystic writers, symbolism acted for Kelly as "a key mystical hermeneutic, reinforcing the authority of Scripture."[97] He focused on key prophetic imagery and used it in his writing. He clearly distinguished between the earthly and heavenly Jerusalem and then immediately switched imagery to talk about the heavenly Jerusalem being the bride of the Lamb.[98] He had a mystic interpretation of the New Jerusalem coming down from heaven.[99] The imagery of divorce and marriage was important to him.[100] As his exegesis of Revelation progressed he distinguished more clearly between the historical Zion as the city of Jerusalem and the spiritual Zion, which he also identified as the Bride of Christ. He spoke of Zion as a symbol but also as a germ or a type—"the Spirit of Christ ever leading on the hearts of the saints to anticipate the full result which the early type promised as it were in the germ."[101] He even distinguished between the references to Zion in Hebrews 12:1 (where he saw it as objective place) and in the Apocalypse (where he saw it as subjective appreciation).[102] As the bride of Christ, Zion was seen by Kelly as being on display to the nations in the millennium, integrating the imagery further.[103]

The combination of bridal imagery and the place of the heavenly Jerusalem placed Kelly within the mystic tradition. Bridal imagery helped Kelly express the desire for mystic intimacy and purity. He called the Church, Christ's "spouse," and the idea of purity arose from the fact that the bride was kept exclusively for the bridegroom without being contaminated by the world.[104] By using the word "affianced," Kelly stressed the affection which the bride should feel for the bridegroom, and encouraged his readers to aspire to this devotion—"Surely this should be our first and last and constant and dearest thought."[105] There was also the sense that the bride

---

96. Ibid., 17.
97. Katz, "The Conservative Character of Mystic Experience," 30.
98. Kelly, *Isaiah*, 34.
99. Ibid., 109.
100. Ibid., 99.
101. Kelly, *Revelation*, 312.
102. Ibid., 397.
103. Ibid., 462.
104. Ibid., 34.
105. Ibid.

was the reward of the redemption which Christ had effected, and this idea combined the intimacy of love and the sense of mysticism—"the great mystery brought out there is the nearness, the love, the intimacy of bridal relationship between Christ and the church."[106] Purity related to the idea that although the Church was presently only affianced, the intimacy of love could be experienced as deeply in the present as when the consummation would eventually take place.[107] Similarly to many mystic writers, Kelly felt the spiritual union with Christ in his present earthly experience to be as great as any physical union, "making them as truly one with Him now as every they will be." Christ was frequently referred to as "the bridegroom" not only for the present day Church but also for the writer of Revelation—"John too looks at Christ as the Bridegroom, at what he is for the heart."[108] Kelly referred to the Gospel parable of the unexpectedness of the bridegroom's coming, to encourage his readers to aspire to the spiritual marriage relationship, and he used deliberately archaic language to do so—"Behold the Bridegroom cometh ; go ye out to meet him."[109]

Light was another key image for Kelly. He associated a growing understanding of future blessedness with the picture of daylight dawning and the day star arising.[110] He was so immersed in the sacred text that he easily transferred biblical imagery to his own writing. Nowhere is this more apparent than in his writing about the verse in Revelation, "I am the bright and morning star." Kelly wrote in highly emotive, aspirational language, extending the imagery within his discourse—"Blessed star of morning before the day comes! We watch not for the day, but for *Him* during the night, and He will give us the morning star, the harbinger of the dawn." He used this imagery to draw his readers into the same intimate spiritual experience as he had—"A blessed place it is—the place of our love and hope: it will never be disappointed of its joy, and the Lord Jesus Christ will surely come, as the bright and morning star to us." It is notable that he used deliberately archaic language—"We may have to tarry somewhat"—and the interdependence of his own phraseology and resonance of biblical phrases drawn from other biblical texts—"but for those who wait for Him and yearn to see Him, the hope might seem to be long deferred. Instead of growing weary and sick,

106. Ibid., 209.
107. Ibid., 394.
108. Ibid., 12.
109. Ibid., 78.
110. Ibid., 45.

may our hearts on the contrary, be filled with the joy and constancy of assurance that the Lord is coming soon." There were frequent exclamations, and a rhythm to the prose; the whole passage ended in a cyclical fashion with the image repeated in the third person—"He is the bright and morning star."[111]

The wilderness became a dominant symbol for Kelly, and the story of the children of Israel passing through the wilderness on the way to the Promised Land became part of his typology. As he wrote, in his exegesis of 1 Peter, "the apostle contemplates the wilderness and our journeying through it," he moved from the Old Testament story to the experience of the Christian within one sentence.[112] He reminded his readers that Moses and Israel had started their journey "with a song of exultation" but had not continued in the same spirit, and he considered that Christians should learn from their mistake.[113] According to Kelly it was always a mistake to forget that we journey through a wilderness world and that it is pre-eminently the scene of temptation.[114] On the one hand, believers needed to be "vigilant and self-judging"; on the other, they should have confidence in God's love for them and should experience joy.[115] The wilderness also came to be a symbol of the place where the Christian was brought in solitude by the Holy Spirit to spend time contemplating Christ and where it was possible to understand real spiritual truth.[116] This has been a common mystic understanding throughout the ages either symbolically or, in the case of the desert fathers, in physical reality. The wilderness was also a clear contrast with the world to come and the symbolism changed at this point, becoming that of "an abiding city, the coming one."[117] The symbol of Sinai, representing the wilderness and the law, was exchanged for Zion. "Zion appears after the utter breakdown of the kingdom under Saul, man's choice."[118] Thus the history of the early nation of Israel was always read by Kelly through the lens of the Christian covenant.

---

111. Kelly, *Revelation*, 498. "Hope deferred, weary and sick" reflects language used in Prov 13:12 (KJV): "hope deferred maketh the heart sick."

112. Kelly, *1 Peter*, 32.

113. Ibid.

114. Ibid., 67, 32–33.

115. Ibid., 72, 31.

116. Kelly, *Revelation*, 359.

117. Kelly, *1 Peter*, 82.

118. Ibid., 133.

Old Testament symbolism was used by Kelly to teach about the mixture of spiritual warfare and rest in the life of the believer. Manna in the wilderness was seen as God's provision before the coming of the law and in the same way Christians could now feed on God's provision.[119] The Sabbath was an extension of this idea, because on the seventh day there was rest— "Christ, the true manna from heaven, who gives eternal life and brings us into *rest*."[120] Kelly accused Fairbairn of being weak in his understanding of this point, and therefore of not understanding the position of rest for the Brethren, but also of showing little understanding of spiritual warfare when it came to writing about the war with Amalek.[121] Reliance on the effectiveness of prayer was important for Kelly because the Brethren must learn "that all their success depends on the hands held up for them above." Thus Moses again became an important type for the Brethren and this was another picture of Christ's role in the Ascension. It was also essential to understand that the Christian could not enter his "full heavenly portion of the church without conflict with the enemy and that is the reason why so many people do not enjoy it."[122] Kelly was able to use typology skillfully to make his spiritual points because of his enormous range of biblical references in his commentary on one key text. Thus his teaching on spiritual warfare was drawn from Revelation 12:7, but within the two pages of his exegesis on this subject he referred to 1 Kings chapter 22, Zechariah chapter 3, Ephesians 6:12, Joshua's wars, Moses' death and Hebrews chapter 9.[123]

Kelly critiqued Fairbairn's second chapter about the law and its six sections in order to provide his own distinctive teaching about the Christian life.[124] He had praise for Fairbairn: "That which has given us most pleasure is the frank acknowledgement in the last section that Christian liberty involves deliverance from the law, not as to justification only, but as to walk and conduct."[125] However in his article about the Tabernacle, he accused him of a great deal of unspiritual discussion about why Moses was instructed in the wisdom of the Egyptians. This touched on an important theme for Kelly—the separation of the Christian from the world—and

119. Kelly, "The Types of Scripture no. iv," 154.
120. Ibid.
121. Ibid.
122. Kelly, *Revelation*, 260.
123. Ibid., 260–61.
124. Fairbairn, *Typology*, 86–194.
125. Kelly, "The Types of Scripture no. iv," 154.

he was critical of Fairbairn's understanding of the Old Testament story. Fairbairn's interpretation of Moses as a leader-in-training who benefited from his secular education in Egypt was clearly not in line with Kelly's own understanding of narrative structure or theological schema. Kelly accused Fairbairn of giving in to "a rationalistic dream."[126] More important, according to Kelly, were the lessons Moses learnt in a solitary place with the flocks of Jethro.[127] Thus we see that Old Testament typology was used by Kelly to draw out the importance of the lonely Christian pathway rather than the benefits of secular, even theological education.

PROPHETIC LANGUAGE WITHIN TYPOLOGY

Somewhat ironically, considering the scope of his own paradigm, Kelly accused Fairbairn of trying to "squeeze the types of Scripture into a human system"; this Kelly saw as being too sympathetic to Reformed Protestant theology, not sufficiently in tune with mystic worship and not clearly pre-millenarian.[128] Kelly felt that Fairbairn's exploration of types and of prophecy was inadequate. In his own biblical exegeses, Kelly's idealism and mystic vision were inspired by his understanding of millenarianism and dispensationalism. Kelly accused Fairbairn of being too influenced by German critics and of having "spiritualizing tendencies, which efface the place of Israel in the future."[129] By this Kelly meant that he disagreed with Fairbairn's paradigm of prophetic typology and believed instead that interpretation of typology should always take into consideration that Israel was to be blessed as a country in the future millennium. He accused Fairbairn of being too absorbed, in his reading of Scripture, in the state of grace now, and of ignoring the difference between dispensations.[130] Although Kelly acknowledged much which was good and valuable in Fairbairn's work, he held that its main fault derived from its author not being a millenarian and not sufficiently proving his eschatological position.[131]

    126. Kelly, "The Types of Scripture no. v," 167.
    127. Ibid.
    128. Kelly, "The Types of Scripture no. i," 106.
    129. Ibid.
    130. Ibid.
    131. Ibid., 106,107. Kelly refers to Fairbairn's lack of understanding that Ephesians often refers to the blessings to come in the future millennium rather than in the present experience of the Christian. Cf. Fairbairn, *Typology*, vol. 1, 61.

As I showed in chapter 6, mysticism often has a sense of secret and eclectic spiritual understanding enjoyed by a few believers but denied to the majority. Typology worked as a secret code for Kelly, allowing him to appreciate the special position of a Christian.[132] It also allowed him to have a mystic appreciation of Christ in the present time, when Christ's authority was not acknowledged by worldly society, and a present understanding of what would only be revealed to the whole world at some time in the future. The Church must know the kingdom in mystery not in manifestation.[133] Thus Kelly's mystical understanding in the present would eventually become a real understanding for everyone else. He had been given a secret understanding of God's purposes. That was why beholding the glory of Christ "now" was a special privilege—as was the inward, eclectic and typological understanding of Scripture. Therefore typology in its prophetic interpretation was far more significant for Kelly than what he regarded as the limited chiliastic understanding of Origen, Jerome and Augustine.[134]

Kelly also saw prophecy as a variety of typology and this is shown quite clearly in his interpretation of Isaiah chapter 53, where the "servant figure" related not only to Israel but also to the coming figure of the Messiah.[135] Kelly clearly differentiated between verses used for one or the other. Thus for example he explained why Matthew chapter 8 took verses 5, 6 and 8 of Isaiah chapter 53, rather than verse 4, to postulate the doctrine of the Atonement. For Kelly, typology was a key way to understand the work of the Messiah as foretold in the Old Testament. Kelly saw the explanation of typology being shown in Scripture itself—"we have to bear in mind that divine interpretation may and does frequently give more than the statement under explanation."[136] Prophecies were important because, like typology, they spoke about present evil but projected it towards the future as well.[137] Interestingly, Kelly saw the Song of Solomon as a prophetic book, although he acknowledged that the Jews saw it as an historical allegory, a picture of Israel being taken out of Egypt.[138] According to Kelly, prophecy was always about departure from the truth, and the Old Testament stories

132. Kelly, *Isaiah*, 41.
133. Ibid., 109.
134. Ibid., 44.
135. Ibid., 60.
136. Ibid., 69.
137. Ibid., 85–86.
138. Kelly, *Song of Solomon*, 14.

about human failure, when interpreted typologically, were also about sin in the future. For example, Achan's sin represented the sin of the people of Israel and also of all who turned against God. Therefore Kelly was able to justify using this typology to talk about the apostasy of the church and the failures of the future before the Messiah came again.[139] According to Kelly, Fairbairn did not sufficiently understand prophecy; Fairbairn's use of the title "The dispensation of primeval and patriarchal times" for his second volume was, for Kelly, inaccurate.[140] In contrast, Kelly gave his own article a more general title—"Primeval Times"—because he believed that the full biblical dispensationalist "system" did not start until after the deluge and therefore, "Dr. Fairbairn gropes in the dark."[141] Fairbairn also limited his references to dispensations to three particular eras—The Fall, the Passover and Christ—thus revealing inadequate understanding of the subject as far as Kelly was concerned.[142]

Israel itself was a significant symbol for Kelly. One of Fairbairn's most important mistakes according to Kelly was the lack of expectation of Israel returning to the land. Kelly accused Fairbairn of "resuming the assault upon the proper hope of Israel, or, as it is there styled, "the church.""[143] This was a very important part of Kelly's mysticism because he claimed that there was a particular attraction of his affections to Israel and that the Christian should love to have an understanding of Israel. "Faith attaches itself to God, *and appreciates and would have part in, the bond that exists between God and His people.*"[144] This affection allowed for attachment to the Old Testament narrative and the perspective of Moses as "the type of Jesus as the deliverer of Israel."[145] This then led to a deep attachment to the books of Moses. In contrast, Fairbairn's exegesis of Exodus chapter 18 was inadequate because it was really about the millennial kingdom and glory. Jethro and Zipporah were types of the Gentiles coming into the blessing.[146]

Kelly's use of symbolism endorses what Katz has observed about mystic writers. He maintained that for them allegory and symbolism were not

139. Kelly, *Isaiah*, 85–86.
140. Fairbairn, *Typology*, 191.
141. Kelly, "The Types of Scripture no. ii," 119.
142. Fairbairn, *Typology*, 192.
143. Kelly, "The Types of Scripture no. iv," 151.
144. Ibid. (Kelly's italics).
145. Ibid., 152.
146. Ibid., 154.

simply interchangeable.[147] He believed that Christian mystic writers were often concerned with allegorical interpretation while Jewish mystics were more occupied with symbol.[148] Such an identity again gives Kelly a particular link with Jewish thinking. Symbolism was important for mystics and Kelly epitomizes this characteristic. Katz has explained the significance of symbolism as being "a fundamental channel of divine teaching through which humankind learns, glimpses, the irreducible Beyond."[149] Kelly in his exegeses not only explored the meaning of biblical symbolism but transferred its inherent power to his own exhortatory writing.

CONCLUSION: THE PURPOSE OF KELLY'S TYPOLOGY

Kelly's typology was always consistent with the theology which undergirded his mysticism—Trinitarian, highly intense and idealistic, and revealing a high Christology. Kelly accused Fairbairn of being more interested in human salvation than in the place of Christ Himself, and of limiting Christ's place in the Holy of Holies and in God's plan of salvation.[150] Typology was particularly useful to Kelly in his high Christology because it was necessarily aspirational and pointing the way forward to Christ, who could never adequately be defined—"no type reaches the mark, because it is not Christ, though it may be a witness of Him."[151]

Surprisingly Kelly used two of his foundational articles about typology to teach about worship. This subject was of the utmost importance to him because the expression of affection was his key motive for worship. He wrote, "We ought not to be satisfied without the full tide of affection going up to Him from us; but let us ever bear in mind that we are accepted because of His holiness." At this point in his article written in May 1857, Kelly became carried away with a whole two pages of writing about worship without even mentioning his argument with Fairbairn. "Worship and service ... [were] part of the path of the people of God. Thus the worship of God's people was acceptable in spite of their infirmity, and holiness was ever before the Lord in the offerings of his house."[152] Kelly said that the

---

147. Katz, "Mysticism and the Interpretation of Scripture," 32.
148. Ibid., 32–33.
149. Ibid., 37.
150. Kelly, "The Types of Scripture no. v," 169.
151. Kelly, *Revelation*, 70.
152. Kelly, "The Types of Scripture no. vi," 185.

Brethren would find it easy to be distracted from the holiness of God by "admiration of fine tones in singing." Instead, there was need for a combination of reverence and joy: "Thus when we worship, we may bow down and look up, not in lightness, indeed, but in happy, holy liberty."[153]

When he came to examine the offerings of Leviticus, Kelly looked primarily at joy. "True worship of the saints, it is (*sic*) joying in God, through the means of the redemption and offering of Jesus; yea, one mind with God, joying with Him in the perfect excellency of this pure and self-devoted victim . . . thus their joy is the joy of Jesus Himself."[154] The peace offering was connected with the communion of saints—often mentioned by the Tractarians and not often connected with the Brethren. Kelly wrote, "the joy of worship necessarily associates itself also with the whole body of the redeemed, viewed as in the heavenly places, whether actually gone before us, or yet in the body below. Hence worship, true worship, cannot thus separate itself from the whole body of the believer."[155] In writing about worship in this way, Kelly was at his most appreciative of other Christians and was prepared to regard Fairbairn's own comments about true worship as being very valuable indeed.[156] Thus not only was Kelly at his most generous in his evaluation of Fairbairn's work when considering the subject of worship but preoccupation with the risen Lord meant that typology became a means of further mystic meditation. Private spirituality and mysticism meant that "blacking a shoe" could be holy, "supposing there is a real connection with Him there; this will assuredly give to what we do a heavenly stamp and impart the truest and highest dignity no matter what we may be about." This philosophy of the spiritual life places Kelly firmly among the writers of the mystic tradition.[157] What was unique in the expression of his mysticism was his use of typology to express an idealized spirituality. "It is happy," Kelly concluded, "when the truth of Christ illuminates consecutive chapters of the Old Testament."[158]

---

153. Ibid., 184.

154. Kelly, "The Types of Scripture no. vii," 201.

155. Ibid., 201.

156. Ibid., 202.

157. Richard Rolle (1290–1349) was known for his exuberant joy in his life and writings and Brother Lawrence (1614–1691) for his practising the presence of God even in the performance of domestic duties.

158. Kelly, *Pentateuch*, 86.

Conclusion
An Assessment of William Kelly's Contribution to Theology

The purpose of this book has been to establish the characteristics of Kelly's theology, how important he was as a Brethren theologian, and what place he might take in the wider stream of Church history. Despite his interest in the accuracy of biblical translation, Kelly was concerned with the whole written text and was fearful of being identified with a particular school of interpretation.[1] Neither did Kelly retreat into an esoteric spiritual experience. Rather than defending "literalism" as a type of theology, he entered into debate with the theologians of the Broad Church, and through the medium of *The Bible Treasury* he encouraged other Brethren writers to do the same. In his major work, *Lectures on the Revelation*, he gave a detailed critique of E.B. Elliot's book *Horae Apocalypticae*, which expounded a historicist pre-millennarian view of eschatology.[2] Kelly was also responding to Elliot's criticisms of himself, so he was clearly involved in reasoned theological argument. It was Reformed theologians, rather than Brethren theologians, who were particularly engaged in "a propositional notion of truth," which later led to the idea of inerrancy.[3] Nor can Kelly be defined simply as a "dispensationalist," even though he was an admirer of Darby. In his sensitivity to literary genre, Kelly has more in common with critical

---

1. Kelly, *Revelation*, xxxv.
2. Ibid., xxxii–xxxiii. Kelly is referring to E.B. Elliot, *Horae Apocalypticae*.
3. Harris, *Fundamentalism and Evangelicals*, 30.

rather than non-critical thinking.[4] Alongside Jewish scholars, Kelly cared more about sense and form than merely about individual words.[5]

As I have demonstrated in chapters 6 and 7, Kelly's interpretation of the biblical text was shaped by his spirituality. In this he can be said to have been theocentric as well as Christocentric. While Kelly saw the dangers of neoplatonism and was cautious about use of the word "mystic," he was nevertheless totally engaged in a Trinitarian, mystic spirituality. He also made a practice of using typology as a way of taking biblical texts out of their historic context and using them to mediate intense spiritual experience. His typology allowed the events of the text, which he accepted as historically accurate, to be thrown forward to future time. Therefore predictive prophecy (a staple of literalist interpretation and much criticized by the higher critics) was also preserved. In the theories of the higher critics, the text was thought to have been written later in Israel's history (exilic) but with reference to events in Israel's past. It emphasized a "present" while incorporating the past. In typology, however, the distant past when the events took place was seen as the time of writing, but its significance was in the future. This approach, adopted by Kelly, led to a more mystic experience, where time was less significant.

Kelly's understanding of biblical symbolic language was not only about hermeneutical analysis. He foregrounded it in his own writing so that biblical metaphor became embedded in his expression of spirituality. He also used emotive language even in biblical exegesis to communicate to his readers the importance of intense spiritual experience. What Kelly contributed in combining literalist, conservative intellectual, and mystic spirituality can best be summed up in his use of the word "portion" in his writings.

Using food imagery, "portion" suggests the idea of spiritual nourishment; this is central to the concept of Kelly "savoring" the nourishment of his soul—"feeding on Him as our portion even now."[6] For Kelly this was far more important than intellectual dissection of the text. There was also the idea of "secret portion," a very special experience which the unenlightened could not understand, and which was linked with the Tractarian idea

---

4. Barton, *The Nature of Biblical Criticism*, 23.

5. Reventlow, *History of Biblical Interpretation*, vol. 2, 237. Reventlow uses the example of Abraham Ben Meier (1089–1161) to show this tendency in Jewish biblical commentators.

6. Kelly, *Revelation*, 451.

of "reserve." It was about identifying with Christ's outcast position. It also provided links with Darby's idea of spiritual degeneration starting from the time of the early Church. This partly explains why John's Gospel was so important to Kelly—"written late and suited to a day of declension."[7] In his use of the word "portion" there was always a sense of contrast with those who seemed to be successful in an "establishment" religious sense. Throughout his work Kelly contrived to own biblical language, to reposition it in his own register and thus to communicate his own spirituality through this foregrounding of language. For example, in order to emphasize the importance of those who are truly spiritual, he took the word "potsherds" from its context in Isaiah and incorporated it in his commentary on Revelation— "but to strive with the potsherds of the earth is beneath those of heavenly birth."[8] The narrative of the Old Testament always created the background for Kelly's own spiritual perspective because it was transformed to mirror the internal spiritual struggles which were the foundation of his mysticism. Down the ages mystics have typically experienced turmoil as they arrived at greater spiritual enlightenment. Kelly used the text of the Old Testament existentially to guide the reader through the details of the spiritual conflict, and typology was a particularly useful means for him to do this.

Kelly also used the word "portion" to signal the differentiation of purpose within the different dispensations, and of the destiny of different people groups. For an evangelical he was surprisingly wide in his interpretation of the way others might know God. He cautioned his readers that they must not assume that "there is only one common blessing for all saints of all times."[9] This differentiation also allowed Kelly to separate the material blessings of the Old Testament from the spiritual blessings of the New, but typology allowed him to read the mysticism of the New into the Old Testament, and to see the materialism of the Old finding its fruition in the millennial prophecies of the New. Although Kelly wanted to defend the historical integrity of the biblical text, he primarily saw the text as a spiritual narrative to be entered into. In common with Paul Ricoeur he wanted to know what the text "did," not merely what it stated.[10]

---

7. Ibid., 68.

8. Ibid., 227. The reference is to Is 45:9 where potsherds (pieces of earthenware) are a symbol of powerless human beings.

9. Ibid., 395.

10. Ricoeur, *The Rule of Metaphor*, 6.

I have claimed that Kelly was a major Brethren theologian in his own right and that, surprisingly, he has been little studied. Kelly admired Darby and edited his work, but he did not follow him blindly. Kelly possessed academic prowess and reputation. He encouraged other Brethren intellectuals and those of a younger generation in his magazine. As Tim Grass has pointed out in writing about F.F. Bruce, "Because Brethren lacked centralized structures and institutions, magazines fulfilled a vital role among them, helping them to maintain coherence by disseminating news and providing sound teaching."[11] By being part of the Moderate Exclusives, Kelly bridged the divide between the Exclusive and Open Brethren and study of his work should help Brethren historians to see that such an intermediary movement was important. Kelly also enjoyed a sufficient reputation in wider ecclesiastical circles to be accepted as a respected representative of Brethren theology. I have shown that the Brethren had more to offer than one would expect from a small, seemingly introverted nineteenth-century sect, and that Kelly was able to mediate the value of the Brethren to the wider Christian world.

Kelly shows us that the Brethren were in line with other movements of the nineteenth century. While, in his intellectual capacity, he was rooted in the arguments of the Enlightenment (though of course rejecting the conclusions of that movement), his work also betrayed the influence of the Romantic Movement. His spirituality found its expression in a different kind of sacramentalism to that of the Tractarians and yet was an interesting parallel to it and, in its devout, focused piety, was perhaps a nineteenth-century evangelical expression of monasticism. The Romantic Movement majored on idealism and the intensity of the poetic imagination. While a secular imagination was not an acceptable option for the Brethren, they excelled in intense spiritualization. Their Old Testament typology allowed for an intensely personal spirituality. Thus the events of the Exodus meant redemption from sin for each individual Christian and Canaan represented a future entrance into glory. In nineteenth-century religion, the Brethren were the sacramentalists of the religious imagination, not of material objects.

The Brethren established a stream of Christianity which was unique in their environment. It was highly aspirational and mediated an exalted Christology which went far beyond ordinary typology. As Kelly argued, "no type reaches the mark, because it is not Christ, though it may be a witness

---

11. Grass, *F.F. Bruce*, 97.

of Him."[12] The living experience of Christ became a way to undergird biblical authority. While this was in tune with the proto–fundamentalist movement, it also served to authorize an existential spiritual experience.[13]

Kelly offered not only a critique of the religious establishment but also, in ecclesiastical terms, an alternative to it which paralleled other nineteenth-century movements. He liked to point out the dangers of replacing the structure of Catholicism with that of Protestantism and of therefore being unable to see the latter's faults.[14] Rather he stood for an independent questioning of the religious establishment, and this was an important strand of Victorian religious experience. Kelly spoke out against the religious establishment because he thought that there was too little submission to God's will in contemporary Christianity.[15] He was a questioner of the religious status quo. He had little time for those Christians in the Broad Church who felt optimism because of human progress. He questioned ecumenical movements because he saw that true Christian unity was very different from "confederacy." The Brethren had individual fellowship with Christians of other denominations, and they saw themselves as valuable because they were outside the denominational system and chose to question it. Kelly dismissed the nineteenth-century debate about disestablishment as being irrelevant to the real purpose of the church. Such an argument was in his opinion, "a great deal too narrow and low a question for a Christian."[16]

There was also a strong polarization between Brethren mysticism and their sense of humanity. Their humanity was strongly reflected in their acceptance of human sinfulness and in their anticipation of the millennium and this is reflected in Kelly's writings. Dispensationalism has often been seen by Church historians as a forerunner of fundamentalism, but it has not been considered as indicating Brethren concern for humanity. I suggest that dispensationalism in Kelly's opus should be considered in this way too. In anticipating a future millennium he affirmed the value of human skills. He was also, despite his transcendent spirituality, in a sense a materialist—he appreciated the reality of the resurrected body, according to Christian

---

12. Ibid., 70.

13. Harris, *Fundamentalism and Evangelicals*, 88. Harris makes reference to Barr and Wenham, *Christ and the Bible*, 2nd ed. for the link between Christ's authority and fundamentalism.

14. Kelly, *Revelation*, 239.

15. Ibid., 50.

16. Ibid., 60.

theology. His materialism him led him to reject the sacramentalism of the Tractarians. The Brethren were industrious in their present lives and were successful in business. They were rebels and individualists, not politically, but against what they considered to be a counterfeit church system. Every time they tried to put their own infrastructure into place, it failed. They recognized and revered individual leaders, but they never formally acknowledged them. Part of the rise of Victorian self-education, they were a grass roots intellectual movement because every member was encouraged to study the Bible and take part in worship and Bible readings.[17] *The Bible Treasury* was widely accessed by members of Brethren assemblies. In their engagement with abstract thought the Brethren rose above the level of the poorly educated. As part of the "age of Atonement," they saw penitence for sin as an essential requisite for conversion, but, unlike other revivalist movements, they did not stay mired in their own sinfulness and they had an experience of both individual and communal joy. They denied the importance of worldly success, but they never made themselves as uncomfortable in the world as some more extreme evangelicals. They did not admire asceticism. In fact they had much more in common with the Jews—cut-off from the world and yet successful within it. It is interesting that it was in the nineteenth century that Jews became particularly prosperous in Europe. The Brethren applied their materialism and their initiative to business success and also to the prospect of being used by God in the millennium. F.F. Bruce was right to claim that the Brethren had a historical identity (emerging out of nineteenth-century Anglicanism) and formed a sociological entity (with roots in the upper–middle classes, yet encouraging the priesthood of all believers).[18] I have only briefly touched on this idea in this book (mainly in chapter 5) but it would be an interesting future line of research into the Brethren.

The links between nineteenth-century futurist premillennarianism and fundamentalism have already been established by Sandeen and Harris. After the 1870s this futurist eschatology offered an option that seemed to heighten faith in the supernatural in an age of skepticism without having to engage in what would be viewed as pseudo–scholarly criticism which would quickly lead to derision.[19] In contrast, historicist pre–millennarianism naturally meshed with historical–critical methods and a more liberal

---

17. Grass, *Gathering to His Name*, 59.
18. Grass, *F.F. Bruce*, 132.
19. Spence, *Heaven on Earth*, 258.

Christianity. Leaders of evangelicalism, especially the holiness movement, became much more populist.[20] However, this was not true of Kelly. He was not part of the historicist school but he was open to argument, intellectual and reflective. His type of conservative scholarly argument disappeared for many years but emerged again in the latter half of the twentieth century.

I have contended that Kelly's place in the continuum of theological history should be acknowledged. Kelly never regarded himself as "the organ of a party important or not": he refused to take "a sectarian place."[21] He claimed that he represented a way of looking at the Bible which was not simply either Protestant or rationalist.[22] He believed that his purpose was to go on to know the Word of God more fully than traditional Protestants.[23]

Kelly had much in common with the approach of his near contemporary, the Dutch theologian Abraham Kuyper (1837–1920) who had an effect on Francis Schaeffer and the moderate form of British evangelicalism personified by John Stott and R. T. France. Like Kelly, Kuyper had a strong belief in sin and regeneration affecting the theory of knowledge.[24] Kuyper's belief that the working of the Spirit on the reader was as important as the details of the written text avoided the later problems of fundamentalism and the narrowing down of the meaning of "inspiration" to dictation and verbal inerrancy.[25] Like Kelly, Kuyper valued form as much as content in the biblical text.[26]

While Kuyper seems not to have been aware of the Brethren heritage of Kelly, twentieth-century Brethren theologians—W. E. Vine (1873–1949), Harold St. John (1876–1957) and Bruce—were. Bruce in his autobiography acknowledged Kelly's "manifest mastery of Greek usage which makes William Kelly's New Testament commentaries, especially those on Paul's epistles, so valuable."[27] They were also in touch with the theological school associated with the Inter Varsity Fellowship, and their influence can be seen

---

20. Ibid., 260.

21. Kelly, *Revelation*, x. vi. Kelly believed that rationalism had its roots in the Reformation and that his own teaching transcended the boundaries of the Reformation.

22. Ibid., vii.

23. Ibid.

24. Ibid., 205.

25. Ibid., 221.

26. Ibid., 227.

27. Bruce, *In Retrospect*, 293.

there. But they cannot be easily pigeon-holed. Bruce, like Kelly, admired Anglican divines such as J.B. Lightfoot and thought that it was Scripture rather than any doctrine or formula which was divinely inspired.[28] Bruce was more open in his attitude to the biblical text than the fundamentalist theologians of the Inter Varsity Fellowship. He stressed the illumination of the Spirit rather than biblical inerrancy, and he suggested that Bible students should look at what the Bible said for itself.[29] Bruce, like Kelly, was wary of systematic theology and he only just tolerated the IVF doctrinal basis and disapproved of evangelical intolerance of Barthian theology.[30] Although Bruce showed a greater acceptance of non-evangelical teaching than Kelly, Kelly showed a wider view of the whole text than literalists. Tim Grass has also suggested that Brethren in the 1920s manifested "a strain of mystic experientialism too," which sometimes influenced their doctrine of Scripture and led to "a divergence of opinion on the issue."[31]

As other mystics of different provenance, Kelly used language as a way of "signing" ultimate realities, including exclamatory and paradoxical language in some of his impassioned writing.[32] Katz has posed the significant question of whether mystics rewrite the text they interpret.[33] Of course Kelly would have been horrified by this notion as applied to his own work because he regarded the text of Scripture as totally "other" and to be revered as the unique Word of God. Nevertheless there is a sense in which any interpretation "rewrites" the original. It does this through a particular hermeneutical interpretation and this is why the Brethren, including Kelly, had a special contribution to make to nineteenth-century theological understanding. Although we see Kelly's endorsement of Brethren teaching, we can also note his humility in referring positively to non-Brethren writers as source material and his acknowledgement of God's Spirit at work amongst Christians of different ecclesiastical background. This has the effect of making him a far less "exclusive" writer than many other Brethren theologians, as well as being a more lucid and articulate writer. That is why he deserves to be better known amongst contemporary Christians. As Barth in the twentieth century, Kelly wanted to look at the whole text and at the

---

28. Grass, *F.F. Bruce*, 222-23.
29. Ibid., 94.
30. Ibid., 152-53.
31. Grass, "How fundamentalist were British Brethren during the 1920s?" 123, 127.
32. Katz, "Mysticism and the Interpretation of Sacred Scripture," 41.
33. Ibid., 70.

completed text rather than the text as a series of redactions.[34] I would like to affirm Kelly as a theologian who contributed to the early conservative evangelical tradition in Britain, rather than to the aggressive fundamentalist school of the USA.[35] Bebbington has suggested that British theological moderation was due to the influence of Romantic thought, and I would link that with Kelly's theological position.[36]

In many respects, Kelly was ahead of his time. Historicism, fashionable in the nineteenth century but unacceptable to Kelly, was rejected by Barth and Brunner in the twentieth century. More recent schools of theology, with writers such as Hans-Georg Gadamer (1900–2002), have felt that Christian assumptions are important for interpretation and they have been critical of higher criticism with its supposed neutral stance.[37] Using Barton's distinction between "meaning" and "significance" in interpreting Scripture, the school of higher biblical criticism in the nineteenth century was mainly concerned with "meaning," while a writer like Kelly, who consciously nourished the spirituality of his readers, majored on the idea of "the significance" of the text.[38] Many writers in the mystic tradition have, like Kelly, rejected nineteenth-century "theories of knowledge."[39] Instead, Scriptural authority is claimed as an authority in its own right, and one which does not need justifying, although in Kelly's exegesis it was thoughtfully defended, as I have shown in this book. Twentieth-century philosophy and hermeneutics have also raised questions about texts which are very much in tune with Kelly's approach. The post-structuralist and feminist writer, Julia Kristeva (b.1941), has pointed out the importance of intertextuality and of understanding the culture-specific nature of codes.[40] Research into speech-act theory by John R. Searle (b. 1932) has highlighted the balance between Divine correction in word-to-world language and promise in world-to-word language.[41] Biderman has shown that performative utterances are part of mystic writing (as well as being part of Scriptural discourse) and it is in

---

34. Barton, *The Nature of Biblical Criticism*, 149.

35. Harris, *Fundamentalism and the Evangelicals*, 47. This examines the divergence between the two streams of theology.

36. Bebbington, *Evangelicalism*, 80–81, 167–69.

37. Ibid., 153.

38. Barton, *The Nature of Biblical Criticism*, 179.

39. Biderman, "Mystical Identity," 78.

40. Kristeva, *Revolution in Poetic Language*, 59–60.

41. Searle, *Speech Acts*, 24, 58.

these performative utterances that "the longed-for presence is declared to be found."[42] It is through such language that Kelly spiritually nourishes his readers. Biderman has affirmed that there is "a close structural parallelism between the profile of 'commentator' and that of 'mystic.'"[43] To use Austin's terminology, even when they use different locutionary acts, they have the same illocutionary force, that is, a desire to be caught up with the presence of God.[44] Hans Penner has seen "mysticism" as a false category because of the "dialectical blending of mysticism and Scripture."[45] Mystical Scriptural exegeses are often a mixture of intellectual sophistication and "emotional exultation" and we can observe this combination in Kelly's work.[46] In Kelly's writing we can ascertain the fourfold sense of Scripture—symbolic, moral, allegorical and anagogic—as initiated by the Medieval mystic writers, even though he is not circumscribed by this method.[47] Traditionally, in anagogical interpretation, we are given to know what to desire, and this aspect of interpretation is very prominent in Kelly's work. He draws out our hearts, yes, in understanding the text, but also inspiring us in the enjoyment of the presence of God. Ricoeur has written about the principle of plenitude in understanding a metaphor, which provides a contextual change of meaning and I believe that in reading Kelly's exegeses we gain from this principle of plenitude. Ricoeur has gone on to analyze the function of biblical hermeneutics in demonstrating the ability of the text to unmask wish-fulfillment and idolatry as well as in providing a process of retrieval which helps us to listen to the power of symbols within it.[48] Such approaches were incorporated into Kelly's whole text response, and, alongside his deep spirituality, they suggest that he should be more widely acknowledged as a theologian and teacher of distinction, one who is worthy of further study, and one who stood "against the trend."

---

42. Biderman, "Mystical Identity," 70.
43. Ibid.
44. Ibid.
45. Ibid., 71, using the work of Penner, "The Mystical Illusion," 89–116.
46. Ibid., 78.
47. Cousins, "The Fourfold Sense," 122–23.
48. Ricoeur, "The Bible and the Imagination," 49–75.

Bibliography

Almond, Philip. *Heaven and Hell in Enlightenment England*. Cambridge: Cambridge University Press, 1994.
Alter, Robert. *The Art of Biblical Narrative*. New York: Basic, 1981.
Barr, James. *Fundamentalism*. London: Student Christian Mission, 1951.
Barton, John. *The Nature of Biblical Criticism*. Louisville: Westminster John Knox, 2007.
Batten, J. E. "Modern Hegelianism Compared with the Old Brahminism." *BT* 1, no.5 (January 1857) 133–34.
———. "The Word of God." *BT* 15, no. 338 (July 1884) 98–101.
Beacon, Richard. "The Impregnable Rock of Holy Scripture." *BT* 18, no. 408 (May 1890) 110–12.
———. "The Impregnable Rock of Holy Scripture." *BT* 18, no. 410 (July 1890) 110–12.
Bebbington, David. *Evangelicalism in Modern Britain: A History from the 1730s to the 1980s*. London: Unwin Hyman, 1989.
Bellett, John Gifford. "The Atonement Money." *BT* 14, no. 325 (June 1883) 273–74.
Bickersteth, Edward. *Yesterday, Today and Forever*. 2nd ed. London: Rivington, 1867.
Brooks, Chris. *Signs for the Times: Symbolic Realism in the Mid-Victorian World*. London: George Allen and Unwin, 1984.
Brown, Ralph. "Evangelical Social Thought." *The Journal of Ecclesiastical History* 60 (2009) 126–36.
———. "Victorian Anglican Evangelicalism: The Radical Legacy of Edward Irving." *The Journal of Ecclesiastical History* 58 (2007) 675–703.
Bruce, Frederick F. *In Retrospect, Remembrance of Things Past*. London: Pickering and Inglis, 1980.
Burnham, Jonathan. *A Story of Conflict: The Controversial Relationship between Benjamin Wills Newton and John Nelson Darby*. Carlisle: Paternoster, 2004.
Bushnell, Horace. *Vicarious Sacrifice*. London: Strahan and Low, 1866.
Campbell, John McLeod. *The Nature of the Atonement*. 3rd ed. London: Macmillan, 1869.
Carson, Donald, and Geoffrey Wenham, eds. *New Bible Commentary: 21st Century Edition*. Leicester: Inter-Varsity, 2000.
Carter, Grayson. *Evangelical Seceders from the Church of England c1800–1850*. Oxford: Oxford University Press, 2001.
Chadwick, Owen. *The Spirit of the Oxford Movement: Tractarian Essays*. Cambridge: Cambridge University Press, 1990.
———. *The Victorian Church, Part Two: 1860–1901*. London: A and C Black, 1972.
Coad, Roy. *A History of the Brethren Movement*. Exeter: Paternoster, 1976.

Bibliography

Colenso, John. *The Pentateuch and Book of Joshua Critically Examined*. London: Longman and Green, 1872.

———. *St. Paul's Epistle to the Romans: Newly Translated, and Explained from a Missionary Point of View*. Cambridge and London: Macmillan, 1861.

Crews, Frederick. "Literary Criticism." http://www.britannica.com.

Cross, Edwin N., *The Irish Saint and Scholar: A Biography of William Kelly 1821-1906*. London: Chapter Two, 2004.

Crowther, Margaret. *Church Embattled: Religious Controversy in Mid-Victorian England*. Devon: David and Charles Archon, 1970.

Darby, John Nelson. "The Atonement." *BT* N6, no. 134 (February 1907) 227-30.

———. "The Atonement." *BT* N6, no. 135 (March 1907) 227-30.

———. *The Collected Writings of J.N. Darby, Ecclesiastical no. 1, Vol.1*, edited by William Kelly. London: Stow Hill Bible and Tract Depot, 1971.

———. *Considerations Addressed to the Archbishop of Dublin and Clergy*. Manchester University Archives: C.W.1.5, 1827.

———. *Dialogues on the 'Essays and Reviews' by One who Values Christianity for its Own Sake and Believes in it as a Revelation from God*. London: W.H. Broom, 1862.

———. "A Few Words on Propitiation or Atonement." *BT* 18, no. 410 (July 1890) 97-98.

———. "Letter 1: On Mysticism." *BT* 6, no. 135 (August 1867) 312.

———. "Propitiation, Substitution and Atonement." *BT* 12, no. 280 (September 1879) 335-36.

———. "The Relative and the Absolute." *BT* 7, no. 152 (January 1869) 198-201.

Davidson, Samuel. *Autobiography*. Edinburgh: T. and T. Clark, 1899.

———. *Introduction to the Old Testament*. London: Williams and Norgate, 1862.

Dickens, Charles. *Barnaby Rudge*. London: Penguin, 1973.

Dickson, Neil, and Thomas J. Marinello, eds. *Culture, Spirituality and the Brethren*. Ayrshire: Brethren Archivists and Historians Network, 2014.

Draper, John. "Colenso's Commentary on Romans: an Exegetical Assessment." In *The Eye of the Storm*, edited by Jonathan Draper, 104-15. London: T. & T. Clark, 2003.

Eagleton, Terry. *Literary Theory: An Introduction*. Oxford: Blackwell, 1983.

Fairbairn, Patrick. *The Typology of Scripture—Viewed in Connection with the Entire Scheme of the Divine Dispensations*. 2nd ed. Philadelphia: Smith and English, 1854.

Farrar, Frederick, W. *Eternal Hope: Five Sermons Preached in Westminster Abbey, November and December, 1877*. London: Macmillan, 1879.

Gladstone, William. *The Impregnable Rock of Holy Scripture*. London: John Wattles, 1890.

Gore, Charles. *Lux Mundi: the Inspiration of the Holy Scriptures*. 10th ed. London: John Murray, 1890.

Grass, Tim. *F. F. Bruce: A Life*. Grand Rapids: Eerdmans, 2012.

———. *Gathering to His Name*. Glasgow: Paternoster, 2006.

———. "How Fundamentalist were the British Brethren during the 1920s?" In *Evangelicalism and Fundamentalism in the United Kingdom during the Twentieth Century*, edited by David Bebbington and David Ceri-Jones, 115-31. Oxford: Oxford University Press, 2014.

Gribben, Crawford, and Andrew R. Holmes, eds. *Protestant Millennialism: Evangelicalism and Irish Society 1790-2005*. Basingstoke: Palgrave Macmillan, 2006.

Harris, Harriet. *Fundamentalism and Evangelicals*. Oxford: Clarendon, 1998.

Hilton, Boyd. *The Age of the Atonement: the Influence of Evangelicalism on Social and Economic Thought 1795-1865*. Oxford: Clarendon, 1988.

———. "Evangelical Attitudes: a Reply to Ralph Brown." *The Journal of Ecclesiastical History* 60 (2009) 119–25.
Hocking, William J. "The Lord's Testimony to the Mosaic Authorship of the Pentateuch." *BT* 19, no. 431 (April 1892) 58–60.
———. "The Lord's Testimony to the Mosaic Authorship of the Pentateuch." *BT* 19, no. 432 (May 1892) 74–76.
———. "The Lord's Testimony to the Mosaic Authorship of the Pentateuch." *BT* 19, no. 433 (June 1892) 90–92.
Hodge, Archibald. *The Atonement*. London: Evangelical, 1867.
Horne, Thomas, et al., *An Introduction to the Study and Knowledge of the Holy Scriptures*, vol.2. *The Text Considered with a Treatise on Sacred Interpretation and a Brief Introduction to the Old Testament Books and the Apocrypha*. 10th ed. London: Longman, Brown, Green, Longmans and Roberts, 1856.
Howard, William. *Religion and the Rise of Historicism*. Cambridge: Cambridge University Press, 2000.
James, William. *The Varieties of Religious Experience*. Edinburgh: Longmans, Green, 1902.
Jay, Elizabeth. *Faith and Doubt in Victorian Britain*. London: Macmillan, 1986.
Jenkins, Michael, "John McLeod Campbell." In *Oxford Dictionary of National Biography* 9: 838–39.
Jobling, David. "Colenso on Myth or Colenso as Myth." In *The Eye of the Storm*, edited by Jonathan A. Draper, 65–102. London: T&T Clark, 2003.
Jowett, Benjamin. *The Epistles of St. Paul to the Thessalonians, Galatians and Philippians*, vol. 2, London: John Murray, 1859.
———. *The Interpretation of Scripture and Other Essays*. London: Library, 1906.
Katz, Steven T., ed. *Mysticism and Language*. Oxford: Oxford University Press, 1992.
———., ed. *Mysticism and Sacred Scripture*. Oxford: Oxford University Press, 2000.
Kelly, William. "The 2 Goats: Lev xvi. 5–10." *BT* 3, no.63 (March 1901) 227–30.
———. "The Absolute." *BT* 6, no. 119 (April 1866) 53–56.
———. *The Advocacy of Christ: A Lecture of 1 John 2.1, 2*. London: T. Weston, 1897.
———. "Appendix 1: The Scapegoat." *BT* 4, no. 80 (August 1902) 114–15.
———. "Appendix 2: Modern Views Subversive of the Atonement." *BT* 4, no. 80 (August 1902) 116–19.
———. "Atonement for Flux Lev xv.13–15." *BT* 4, no. 78 (June 1902) 82–83.
———. "Azazel or the People's Lot." *BT* 3, no. 70 (October 1901) 323–26; 339–42.
———. "Azazel or the People's Lot." *BT* 4, no. 73 (January 1902) 3–6.
———. "Baptism." *BT* 9, no. 202 (March 1873) 240.
———. *Bible Treasury, A Monthly Magazine of Papers on Scriptural Subjects Edited by William Kelly*. Winschoten: H.L. Heijkoop, 1885–1920.
———. "The Bride Called for Isaac (Gen xxiv.1–9)." *BT* 2, no. 45 (September 1890) 321–23.
———. *Brief Notice of G. Cox's 'The Thirty-Six Reasons Against the Immortality of the Soul'*. London: R.L. Allan, n/d.
———. "The Call of the Bride: The Substance of a Lecture on Genesis xxiv." *BT* 9, no. 210 (November 1873) 359–66.
———. "The Catholic Apostolic Body Chapter iv: Doctrine." *BT* 1, no. 5 (February 1857) 44–47.
———. "The Catholic Apostolic Body or Irvingites. Chapter iv: Doctrine} 5 The Atonement etc." *BT* 18, no. 409 (June 1890) 93–95.

Bibliography

———. "Charges Against Mr. Davidson." *BT* 1, no. 5 (April 1857) 186.
———. *The Coming of the Day of the Lord*. London: T. Weston, 1903.
———. "Correspondence: Recent Baptismal Agitation." *BT* 9, no. 188 (January 1872) 14–16.
———. "The Day of Atonement: Azazel or the People's Lot Lev. vi.20-26." *BT* 3, no. 69 (September 1901) 323–28.
———. "The Day of Atonement: Concluding Remarks." *BT* 4, no. 75 (March 1902) 35–36.
———. "The Day of Atonement: The Incense and the Bullock (concluded)." *BT* 3, no. 68 (August 1901) 307–12.
———. "The Day of Atonement: The Principle." *BT* 3, no. 60 (November 1900) 179–83.
———. *The Doctrine of Christ and Bethesdaism*. London: Weston, 1906.
———. "The Double Document Notion of Sceptics." *BT* 6, no. 138 (November 1867) 356–60.
———. "Drummond's Natural Law in the Spiritual World." *BT* 15, no. 345 (February 1885) 220–23.
———. "The Early Chapters of Genesis. Chapter iii} 1." *BT* 19, no. 436 (September 1892) 129–30.
———. "Eternal Life: Notes on a Lecture." *BT* 5, no. 100 (April 1904) 61–62.
———. *An Exposition of the Book of Isaiah*. 3rd ed. London: F.E. Race, 1916.
———. *An Exposition of the Epistle to the Hebrews with a New Version*. London: T. Weston, 1905.
———. *An Exposition of the Gospel of John*. London: C.A. Hammond Trust Bible Depot, 1898.
———. *An Exposition of the Gospel of Luke*. Glasgow: Pickering and Inglis, 1903.
———. *An Exposition of the Gospel of Mark*. London: C.A. Hammond, 1934.
———. "The Fall of Man." *BT* 20, no. 452 (January 1894) 56–57.
———. "The Feasts of Jehovah: The Day of Atonement." *BT* 16, no. 363 (August 1886) 113–14.
———. "FER Heterodox on the Person of Christ." *BT* N4, no. 77 (May 1902) 78–82.
———. *The First Epistle of Peter*. London: T. Weston, 1904.
———. *God's Inspiration of the Scriptures*. London: Weston, 1903.
———. "The Gospel and the Church. Viii. The Snares in the Paths of its Ministers." *BT* 18, no. 416 (January 1891) 205–7.
———. "The Higher Criticism." *BT* 5, no. 120 (December 1905) 374–79.
———. *The Higher Criticism*. 2nd ed. London: T. Weston, 1906.
———. "The Higher Criticism (continued)." *BT* 6, no. 121 (January 1906) 7–15.
———. "The Higher Criticism (continued)." *BT* 6, no. 122 (February 1906) 26–29.
———. "The Higher Criticism (continued)." *BT* 6, no. 123 (March 1906) 43–46.
———. "Hope of Christ's Coming Again and its Relation to the Question of Time: no. ii." *BT* 1, no. 5 (September 1856) 57–61.
———. "The Importance of the First Resurrection as a Hope of the Church." *BT* 1, no. 5 (January 1857) 79–81.
———. "The Incense and the Bullock: Lev xvi.11-19." *BT* 3, no. 66 (June 1901) 275–78.
———. "The Inspiration of the Scriptures. Chapter ii: Apostasy and Authority." *BT* (April 1898) 59–61.
———. "The Intermediate State." *BT* 3, no. 53 (May 1900) 80.
———. *Introductory Lectures to the Epistle to the Romans*. Illinois: Bible Truth, n/d.
———. *J.N.D. as I Knew him*. Belfast: Words of Truth, 1986.

———. "The Judgment and the Eternal State: No. vii." *BT* 1 (May 1857) 185–87.
———. "The Kingdom: No. v." *BT* 1, no. 5 (January 1857) 122–26.
———. *Lectures Introductory to the Earlier Historical Books*. London: Hammond Trust, 1874.
———. *Lectures Introductory to the Pentateuch*. London: W.H. Broom, 1871.
———. *Lectures Introductory to the Study of the Minor Prophets*. 5th ed. London: G. Morrish, n/d.
———. *Lectures on the Book of Daniel*. 2nd ed. London: G. Morrish, n/d.
———. *Lectures on the Book of Revelation*. London: G. Morrish, 1869.
———. *Lectures on the Church of God*. 7th ed. London: Broom and Rouse, 1897.
———. *Lectures on the Epistle of Paul the Apostle to the Colossians with a New Translation*. London: G. Morrish, n/d.
———. *Lectures on the Epistle of Paul the Apostle to the Ephesians with a New Translation*. London: G. Morrish, n/d.
———. *Lectures on the Epistle of Paul the Apostle to the Galatians with a New Translation*. London: G. Morrish, n/d.
———. *Lectures on the Epistle of Paul the Apostle to the Philippians with a New Translation*. London: G. Morrish, n/d.
———. *Lectures on the Gospel of Matthew*. London: Morrish and Allan, 1868.
———. *Lectures on the New Testament Doctrine of the Holy Spirit*. London: W. H. Broom, 1860.
———. *Lectures on the Second Coming and Kingdom of the Lord and Saviour Jesus Christ*. London: T. Weston, n/d.
———. *Letters*. (1844–1906). Box 30, Christian Brethren Archives, The John Rylands Library, Manchester University, Manchester, UK. Unpublished.
———. "Life and Death." *BT* 5, no. 98 (February 1904) 27–29.
———. "Life Eternal Denied." *BT* 4, no. 74 (February 1902) 23–27.
———. "Life Eternal Denied by FER." *BT* 4, no. 73 (January 1902) 10–16.
———. "Life Eternal Denied by FER." *BT* 4, no. 77 (May 1902) 73–77.
———. "Names of God in the Psalms." *BT* 18, no. 406 (March 1890) 48.
———. "New Testament Millenarianism." *BT* 1, no. 5 (October 1856) 71–73.
———. "Notes on Scripture. No. v: Our Joy in Heaven. Luke ix.28–36." *BT* 1, no. 5 (May 1857) 188.
———. *Notes on the Epistle of Paul the Apostle to the Romans*. No publication details, 1873.
———. "Notes of the Month." *BT* 1, no. 5 (October 1856) 70.
———. "On Inspiration." *BT* 4, no. 89 (October 1863) 350–52.
———. *The Pentateuch and its Critics*. 1st ed. 1877. London: Broom and Race, 1913.
———. "The Pre-Millennial Advent in Relation to the Agencies of Salvation: no. iv." *BT* 1, no. 5 (November 1856) 92–94.
———. "Pre-Millennialism Consistent with the Completeness of the Church at Christ's Coming Again." *BT* 1, no. 5 (October 1856) 75–79.
———. *Propitiation—A Valuable Reply to CES by W. Kelly*. London: C.A. Hammond, n/d.
———. "Scripture Queries and Answers." *BT* 6, no. 128 (January 1867) 206–8.
———. "Scripture Queries and Answers." *BT* 8, no. 176 (January 1871) 207–8.
———. "Scripture Queries and Answers." *BT* 2, no. 32 (August 1898) 127–28.
———. "Scripture Queries and Answers." *BT* 2, no. 35 (November 1898) 175–76.
———. "Scripture Queries and Answers." *BT* 2, no. 32 (January 1899) 208.

Bibliography

———. "Scripture Queries and Answers." *BT* 2, no. 40 (April 1899) 256.
———. "Scripture Queries and Answers." *BT* 5, no. 100 (April 1904) 62-64.
———. *The Second Epistle of Peter*. London: T. Weston, 1906.
———. "The Separate State and the Resurrection." *BT* 1, no. 15 (March 1897) 239-40.
———. "The Serpent and the Woman's Seed." *BT* 20, no. 459 (August 1894) 127-28.
———. "The Soul Neither Mortal Nor to Sleep." *BT* 20, no. 458 (July 1894) 110-12.
———. *Tracts*, London: W.H. Broom, 1854.
———. *Tracts*, London: T. Weston, 1905.
———. *Two Lectures on the Song of Solomon*. London: F.E. Race, 1917.
———. "The Types of Scripture No. i: Historical Glance and General Principles." *BT* 1, no. 5 (December 1856) 103-7.
———. "The Types of Scripture No. ii: Primeval Times." *BT* 1, no. 5 (January 1857) 119-22.
———. "The Types of Scripture No. iii: Typical Persons and Things in the Book of Genesis." *BT* 1, no. 5 (February 1857) 135-38.
———. "The Types of Scripture No. iv: The Histories of Exodus." *BT* 1, no. 5 (March 1857) 151-55.
———. "The Types of Scripture No. v: The Tabernacle and its Vessels." *BT* 1, no. 5 (April 1857) 167-70.
———. "The Types of Scripture No. vi: The Priesthood." *BT* 1, no. 5 (May 1857) 183-85.
———. "The Types of Scripture No. viii: The Offerings of Leviticus." *BT* 1, no. 5 (June 1857) 199-202.
———. "What is a Succession a Succession of? Or the Apostasy." *BT* 16, no. 396 (May 1887) 266-67.
———. "The Word of God." *BT* 15, no. 339 (August 1884) 117-22.
Kirkpatrick, A.F. and S.R. Driver. *The Higher Criticism*. New York: Hodder and Stoughton, 1912.
Landow, George. *Victorian Types, Victorian Shadows: Biblical Typology in Victorian Literature, Art and Thought*. London: Routledge and Kegan Paul, 1980.
Larsen, Timothy. "Bishop Colenso and his Critics: the Strange Emergence of Biblical Criticism in Victorian Britain." In *The Eye of the Storm*, edited by Jonathan Draper, 42-59. London: T. & T. Clark, 2003.
———. *Crisis of Doubt—Honest Faith in Nineteenth Century England*. Oxford: Oxford University Press, 2008.
Law, David. *Inspiration*. London: Continuum, 2001.
Locke, John. *An Essay Concerning Human Understanding*. New York: J. & J. Harper. 1824.
———. *The Reasonableness of Christianity as Delivered in the Scriptures*. London: Rivington. 1824.
Louth, Andrew. *The Origins of the Christian Mystical Tradition, from Plato to Denys*. Oxford: Clarendon, 1981.
Mackintosh, Robert. *Historic Theories of Atonement with Comments*. London: Hodder and Stoughton, 1920.
Maurice, Francis D. *The Doctrine of Sacrifice*. Cambridge: Macmillan, 1854.
———. *Theological Essays*, 2nd ed. Cambridge: Macmillan, 1853.
McGrath, Alister. *Christianity's Dangerous Idea: The Protestant Revolution*. London: SPCK, 2007.
Moberley, R. Walter. *At the Mountain of God*. Sheffield: JSOT, 1983.

BIBLIOGRAPHY

Morris, John. *F.D. Maurice and the Crisis of Christian Authority*. Oxford: Oxford University Press, 2005.

Newman, Francis W. *The History of the Hebrew Monarchy from the Administration of Samuel to the Babylonish Captivity*. London: Chapman, 1847.

———. *Phases of Faith or Passages from the History of my Creed*. London: Rubner, 1874.

Newman, John H. *An Essay on the Development of Christian Doctrine*. 5th ed. London: Longman, Green, 1887.

Noel, Napoleon. *The History of the Brethren*, vols 1 and 2. Edited by William Knapp. Colorado: W.F. Knapp, 1936.

Norman, Edward R. *Church and Society in England 1770–1970: A Historical Study*. Oxford: Clarendon, 1976.

Orchard, Stephen. "English Evangelical Eschatology 1790–1850." PhD thesis, Cambridge University, 1969.

Pickering, Henry. *Chief Men Among the Brethren, a Series of Brief Records of Brethren Beloved*. Glasgow: Pickering and Inglis, n/d.

Quiller-Couch, Arthur, ed. *Oxford Book of English Verse 1250–1918*. Oxford: Clarendon, 1968.

Quinna, Philip L. "The Atonement." In *The Oxford Companion to Christian Thought*, edited by Adrian Hastings, Alistair Mason, and Hugh Pyper, 51–52. Oxford: Oxford University Press, 2000.

Reardon, Bernard. *From Coleridge to Gore*. London: Longman, 1971.

Reventlow, Henning Graf. *History of Biblical Interpretation: Vol. 2, From Late Antiquity to the Middle Ages*. Translated by James Duke. Atlanta: Society of Biblical Literature, 2009.

———. *History of Biblical Interpretation: Vol. 4, From the Enlightenment to the Twentieth Century*. Translated by Leo Perdue. Atlanta: Society of Biblical Literature, 2010.

———. "The Role of the Old Testament in the German Liberal Protestant Theology of the Nineteenth Century." In *Biblical Studies and the Shifting of Paradigms 1850–1914*, edited by Henning Graf Reventlow and William Farmer, 132–38. Sheffield: Sheffield Academic, 1995.

Ricoeur, Paul. "The Bible and the Imagination" in *The Bible as a Document of the University*, Hans Dieter Betz. Chico: Scholars, 1981.

———. *Freud and Philosophy. An Essay on Interpretations*. New Haven: Yale University Press, 1970.

———. *The Rule of Metaphor. Multi-Disciplinary Studies of the Creation of Meaning in Language*. London: Routledge and Kegan Paul, 1978.

Rigg, James H. *Modern Anglican Theology*. London: Heylu, 1857.

Ritchie, Lionel Arthur. "Patrick Fairbairn." In *Oxford Dictionary of National Biography*, 2004. Accessed July 12, 2014. www.oxforddnb.com/view/article/9065

Robertson, Frederick W. *Sermons on Christian Doctrine*. Boston: Fields, Osgood, 1869.

Rogerson, John. *Old Testament Criticism in the Nineteenth Century. England and Germany*. London: SPCK, 1984.

———. *W.L.M. de Wette, Founder of Modern Biblical Criticism: An Intellectual Biography*. Sheffield: JSOT, 1991.

Rowell, Geoffrey. *Hell and the Victorians*. Oxford: Clarendon, 1974.

Sandeen, Ernest. *The Roots of Fundamentalism*. London: University of Chicago Press, 1970.

Bibliography

Scott, Thomas. *Essays on the Most Important Subjects in Religion.* 9th ed. London: L.B. Seeley, 1822.

Searle, John R. *Speech Acts. An Essay in the Philosophy of Language.* Cambridge: Cambridge University Press, 1969.

Shea, Victor, and William Whitla, eds. *Essays and Reviews: The 1860 Text and its Reading.* Charlottesville: University Press of Virginia, 2000.

Spence, Martin. *Heaven on Earth. Reimagining Time and Eternity in Nineteenth-Century British Evangelicalism.* Oregon: Pickwick, 2015.

―――. "The Renewal of Time and Space: The Missing Element of Discussions about Nineteenth-Century Premillennialism." *The Journal of Ecclesiastical History* 63 (2012) 81–101.

Stunt, Timothy C.F. *Early Brethren and the Society of Friends.* CBRF Occasional Paper no 3, Pinner, Middlesex: Christian Brethren Research Fellowship, 1970.

―――. "John Nelson Darby (1800–1882), Member of the So-Called (Plymouth) Brethren." *Oxford Dictionary of National Biography.* 2004–14. Accessed 11 November, 2013.

―――. "Two Nineteenth-Century Movements." *The Evangelical Quarterly* 37 (1965) 221–31.

Taylor, Malcolm L. "Born for the Universe: William Kelly and the Brethren Mind in Victorian England (Aspects of the Relationship between Science and Theology)." MPhil thesis, University of Teesside, 1993.

Tennyson, Alfred. *In Memoriam.* Edited by Susan Shatto and Marion Shaw. Oxford: Clarendon, 1982.

Thiselton, Anthony C. *New Horizons in Hermeneutics.* London: HarperCollins, 1992.

Thomson, William. *The Atoning Work of Christ, Viewed in Relation to Some Current Theories.* Oxford: Longman, Brown, Green and Longmans, 1853.

Tillotson, John. *The Works of the Most Reverend Dr. John Tillotson, Late Lord Bishop of Canterbury. In Ten Volumes.* London: J.F. Dove, 1820.

Toon, Peter. *Evangelical Theology 1833–1856, a Response to Tractarianism.* London: Marshall, Morgan and Scott, 1979.

Turner, W.G. *William Kelly as I Knew Him.* London: C.A. Hammond, n/d.

Underhill, Evelyn. *The Mystics of the Church.* London: Clarke, 1925.

Walker, David P. *The Decline of Hell.* London: Routledge and Kegan Paul, 1964.

Weremchuk, Max. *John Nelson Darby: A Biography.* Neptune, NJ: Loiseaux Brothers. English edition, 1992.

Wette, W.M.L. de. trans. Theodore Parker. *A Critical and Historical Introduction to the Canonical Scriptures of the Old Testament*, vol. 1. Boston: Little and Brown, 1843.

―――. trans. Theodore Parker, *Introduction to the Old Testament*, vol. 2. Edinburgh: T. & T. Clark, 1892.

Wheeler, Michael. *Death and the Future Life in Victorian Literature and Theology.* Cambridge: Cambridge University Press, 1990.

White, Vernon. *Atonement and Incarnation, an Essay in Universalism and Particularity.* Cambridge: Cambridge University Press, 1991.

Wilkinson, Paul Richard. *For Zion's Sake: Christian Zionism and the Role of John Nelson Darby.* Milton Keynes, UK: Paternoster, 2007.

Williams, Norman Powell. *The Ideas of the Fall and of Original Sin.* London: Longmans, Green, 1927.

Wilson, H.B. *The Communion of Saints, an Attempt to Illustrate the True Principles of Christian Union in 8 Lectures*. Oxford: William Graham, Hatchard and Son, 1851.

Wreford, Heyman. *Memories of the Life and Last Days of William Kelly*. London: T. Weston, 1906.

YOD. "Dummond on Evolution (Second Letter)." Bible Treasury 19, no. 448 (September 1893) 334.

Young, John. *The Life and Light of Men*. London: Alexander Strahan, 1866.

www.ingramcontent.com/pod-product-compliance
Lightning Source LLC
Chambersburg PA
CBHW052339230426
43664CB00041B/2489